Born in Hamilton, New Zealand, in 1963, Warren Gatland played rugby for the provincial side Waikato for eight years, and made 17 appearances for the All Blacks, before turning to coaching.

He was the Head Coach of the British & Irish Lions squad which recorded an epic and thrilling Test series draw against the mighty All Blacks in 2017. The result was the first time the Lions had not lost a series in New Zealand since 1971. Gatland also led the Lions on their triumphant tour of Australia in 2013, and he served as Assistant Coach on the 2009 tour of South Africa.

After a dozen years at the helm, Gatland left his post as Head Coach of Wales after the 2019 World Cup. In that time, the Welsh have reached two World Cup semi-finals and won three Grand Slams and the Six Nations four times. During his career, Gatland has also coached Connacht and the Irish national team, as well as Waikato and Wasps. He is currently Head Coach of the Chiefs in New Zealand's Super Rugby.

Also by Warren Gatland and available from Headline

In The Line of Fire

WARREN GATLAND

PRIDE AND PASSION

MY AUTOBIOGRAPHY

HEADLINE

First published in 2019 by
HEADLINE PUBLISHING GROUP

First published in paperback in 2020 by
HEADLINE PUBLISHING GROUP

1

Cataloguing in Publication Data is available from the British Library

ISBN 978 1 4722 5246 3

Typeset in Warnock Pro by
Palimpsest Book Production Ltd, Falkirk, Stirlingshire

Printed and bound in Great Britain by Clays Ltd, Elcograf S.p.A.

Headline's policy is to use papers that are natural, renewable and recyclable
products and made from wood grown in well-managed forests and other controlled
sources. The logging and manufacturing processes are expected to conform to the
environmental regulations of the country of origin.

HEADLINE PUBLISHING GROUP
An Hachette UK Company
Carmelite House
50 Victoria Embankment
London
EC4Y 0DZ

www.headline.co.uk
www.hachette.co.uk

I dedicate this book to the three most
important people in my life — Trudi, Gabby and Bryn.
I love you so much, Big Much, and there's nothing greater than that.

CONTENTS

Prologue

SEVENTEEN MILES
AND A WHOLE WORLD AWAY

1st November 2019: Tokyo

There is a full house of almost 50,000 in the Tokyo Stadium tonight to watch Wales, my team, take on New Zealand, my country, at the Rugby World Cup. It is one of the great rivalries in the sport and in any other context, it would be a moment to savour. Sadly, this is a case of wrong place, wrong time. They call it a final, but it's the Bronze Medal final. The real final is being played tomorrow, an hour's drive down the road in Yokohama, and by the time South Africa and England take the field, my post-Wales life will already be a day old.

What can I expect from this evening's game, my last after twelve years as head coach? Tough question. The All Blacks will be on the rebound after finishing a distant second to England six days ago and as I watch them warming up on the far side of the halfway line, I see some of rugby's super-elite – Kieran Read, Brodie Retallick, Sonny Bill Williams, Ben Smith, Beauden Barrett – going about their preparations with a glint in their eyes. They're not here to mess around. They're here to right some wrongs.

As for us, we're suffering. We've had a short turnaround from a brutal semi-final against the Springboks and we're held together by bandages, sticky tape, blind faith and bottomless reserves of desire. We were short on numbers when we faced the South Africans and we're even shorter now. Leigh Halfpenny, George North, Tomas Francis, Aaron Wainwright: they all joined the injury list last weekend and were declared unavailable for selection.

I'm not the only member of the coaching staff moving on after this tournament, so in the team meeting I ask Alan Phillips, Shaun Edwards and Robin McBryde to mark the moment in their own way. Alan, our long-serving manager, is very emotional. Like me, he played international rugby in the hard position of hooker; like me, he has a soft side. When he speaks, he cannot hide his emotions. Shaun, a true trail-blazer in the ever-evolving science of defence strategy, is incredibly generous with his words, pointing out that apart from our captain Alun Wyn Jones, every player in the room is an international because I made him one. I swallow hard at that. Robin speaks brilliantly. He has become a real force as forwards coach, increasingly influential as a talker and the very embodiment of commitment to the cause. His mother passed away during this tournament, yet he stayed the course because he felt it was his duty. 'It's what she would have wanted,' he told me. Astonishing. When he talks, incredibly positively, he makes the players laugh. Good on him.

Me? I don't say much about the game. I concentrate on what we have going for us as a group. 'One of the enduring characteristics of this team over the last few years is our complete refusal to give up,' I say. 'We never, ever give up.'

And as I watch from the coaching box, there is not the slightest whiff of a capitulation. We concede two early tries and when that happens against an All Blacks team with a point to prove, the phrase 'long day at the office' springs to mind. But we dig in. We work our way back to 14–10 with a try from Hallam Amos and five points from the boot of Rhys Patchell, who is playing with great skill and no little authority at fly-half and looks ready to fulfil his potential as a genuine Test No 10.

There is a lot of guts on show out there. Jonathan Davies, our Lions centre, isn't even close to being fully fit and I know that some of our tight forwards, like Alun Wyn and Ken Owens, have emptied themselves over the course of the tournament and are almost playing on memory alone. Yet they're giving whatever they still have to give. I'm incredibly proud of them.

Ever the optimist, I'm thinking we can stay in this game if things fall right for us. Even when Ben Smith scores a brilliant solo try to give New Zealand an eleven-point lead, I have a good feeling about the rest of the match. If we can just hold them to this until the break . . .

But we don't hold them. Ben Smith scores again with the last move of the half and two minutes after the restart,

Sonny Bill reaches into his bag of party tricks to create a try for Ryan Crotty. This is the best I've seen Sonny Bill play for quite a while. Trust him to choose tonight. If we continue to give him the run of the field, 35–10 could become 65–10 almost without us noticing. Yet even now, with the game gone and an unnerving amount of time left on the clock, we keep playing, keep asking questions, keep refusing to roll over. This is what I spoke about in the meeting. This is what counts.

At the final whistle, we've lost 40–17. As Alun Wyn says to me when I join him on the field, it would have been a whole lot worse but for the spirit in our team. Sonny Bill walks across to me and, out of the blue, shakes me by the hand and says: 'Warren, I have a huge amount of respect for you as a coach.' I thank him for his kind words.

In the changing sheds afterwards, 'respect' very much captures the mood of the occasion. Coaches and players intermingle in each other's dressing rooms, swapping jerseys and sharing thoughts and stories along with the obligatory end-of-tournament beers. It is a happy moment for me, even in defeat. Rival teams do not always share this kind of intimacy, so it is a mark of mutual respect that we can feel so relaxed together.

There will be more beers tomorrow, for sure. We will find ourselves a bar in town and say our fond farewells while the World Cup final is played out elsewhere. We would have loved to have been where South Africa and England are, but Wales will have to wait until 2023 for another shot at the ultimate prize. I'll be doing other things, and those other things start next week. On Wednesday, I have a business meeting with my new employers, the Chiefs, in Hamilton, Waikato. Which is where it all began.

1

BAREFOOT IN THE FROST

Sometimes, it's the small things that loom largest in the mind's eye. My rugby life has already spanned more than half a century – I was just five when my father introduced me to the game by taking me to a junior boys' muster session at the Eastern Suburbs club, just around the corner from our home in Hamilton – and my memory is full of big sporting moments jostling for space: my first provincial game for Waikato, my first training run with the All Blacks, my Ranfurly Shield victories, guiding Wasps to their first European title, winning Grand Slams with Wales, beating the British and Irish Lions as a player and then coaching them to a series victory in Australia and a bitterly fought draw in my own country. Yet I'm not sure if I ever felt prouder or more excited than when I was given my first pair of boots.

I would have been ten, maybe eleven, and for the previous few years, I'd played my rugby in bare feet. It didn't matter whether the pitch was as wet as slush or as dry as a desert; it made no difference whether it was ankle deep in mud or glistening with winter frost. Kids from my corner of Hamilton, which was far from the most prosperous part of town, were not accustomed to playing in boots until they were leaving childhood behind and heading towards high school. Not that it mattered to us. Every boy in the neighbourhood wanted to be an All Black, and to be an All Black you had to play rugby. Proper rugby. Whatever it was we played on a Saturday morning in the late 1960s, it wasn't 'tag' or 'touch' or ten-a-side. There were always fifteen players on each team, every one of them knocking lumps out of the next kid while busily honeypotting around the ball; and if you happened to get your hands on it, you'd run as fast and as hard as you could. It was rough and it was tough, like a game of 'Bullrush' – I think they call it 'British Bulldog' in the UK – with just a faint hint of rugby about it. And if it hadn't been for the weigh-in system, which went at least some way to ensuring that the physical disparities weren't so great as to leave large numbers of local youngsters at serious risk of orthopaedic trauma, the hospital wards might have had more weekend business than they could handle. Some kids grow faster than others and many of my friends from the local Maori community looked like giants as they mounted the scales in the clubhouse and waited for their team allocation. The rugby may have been pretty wild, but it was underpinned by a good deal of logic and common sense.

By the time I received that heaven-sent gift of a pair of boots, my head was full of rugby. As I moved through the grades as a single-minded and confident footballing No 8 – yes, really – and started playing competitive matches on a Saturday, the sport became all-consuming. Friday night was the most exciting night of the week because it was just hours from kick-off. It was the one time my mum could persuade me to go to sleep early, and I would lie there with my black and white Eastern Suburbs shirt folded neatly on the end of the bed. The boots? They would be at my side, the leather lovingly polished and the laces washed clean. I treasured them. They weren't the most up-to-date model – if they didn't quite have hobnails rather than studs, they were definitely traditional rather than futuristic – but they meant the world to me. It was not a time of plenty for us as a family in Hamilton, but my parents did their best to provide for us with the support of my grandparents.

I was the eldest child in what would become a pretty substantial family. My sister Kim was a couple of years younger than me; then came my brother Paul, another brother, Ryan, and then after another few years, my sister who was twenty-one years younger than me, Micharn. My dad Dave was a car salesman, although I have an idea in the back of my mind that he started out selling sewing machines. Remember them? They seem almost as prehistoric as hobnail rugby boots. Dad was a sportsman – a good enough back-rower to have played senior club rugby in Hamilton, which to all intents and purposes was the grade below Waikato provincial selection. My first memories are of us living in a house in a suburb called Chartwell, and thanks to Dad's job, we were never in need of a car of our own to get around: he would always arrive home with something decent in the wheels department and it felt good, being driven here and there in something brand spanking new.

As Dad was also an excellent water polo player, it goes without saying that he was very strong in the water: a talent shared by my mum Kay, who swam in the best local competitions and held a variety of records. She was a lively, positive individual who enjoyed her social life and had all the energy required to hold down a hairdressing job while raising an ever-growing family. I can't remember her not working to help make ends meet – apart from the enviable line in cars, our lifestyle was a long way short of flashy – and her absences during the working day or as part of a young married couple socialising meant that I spent a lot of time with my maternal grandparents, who had always supported their daughter as best they could. Not least when she fell pregnant with me at the age of eighteen, before she was married.

My grandfather was a particularly fascinating character. A keen photographer who showed some genuine talent in the field, he had fought in the deserts of North Africa and the Middle East during World War II and put together an album of pictures from that terrible time that I hold dear to this day. He developed emphysema, which he blamed on the sand inhaled during his tour of duty, and was a very sick man by the time I got to spend time with him. Despite his discomfort, he would happily sit for hours, breathing oxygen through his mask while telling me the stories associated with his pictures. He wasn't too fond of many of the things he saw during the war years, and I remember him saying sadly that if his experience in the region was anything to go by, there would never be peace in the Middle East (quite a premonition, as it turns out). At the same time, many of his tales were inspiring and all of them compelling. Those discussions gave me an abiding interest in history that sustained me through my school years and remains a passion to this day.

Money was tight more often than not, but my dad had ambitions of building a car sales franchise of his own as a means of improving the family fortunes. My parents sold the house in Chartwell to free up some money to invest in the new business, but from what I can recall, the venture never really threatened to take off. After a couple of years, Dad was back working for someone else, which must have been hard for him to take. As a family we moved quite a bit from one rental home to another before moving in with my grandparents for a few years. That meant changes of school, too, and when I was about twelve, I found myself moving out of my home town for the first time in my life and attending school in nearby Te Awamutu, where Dad had signed up for his latest job. I'd set my heart on attending Hamilton Boys' High School – a serious rugby and sporting establishment, over and above everything else – and had been accepted, but events conspired against me. It was Te Awamutu College, or nothing.

This was a big change for me and if it hadn't been for sport, which provided me with the solid ground I needed, I'm not sure how I would have developed. I felt I was a good student, motivated and committed in the classroom as well as in the rough and tumble of the sporting environment, but later in one of my school reports, the teacher wrote: 'Warren, life is not a rugby field!' Had I been expected to write a reply, I'd probably have said: 'You're right. The school has a cricket pitch too.' Basically, I loved any activity with a competitive edge to it. If I have one regret about my sports upbringing, it's that I didn't follow my parents' example in getting the most out of my swimming. Partly, that was down to Mum. Training in the pool is notoriously hard on kids from a very early age, and having been through the mill herself, she wasn't exactly desperate to see her children go through the same thing. But like my sister Kim and brother Paul, I was pretty capable in the water. Paul went on to compete at quite a high level.

That teacher was right, of course: rugby was an amateur game back then, and somewhere along the line, I would find myself in need of a job. A proper job. But I was a sports nut of a kid in a sports-nut country, captaining the first XV at school, winning honours in the big age-group competitions and starting to win some representative recognition at provincial level. As I got older I didn't pay enough attention to my studies as I was too occupied with sport. Throw in the cricket as an extra – I made the top team at Te Awamutu a year before others in my age group and scored a good few runs in my first season – and it's fair to say there was plenty to distract me from my studies. It wasn't a big issue: I didn't neglect my academic work completely and my performance levels didn't fall off a cliff. But when I looked to the future, the first thing I saw was an All Black shirt with my number on it. I knew from a pretty tender age that I wanted to take a proper shot at big-time rugby but I also loved my cricket and was making representative teams there too.

Funnily enough, it was cricket that gave me my chance. Some friends of mine who were students at Hamilton Boys' High invited me to play in a tournament during the school holidays and things went well for me with both bat and ball. I could play a few shots all around the wicket and while I wasn't as quick a bowler as I imagined myself to be – my delusions of Michael Holding-esque grandeur disappeared when opposition batsmen of a good standard started exposing my medium-paced inswingers for what they were – I could fight my corner well enough. After that tournament, I told my parents that I wanted to leave Te Awamutu College and go to Hamilton Boys' High, which had been my first choice all along. They saw what it meant to me and agreed that I should move back into town and live with my grandmother Nora. At long last, I was where I wanted to be.

The principal at Hamilton Boys' High was Tony Steel, an All Black who had played nine Tests on the wing just a few years previously – the first four of them against the Lions in the 1966 'blackwash' – and notched up seven tries (not to mention another thirteen in non-international appearances, at the rate of almost one a match). For a teenager like me, finally enrolling at the school I had always wanted to attend, this was really something. Back then, our rugby internationals were very much a part of the community, right in the thick of daily life, as well as being 24-carat heroes. Waikato rugby folk, by which I mean virtually the entire population, felt their presence deeply and took enormous pride in the All Blacks we produced. I was no exception. During my time playing rugby there, I got to know some of the greatest players in the history of the province: Has Catley from Taupiri, a country club where I was to play and coach, was as good a hooker as any to wear the silver fern, and the Clarke brothers, goal-kicking Don and hard-scrummaging Ian. They were our people and they meant the world to us, especially as we always believed we were in the shadow of Auckland over the Bombay Hills and were considered by the big-city types to be country cousins at best and second-class citizens at worst. They had a saying in Auckland: 'Nothing happens south of the Bombays' – meaning the Bombay Hills. No wonder we awaited the Queen's Birthday weekend with a serious degree of relish, because that was when the annual Waikato–Auckland fixture was traditionally played. There is a famous local story of Ian Clarke refereeing the game after his retirement as a player and growing so despondent at the scale of the drubbing being inflicted on his successors that he was heard to say after yet another Auckland try: 'Come on, boys. I'll give you a hand.'

In truth, Tony Steel was not one of ours. Far from it. He hailed from the South Island – born in Greymouth, educated in Christchurch – and had played all his provincial rugby for Canterbury. His life in Hamilton was about teaching, not about upbringing. But he was right up my street in the rugby sense. It is widely assumed that all New Zealanders of my age regarded Colin Meads, the great second-row superman of the All Black pack and the so-called 'Godfather' of world rugby, as the main attraction, our hero of heroes. He was certainly an iconic figure, in the days when 'iconic' was simply a word rather than a cliché, and he was representative of a certain kind of Kiwi: the farmer, the outdoors guy, the strong and silent type who could run uphill with a pile of fence posts on one shoulder and a fully-grown sheep on the other. It's also important to say that, by any reckoning, he was an exceptional player. But one of the reasons I held Tony Steel in such high regard was that despite being a back-rower, I found the glamour positions of rugby more fascinating than the muck-and-bullets side of the game, which is quite an admission from someone who ended up at the very sharpest point of the forward contest. My All Black heroes were to be found way out there on the wing: trailblazing Bryan Williams, an Aucklander of Samoan descent who did as much as anyone in history to give the Pacific Islanders a proper stake in New Zealand rugby, was one of them; and feisty little Grant Batty, who brought his small stature to bear on some extremely substantial opponents, was the other. These were the guys who caught my eye and captured my imagination. A little later, Bernie Fraser and Bruce Robertson created the magic that left me spellbound. They were backs, too. It may well come as a shock to those critics who like to accuse me of one-dimensional coaching (people repeatedly describe my tactical approach as 'Warrenball', whatever that means) but running rugby has always been my thing.

If I can't say I was personally coached by Tony Steel after I arrived as a fifth-former and before he launched a successful career in politics, I can definitely attest to the fact that under his leadership, Hamilton Boys' High started to become a real power school in the land. This has been further enhanced by the leadership of Sue Hassall, the first woman principal at the school, who has been in charge for a long time. While the private schools made their mark on the New Zealand age-group scene, it was Hamilton Boys' and the other leading state schools, from Auckland Grammar to Christchurch Boys', who were top of the pile. They may have been non-selective, with admission governed first and foremost by catchment area, but they had pupil numbers on their side, and as rugby was the game of the people, that was a big advantage. The rugby I played there was ferociously compet-itive right the way through the grades: full-on training twice a week was followed by Saturday fixtures around the North Island, with Palmerston North Boys', Gisborne Boys' and New Plymouth Boys' on the traditional fixture list as well as Auckland Grammar. They might as well have been All Black matches, such was my nervous excitement on the eve of a game, and I discovered something about myself as the seasons unfolded: namely, that I enjoyed being on edge. I found that pressure, self-imposed as well as applied from outside, brought the best out of me. Such was my progress, I was asked to captain the first XV and held the job for two years rather than the customary one. It meant the world to me.

It was Glenn Ross – the same Glenn Ross who would eventually coach at professional level in Europe with the likes of Sale, Northampton and Connacht – who guided me through my rugby years at Hamilton Boys' High and I owe him a debt of gratitude. I was still playing as a No 8 and fancied myself as not a bad loose forward, especially when I was picked to represent Waikato Schools and then made the cut for the Northern Region XV. Can I remember the name of the bloke I beat to a place in the team? Just about. His name was Michael Jones. Yes, you heard it right. *The* Michael Jones, revered to this day as one of the greatest loose forwards ever gifted to the rugby world by a country where numbers 6, 7 and 8 have ruled the roost since time immemorial. If he wasn't half bad as a player at the time, he was beyond brilliant five years or so later when New Zealand won the 1987 World Cup. Did I put him firmly in his place as we chased that spot in the Northern Region team? I wouldn't quite say that, but it wasn't long before he shifted from No 8 to the open-side flank, so maybe he knew when he was beaten! We laugh about it now because it seems so ridiculous. As Waikato Schools had won the Northern Region competition and I was captain, it was probably the reason I was selected ahead of him. A short while after the World Cup victory, when things had been restored to their proper order, I found myself playing alongside him in an invitation fixture up in Whangarei. I remember him receiving the ball on halfway, holding it under his left arm while fending off three opponents with his right hand, pirouetting past a couple more defenders on the 10-metre line and then sprinting forty metres for a try under the posts. I've racked my brains, but I don't remember ever registering a try quite like that.

My representative schools rugby was played in the early 1980s, which was when I first saw the All Blacks play live. I'd seen Waikato play a good few times, starting at the age of eight or nine: the first game I remember attending was the 1977 match against the touring Lions. They won 18–13 in front of a full house at Rugby Park, which was situated all of a third of a mile away from my grandmother's house and that day hosted some of the biggest names in the sport: Andy Irvine at full-back, Ian McGeechan in the centre, Phil Bennett at outside-half, Peter Wheeler at hooker and a seriously combative all-Welsh back row of Jeff Squire, Terry Cobner and Derek Quinnell. Yet however star-studded they may have been, I'm not sure the quality of their players registered with me. Life in New Zealand at that time was narrowly focused, if I'm being honest about it. While the All Blacks and the Waikato regulars could not have been more familiar to me, the rest of the world was both a mystery and an irrelevance.

Things were very different four years later when the Springboks came to town. Different for everyone – everyone I knew, everyone in Hamilton, everyone in the country – and not in a good way. There was no mystery about things now, because the arrival of the South Africans on our shores was overwhelmingly the biggest political issue of the day as well as the biggest sporting one, and as it tore at the fabric of New Zealand society, it could hardly have been more relevant. Forget Brexit and the disharmony it has created in the United Kingdom; this has been small beer by comparison. The Springbok tour of New Zealand in 1981 split families down the middle, put protestors on the streets in numbers few of us Kiwis imagined possible and brought civil unrest into our lives, front and centre. I remember the events of those few weeks as vividly as anything that happened in my young life, not least because I found myself present at two pivotal moments: the game against Waikato in Hamilton and the deciding game in the three-Test series against the All Blacks at Eden Park in Auckland.

In sporting terms, as in many other walks of life, the South Africans had become pariahs because of the apartheid policy of their government, and there was growing pressure on all rugby-playing countries to cut ties with them. The All Black tour down there in 1976, supported by our newly-elected Prime Minister Robert Muldoon, had led directly to a mass African boycott of the Olympic Games in Montreal later that year, and despite the signing by Commonwealth nations of the Gleneagles Agreement, which described apartheid in sport as an 'abomination' and sought to discourage contact with South Africa, Rob Muldoon stuck to his 'no politics in sport' position and allowed the '81 tour to proceed. The vast majority of elder statesmen and chief power brokers on the New Zealand Rugby Football Union were right behind the decision, yet Graham Mourie, the inspirational Taranaki flanker who had skippered the All Blacks to a first Grand Slam on the 1978 tour of the British Isles and was regarded as a serious thinker on the game, came out against the union's call and refused to play for reasons of conscience. So too did Bruce Robertson, one of my heroes. That alone gives you an idea of the rift that opened up in our rugby. I was soon to discover that the rift was a whole lot wider, and far more damaging, than a simple difference of opinion between a couple of big-name players and the board.

I was eighteen by now and I was trying to find my own way in the world, playing rugby for the Hamilton Old Boys club and living in a flat in town. When the Boks arrived for the Waikato match in late July – only the second game of the tour – I went to Rugby Park with some friends well ahead of kick-off and found a place on the terraces. There had been an anti-tour demonstration at the first game, against Poverty Bay in Gisborne, and some protestors found their way on to the pitch, only to be manhandled straight back off it again by spectators and security men. The trouble in Hamilton was of a different magnitude. The ground was jam-packed and it seemed the match would start on time, but just before the teams were due to take the field a bunch of protesters pushed through the fence, linked arms and walked on to the grass. In no time at all, there were hundreds of them. The mood wasn't the best: there were police with batons surrounding the intruders on the field and I remember people around me baying for blood, shouting and chanting and pelting the demonstrators with full cans of beer and a variety of less valuable missiles. What none of us realised immediately was that there had been some pretty serious trouble outside the ground and that once they'd made it into Rugby Park, the protestors had thrown sharp objects – tacks and nails, primarily – on to the playing surface. It was a mess, the whole thing, and as the mood darkened by the minute, there was an announcement on the sound system. The game was off. At that point, the mood was not just dark, but ugly. It stayed that way. One of my flatmates was so furious, he went into the bars that night looking for protestors, with the stated intention of giving them a hiding. He wasn't the only one with that in mind: there were a whole stack of rugby nuts feeling betrayed and prowling around town in search of someone to blame. If you happened to have been out and about in Hamilton that evening and you looked like someone who was celebrating the cancellation of the match . . . well, you were in an ocean of trouble.

What did I feel? I'd paid to go to the game and I was certainly disappointed that it failed to go ahead, so I guess that puts me in the pro-tour camp. In so far as I gave the subject any thought back then, I bought the argument that sport and politics were two different things. It wasn't a matter of being brainwashed by anyone, any more than it was a case of being ignorant of apartheid. I was as familiar with the issue as any other average guy in the street. Looking at it now, part of me sees it almost as a subconscious thing – a deep-seated assumption that as important people had made the decision to allow the tour to go ahead, life would go on as normal. Another part of me thinks it was simply a question of falling on one side of the argument or the other, depending on personal circumstances. It sounds naïve now, I accept: almost forty years on, we all know that sport and politics go hand in hand. But back then, I was just a sports-mad teenager with a ticket for the big match.

If the match in question failed to happen, a much bigger one went ahead as planned. Sort of. My dad had somehow sourced a pair of tickets for the Eden Park Test and as I'd never seen the All Blacks play live, I was well up for the occasion. We had to go through security barriers to gain access to the ground – unheard of in New Zealand in that innocent age – and however unexercised I was about the broader questions over whether or not this event should be happening, I was all too aware of the protestors congregated on the sides of the roads leading to the stadium. At one point, we passed a flatbed truck full of demonstrators. Among them was a girl, more or less my age. 'Enjoy the game, you w***ers!' she screamed as I walked past with my dad. It set the tone quite nicely: even though the game itself was a classic, with the Boks storming back into contention late on after falling a long way behind in a one-sided first half, the overriding feeling was one of siege. There were police in riot gear all over the place, determined to prevent a second Hamilton. What they couldn't prevent was an aerial bombardment from protestors in a light aircraft circling over the ground. Their weapon of choice was the flour bomb, dropped from a height of several hundred feet, and one of them landed on the All Black prop Gary Knight, who hit the deck with an almighty thump. It must have been flour of the self-raising variety, for Gary somehow managed to get back up. After a little on-field treatment, which amounted to nothing more than a dusting down, he played on. Today, he would have been an automatic candidate for a Head Injury Assessment. You can just hear the late Sir Colin Meads complaining that the game has gone soft!

Under the circumstances, it was entirely appropriate that the contest should end on a controversial note. We were standing directly behind the posts as Clive Norling, the Welsh referee, awarded a highly dubious penalty to 'us' in the fifth minute of injury time, with the scores locked at 22-all. The fate of the series rested on the narrow shoulders of the New Zealand full-back Allan Hewson and as he kicked for goal, I initially feared he'd fluffed it. But the ball changed direction on the wind and shaved its way inside the upright. It was a moment to remember, even amid all the other things about that afternoon that are difficult to forget. So ended my first direct contact with the All Blacks. The next time I watched them live, I was in the squad.

Sharing that Eden Park experience with my dad was a special thing for me. He was always very supportive of my rugby, as was my mum: they made every effort to watch me play right the way through my high school years, even if there was a lengthy trip involved. But Dad wasn't a demonstrative sort and he didn't find it easy to hand out a whole lot of praise. Even when I played pretty well, he didn't have much to say on the subject. I don't suppose this was unusual in the New Zealand of that time, where the deal seemed to be that kids were brought up macho-style, with emotional attachment kept hidden a long way beneath the surface. It didn't occur to me until I reflected on it much later on, but what I really craved as a teenager was precisely the openness that Dad didn't feel able to show. I wanted to impress him; I wanted him to acknowledge the fact that I was out there trying my hardest and doing everything I could to make him proud. On the few occasions he gave me a heartfelt 'well done', it meant everything to me. But I don't recall him ever hugging me and telling me he loved me. When I was blessed with my own children, I hugged and kissed them every day they were growing up. I still do it now, even though Bryn, my son, is a fully-fledged professional rugby player, easily fit and strong enough to throw me around like a rag doll. When, during the family beach holiday we took after the Lions tour of New Zealand in 2017, he picked me up with the intention of chucking me straight into the sea, I could be heard squealing like a pig. 'You're hurting my neck . . . seriously, you're hurting my neck.' I played in the front row with all the tough guys; Bryn is a modern day outside-half. Owning up to my physical inferiority hurts me even more, but that's modern rugby for you. These blokes are beasts.

Towards the end of my time at Hamilton Boys' High

School, I was guilty for the first and only time of allowing sport to dominate my life at the expense of my studies. If I was to stand any chance of landing a decent job for myself, higher education was the key. To get into higher education, I needed a better set of results than I'd managed in my final examinations. My history was still well up to scratch – it was the one academic subject I truly loved – but as mathematics had almost completely passed me by, my chances of making a name for myself as a theoretical physicist were fairly remote. I know now that learning stuff that doesn't come naturally to you requires maturity, and I hadn't shown enough of it. So I stayed on for another year, attending classes for one part of the day and rolling the cricket pitch for the other part. Late in the year, I had a discussion with my history teacher Peter Skerman, who also happened to be assistant coach of the rugby team. 'What are you going to do, Warren?' he asked. I didn't have much of a clue, so I just threw out the word 'university'. Peter suggested teacher training college as a practical alternative. This was something that hadn't crossed my mind, but it made perfect sense: it was a government-paid job with good holidays, and if I ever proved good enough as a rugby player to make it into a top team and go on tour, my salary would be secure. I applied for two roles – primary school teacher and secondary school history teacher – and landed the first of them. Off I went to teacher training college, happy in the knowledge that my fledgling rugby career wouldn't miss a beat.

I finished my three years of teacher training with a

diploma, a busted ankle – I did it while playing sevens – and Trudi, who has been my wife for thirty years. She was in my year at college, and as we vaguely knew each other, I pinched her on the bottom on the first day back of the third year as we were standing at the noticeboard checking out our time-table. 'Hi, how was your summer?' I asked, my bold streak disappearing rapidly into the mists of shyness, which came far more naturally to me when it came to talking with girls. There followed a spell of cat and mouse until I summoned the courage to phone her. No answer. I kept ringing for six hours and might still be ringing now if the realisation hadn't dawned on me. I had misread one of the digits. When I finally got through to Trudi, I invited her to a party. Two days later, I picked her up and stopped at an off licence to buy a bottle of wine. It was closed because of industrial action, so I found a shop and bought two bottles of Coca-Cola instead. Classy stuff. Yet despite my obvious failure to sweep her off her feet, we really hit it off. We both spoke the language of sport, which helped: Trudi was a good netball player while her father, Terry Shaw, had played full-back for Thames Valley when they beat the Wallabies in 1962 and dropped the winning goal – the most celebrated sporting moment in the history of the province. He had also played cricket for Northern Districts so was a very talented sportsman. She had two rugby-playing brothers into the bargain, Clif and Paddy, both of whom played for the NZ Secondary Schools team; Paddy played with the likes of Jeff Wilson, Carlos Spencer and Jonah Lomu, no less. If success really comes down to the company you keep, I was in good company.

Finally, there came a moment when Trudi and I were walking home one day, wheeling our bikes and I asked: 'I couldn't have a kiss, could I?' She leaned forward and . . . tripped over her bike, landing awkwardly on top of it. I helped her to her feet, as any gentleman would, so in the most literal sense, I had truly picked her up. We often talk about that first kiss.

Right the way through my time at college, I played for Hamilton Old Boys – a very strong club, one of the best around – and it was during my time in the Under-21s that a guy called George Simpkin suggested I might make it as a hooker if I made the switch from No 8. His logic was that while I had good skills, I would never be the tallest or the quickest. Why listen to George? There was one very good reason: he was coaching the Waikato provincial team at the time and was therefore a pretty big fish in the local pond. It was a serious suggestion from a serious rugby man and I treated it as such. I believed I was a good No 8, but was I good enough to be special? The honest answer was: 'Probably not.' The hooking role, on the other hand, opened up some new possibilities. I already had the skills and the hands, and while I didn't run around trying to beat people up, I was as intensely competitive as anyone I'd come up against. As for the technical side of scrummaging and line-out throwing . . . well, I could learn that stuff. The more I considered it, the bigger an opportunity it seemed. After a few positional dabbles in 1983, I made the leap in '84. It was a challenge – everything in the front row was a challenge of mind, body and spirit in those days and I don't think it's much different now – but the moment I committed myself to making a go of it, I couldn't get enough of the No 2 shirt.

I had to bide my time and show patience. There was no coming straight in from the age-groups and ruling the roost, as the better players do now. At Hamilton Old Boys, there were players in their thirties showing no sign of moving aside for some spotty kid with ideas above his station. Not to put too fine a point on it, there were real live All Blacks playing club rugby in Hamilton. But I knuckled down, trained hard, soaked up every last snippet of information about the art of set-piece survival – rule number one: if the scrum is collapsing, go face down in the mud rather than tuck your head under and break your neck – and waited for a chance. It came in a game against Tokoroa, renowned home town of such World Cup combatants as Walter Little, Richard Kahui and Quade Cooper, among others. From a Tokoroa scrum, their backs moved the ball straight along the line, at which point I smashed their wing into touch having ripped across the field like a proper athlete. The No 7 actually said to me: 'Jeez, where the hell did *you* come from?' A short while later, I was the senior hooker at Hamilton Old Boys.

Sports people talk a lot these days about 'steep learning curves'. Looking back at that early point in my hooking career, the curve was as steep as the upper reaches of Mount Taranaki. At school under Glenn Ross, we'd gone through a whole season without kicking the ball, such was our desire to play fast, positive, attractive rugby. (The fact that four of our threequarters had not only run in the New Zealand Schools sprint relay final but had actually won it may have convinced Glenn that this was the way forward.) Now, playing with the grown-ups, it was all about territory. This took some getting used to, but I adjusted to the new reality quickly enough. So quickly, in fact, that I was selected for Waikato in 1985, a year after converting to hooker. Bruce Hodder, a bigger forward than me and technically sound, was the main man and he kept me sitting on the bench for the whole of my first season at provincial level. Which was a disappointment, not least because Waikato struggled badly and ended up being relegated from the top division. I almost got on against Manawatu, but as I'd popped a shoulder joint in training on the eve of the game and would have had to do my line-out throwing underarm, I was pleased to be overlooked. When the final match of the season came around, against Taranaki, I was absolutely desperate for a run and couldn't help wondering why the selectors went for Bruce yet again. What harm would it have done to play me, given the circumstances?

Just before kick-off, Bruce approached me and offered to feign an injury midway through the contest. It was his way of helping me out. My reply? 'Thanks, but please don't do that. When my first game comes, I want to feel I've deserved it.' I wouldn't have long to wait.

2

A MOOLOO MAN DOES THE HAKA

As anyone who has ever thrown a ball into a line-out will confirm without thinking twice, timing is everything. Just as I was on the rise as a potential successor to Bruce Hodder as the number one hooker in Waikato, the team were on the slide into the second tier of provincial rugby in New Zealand – absolutely not the place where the loyal local supporters wanted or expected us to be. Relegation hurt so badly, and there was a deep feeling in and around Rugby Park that we were at a crossroads. Which meant possible changes of focus and direction. If I could improve the weaker areas of my game while building on my strengths, I would be in a perfect position to seize the moment.

If I'd designed the 1986 season to my own specifications, it couldn't have gone better. I was selected to start a pre-season game against Taranaki, which we won: no mean feat, as the New Plymouth crew were a first division outfit. Bruce decided to call it quits in Hamilton and head off overseas so I was selected as the number one hooker. As for the second division games themselves, we were too good for the opposition and won each and every contest, generally by a good margin. The one close shave was the promotion decider with North Harbour, who had a loose forward by the name of Wayne Shelford. 'Buck', as he was known by everyone from Whangarei to Invercargill, was a New Zealand captain in waiting and a very formidable opponent indeed. In front of our own full-house crowd, we won by a point. I remember us defending for our lives in our 22, behind on the scoreboard and up against the clock, when we snaffled one last piece of possession and went the length. Daryl Halligan, a wing who went on to forge a professional career in rugby league, was the man who touched down. Pretty much everyone in the ground was ecstatic, including one of the 'home town' touch judges, who jumped in the air with joy as the try was completed. In those days, the neutrality of officials was not always guaranteed.

That victory was the start of something for Waikato because we knew there were some strong-willed and talented players heading towards the first team, most of them local products, the rest from rival provinces. During that promotion run, we had Ian Foster (a World Cup-winning assistant coach with the All Blacks in 2015) at first five and John Mitchell, a familiar rugby face around the globe, at No 8. The following season, the brilliant breakaway Duane Monkley – quite possibly the best player never to win a New Zealand Test cap – laid claim to the No 7 shirt. In '88, we added Steve Gordon and Brett Anderson to our engine room options and introduced Richard Jerram on the blind-side flank; in '90, the back division was bolstered by players as good as Matthew Cooper at full-back or centre, Rhys Ellison in midfield and Simon Crabb at half-back. This was the backbone of the side who would win a first NPC title for the province in 1992 and beat the British and Irish Lions a year later. It was an exercise in team-building, drawing together like-minded people who wanted nothing more than to compete with Auckland, who had a stranglehold on New Zealand rugby affairs.

If those years of gathering momentum meant the world to the 'Mooloo' folk among whom I'd grown up (the term Mooloo goes back to 1951 and refers to when the ceremonial cow was anointed as the club's first official mascot), it was nothing to the bliss I felt being a first-choice member of the front row. Especially given the way we played. With the single exception of Auckland, who were very strong up front and knew how to mix it at close quarters, we felt we could dominate our opponents at scrum time and maul them into oblivion. During one game against Wellington, played in the kind of gale-force conditions for which that city is notorious, we rolled a maul seventy metres to the goal-line: churning it up, breaking round the edges, churning it up again, all the way home. Opponents knew how to stop us in the theoretical sense. In practice, it was a different matter entirely. As a pack of forwards, we revelled in our supremacy. Country cousins? We wanted to beat Auckland as they were the benchmark and probably the best team in the world at the time.

After two seasons in the senior team, I was awarded the captaincy. There were people who had been in the side longer than me, but I was twenty-five, ambitious both for myself and for the province, and I felt I had enough leadership experience to justify the decision of Duncan Dysart, the head coach at the time. I had spent a good chunk of my age-group rugby being the first out of the shed and ended up skippering Hamilton Old Boys into the bargain. Never once had it fazed me. In fact, I'd loved the responsibility of captaincy and, looking back, I think it hot-housed me in terms of game understanding. But that experience in '88 was anything but fulfilling and at the end of my stint, I promised myself I'd never do it again.

Why? If I'm being honest, I felt undermined by one of our best-known and most successful players, Richard Loe. Richard was not a local – a South Islander, he had played for Canterbury and Marlborough before joining us – but he was a major contributor to Waikato's recovery from the relegation season and our drive towards major honours. He was also my front-row mucker – a prop with a well-earned reputation for iron strength, allied to a ruthless streak that made tough men think twice about crossing him. He had his fair share of disciplinary trouble over the course of a long career and ended up being regarded far and wide as one of rugby's 'bogey men'. None of that worried me. What *did* concern me during my year as captain was his attitude. He was already an All Black and a man of forthright views. On a bad day, he was more than forthright, to the point of being antagonistic. He wasn't the easiest to get along with, basically, and I eventually decided it might be better to concentrate on my hooking and leave the arguing to someone else.

That someone else turned out to be John Mitchell, who succeeded me as captain and ended up doing the job through the glory years, although Richard was also given a chance to lead by Glenn Ross, who took over as our coach in the late 1980s. I thought it was a clever idea to appoint Richard, on the basis that school bullies can often make the best prefects, but there was a game against Canterbury where we were thumped by almost fifty points and it brought out the worst in him. I remember standing behind the posts late in the game, feeling thoroughly miserable, when I heard Richard berating people about costing him his latest shot at All Black selection. It was one of those 'Whooooaaa . . ' moments. Together with my good friend Andrew Strawbridge, a goal-kicking regular in the team, we told Glenn that the atmosphere was becoming rotten. Glenn sent Richard home mid tour and asked me if I'd consider another shot at the captaincy. I declined. I'd promised myself I would never go there again and I'm as stubborn as a mule. But in the spirit of co-operation, I added that John was the best man for the job anyway. Under Mitch, we would soon win our first NPC title, enjoy an exquisite taste of Ranfurly Shield glory and luxuriate in that great win over the Lions. Something tells me it was one of my better suggestions.

I played a lot of rugby with Mitch – and against him too, whenever Hamilton Old Boys took on Fraser Tech in the most hotly-contested club derby in town. In fact, I saw him on a daily basis during my teacher training years, for the very good reason that we shared a flat. My old friend Karl, the protestor-hunting vigilante circa 1981, was also a tenant. Of the three of us, I was by an interstellar distance the tidiest, to the extent that I felt like a house mum. We had one of those old agitator washing machines – the top-loading type that saved you money on the bills while shortening the lifespan of your clothing, thereby leaving you with a delicate cost-benefit calculation. Not that it was too delicate in our case. I remember going away for a weekend, leaving Mitch and Karl to look after themselves. Big mistake. When I returned on the Monday, that bloody washing machine had been going nonstop for the best part of seventy-two hours . . . with the same load. Needless to say, the clothes inside were as black as soot. As I wasn't naturally suited to clearing up after people, my mood was every bit as dark.

If Mitch went about his rugby in a hard, cold-eyed way, underpinned by outstanding athleticism – he played basketball to a high level, as well as union – and a very high level of fitness for those times, Duane Monkley was one of those utterly dependable performers who never seemed to let his standards slip. The '93 Lions had never heard of him when they arrived in Hamilton for the penultimate game of their tour, but they didn't remain ignorant for long. By the time they boarded their bus and headed for Auckland for the final Test, none of them could work out why they wouldn't be facing him at Eden Park. Duane was fit, committed, a master of the full range of back-row arts and off-the-scale tough. I remember him playing for Waikato with a badly broken hand. Even though he couldn't flex it even a fraction of a degree, he simply strapped it up before kick-off and got on with the job. How hard is that? As a No 7, you spend half your life on the floor in search of a ball to steal and the other half tearing around the field in search of opponents to tackle. The ability to transition between the two – to get off the deck in the twinkling of an eye and reach the next port of call ahead of everyone else – is the key skill for an open-side specialist. That day, Duane could use only one of his hands to push himself back to his feet. Did anyone notice? It certainly didn't register with me, and I was as close to him as most.

Why did the national selectors ignore him? We may never know. He wasn't the tallest player, and in the days before line-out lifting, height tended to be a factor in piecing together a back-row unit. But Duane made up for it in so many ways, it is not a satisfactory explanation. He deserved so much more.

Progress is never as rapid as you'd like it to be, especially when you're young and impatient, and we had our knockbacks. Our Ranfurly Shield game against Auckland in 1987 certainly didn't go to plan. They had all the big names strutting their stuff – Grant Fox, Alan Whetton, Zinzan Brooke, you name them – and put thirty points on us. It underlined the fact that the big population centres still held sway and we'd have to shift heaven and earth to break up the urban domination. Yet on the other hand, I loved playing in that game. It was painful, yes, but I had an insatiable thirst for knowledge and there was no better way of learning than going up against the people setting the standard. Sure enough, things finally shifted in our direction. We beat Auckland away from home in 1992 and again in '93, and they didn't cross our line in either match. The first game was an NPC semi-final and we were the ones who scored the tries, Simon Crabb bagging two and Wayne Warlow the other. Auckland responded only through the Fox boot, yet even then they kept their swagger. 'If that had been a Shield game,' Zinzan said to me at full-time, 'you wouldn't have won.' I tucked that comment away in the corner of my mind reserved for thoughts of the next encounter.

When we went to Eden Park the following year, the Shield *was* at stake. Auckland had been in possession of the Log o' Wood for eight long years, defending it on more than sixty occasions. It was an astonishing record, so for us to beat them 17–6 on their own dirt – Ian Foster scored the game's only try and also dropped a goal, with Matt Cooper adding the rest in penalties – was special. I didn't remind Zinzan of his remark – not because I was too polite, but because I didn't happen to stumble across him amid the bedlam following the full-time whistle – but I do remember saying to his great back-row partner Michael Jones: 'Come on, Michael, you've held it for long enough.' I was so tired at the end, I didn't go up for the presentation ceremony. I went straight to the changing rooms instead and spent a few minutes by myself, trying to make sense of what we'd achieved. Then we all travelled back to Hamilton on the team bus, stopped off at Rugby Park for a beer or two . . . and found 15,000 locals waiting for us. It was a pinnacle moment for me, maybe the most rewarding of all in my time as a player. And when I reflected on it afterwards, I admitted to myself that I owed Auckland a debt of gratitude. They had been the benchmark down the years and they'd shaped my rugby thinking. They taught me how to play the situation and the referee, where to find the short cuts, how to 'cheat' creatively, how to turn guilt into innocence. In other words, I learned the craft of rugby by playing against them. It was a priceless education.

I don't suppose I would have come under consideration for a place among the All Black elite if I hadn't demonstrated an ability to perform against the very best the New Zealand provincial game had to offer, but it wasn't a meeting with Auckland that propelled me towards a shot at Test rugby. My year as captain coincided with the 1988 Wales tour of New Zealand and if there were some high-calibre players in the visiting party – Ieuan Evans, Jonathan Davies, Robert Jones and Dai Young had all blossomed at the inaugural World Cup the previous year, while the likes of Staff Jones and Bob Norster had been Test Lions against the All Blacks in 1983 – they didn't add up to much on this occasion. We hosted the opening game of the eight-match programme and won 28–19. For me, it was one of those wonderful days when the ball repeatedly came my way. I must have contributed a dozen carries, fifteen maybe, and when that happens to any hooker he tends to catch the eye. The invitation to an All Black trial was immediate and with Sean Fitzpatrick cemented in as first choice, I found myself up against Hika Reid, a fully-fledged international from the Bay of Plenty who had been around the block more than once and knew what was what. 'You win your ball, I'll win mine,' he said to me at the first scrum. I wasn't having any of it. Here was an old fella chasing his last hurrah and trying to play me. I decided to decline his generous offer and went after him with all the energy I could muster. It worked. I was duly picked for the forthcoming trip to Australia.

Had I stopped to think about it, I might have been a little unnerved: after all, this had come to me fast, in only my third season as a provincial front-rower. But there was precious little time for thought. Right ahead of me was a thirteen-match road trip on the far side of the Tasman and I'd be a busy boy. Back then, tour parties were tiny: twenty-six players, one coach, a manager, a doctor and a physio. That was it. Tough as he was, not even Sean Fitzpatrick could play all eighty minutes of each and every fixture. This was a massive opportunity for me and when I arrived in the Takapuna area of Auckland for the pre-departure training stint, I was mentally on edge and physically prepared. The long and short of it was this: I felt I deserved to be there. Not that there weren't some shocks in store. Alex Wyllie – 'Grizz' to those who knew him, which included the entire New Zealand rugby community and countless other union followers around the world – was the coach and he was not in a mood to dilute his reputation as the hardest of hard men by going soft on his squad. The training was tougher, miles tougher, than anything I'd experienced even with Waikato, where I'd seen grown men cry with the pain. I considered myself to be as fit as anyone, but believe me, there were moments in those sessions when I didn't know which way was up.

Two things helped me through. The first was the pride I felt in being an All Black, with my photograph in the *New Zealand Herald* and my silver-ferned training gear in my kitbag. The second was peer pressure. If Grizz told you to run to the line in the warm-up, that's what you did. You didn't stop six inches short. If he ordered you to run a lap of the field, you didn't take a metre off the corner. Those were the values and to a man, the senior players upheld them. They knew that when it came down to the last five minutes in a big match, it was always the discipline that counted. The moment John Kirwan or Grant Fox or our captain Buck Shelford spotted someone going easy on himself, they would dish out the mother and father of a bollocking, right to his face in front of everyone else. If you wanted to hang with the All Blacks, you didn't take the same liberty twice.

Then there were the team meetings, held in the absence of Grizz and the management. Time and again, the newcomers were reminded of the importance of the jersey, the responsibility it carried, the depth of ambition we were all expected to share. Who did the talking? Buck's was the major voice, but Foxy was big into it too. John Kirwan and Gary Whetton were also towering figures in the squad, while another small group – Alan Whetton, Michael Jones and Steve McDowell – were a little quieter but still highly influential. It was fascinating to see them up close. Buck never lost a game as All Black captain, and looking back on his tenure from a distance, it is easy to see why: he wasn't the greatest rugby player in the world in the technical sense, but when it came to putting his body on the line, running through a brick wall, never complaining, leading from the front, setting an example . . . there was no better person on earth to do those things. By comparison, a wondrously gifted footballing forward like Gary Whetton was nowhere near as driven. In moments of strife, all of us, seasoned internationals and newcomers, turned to Buck. I had, and retain to this day, the greatest respect for him.

We flew from Auckland to Perth, where I was due to make my debut in the tour opener against Western Australia. After six or seven hours in the air, the doctor John Mayhew told us we should check into the hotel and head straight down to a big grassy space on the bank of the Swan River and prepare ourselves for a light run and a stretch. Some light run, some stretch. Grizz flogged the hell out of us for an hour and a half. John Kirwan, in particular, went off his nut. We'd trained exceptionally hard in Auckland and now this, just before the game. Yet there was method in the Wyllie madness. He always identified the games we could go into tired and still win, and Western Australia was one of them.

It quickly dawned on me that this was longer-term, big-picture stuff. In the week of a genuinely big game, he was happy to back off. Having said that, I'm not sure that eve-of-match session did me any favours. We put sixty points on the opposition, but my hamstrings were tight and my legs felt dead right from the start. I was bitterly disappointed. All game, I kept thinking to myself: 'I'm running around this bloody field, trying as hard as I've ever tried, and the game is passing me by.'

On reflection, it wasn't merely the Wyllie approach to training that left me for dead that day. The haka was equally to blame. I was more nervous and afraid of participating in the most celebrated pre-match ceremonial act in the whole wide world of sport than I was of anything else, including my first line-out throw. It was All Black ritual for debutants to perform it for the rest of the team the evening before the game. They would decide if I was passing muster and left me in no doubt that there would be some serious consequences if I came up short. Every minute of my spare time seemed to go on rehearsing the damned thing until it became almost second nature. The Friday-night team meeting was the critical moment and I was in a right old state beforehand. It wasn't simply a fear of having the piss taken out of me. It was far more serious than that. There was an onus on me to get it absolutely right: the actions, the words, the pauses, every last comma and full stop. No wonder my legs were heavy straight from kick-off. I'd spent days squatting down in my room yelling 'Ka Mate!' at the top of my voice.

Buck was central to haka affairs. Before he came into the side, the traditional Maori war dance had been performed only before matches in other parts of the world. From 1986 onwards, it played a part in our home games too. It wasn't merely a case of greater frequency, either. Under Buck, the haka became a different animal entirely: there was more aggression, more attitude, more feeling. His Maori background gave him a deep understanding of the haka tradition, of the nature of the thing, and he saw it as an essential part of our make-up – an expression of our intensity and a way of imposing ourselves on the opposition. In short, he weaponised the haka. This suited me perfectly. As I'd played with and against the Maori all my rugby life and developed a good many friendships with people from that community, I was completely comfortable with the greater emphasis Buck placed on this aspect of All Black life.

I played six games on that Aussie tour and came home thinking I'd done myself a bit of good, but I wouldn't wear the black shirt on the field again until the following year, when we toured Wales and Ireland. One reason was that in the days of the six-man replacements' bench, we didn't always include a specialist hooker. Steve McDowell, a brilliant prop, felt he could play across the front row in emergency situations and that allowed the selectors to stack up on locks and loose forwards. The main reason, however, was Sean Fitzpatrick and his remarkable physical resilience, bordering on indestructability.

He was such a tough opponent: hard, cunning, edgy,

ruthless, a master of the wind-up and, in the best possible way, a bit of a chancer. He scored more than his fair share of tries running those 'goal-hanger' lines in the wide areas of the field and loved every second of his time with the ball in his hands. He was a good scrummager, too, and we had some rare old battles in that department. I did, however, consider myself to be the better line-out thrower – the skill at the top of my 'work-on' list throughout my years in top-flight rugby. I wasn't alone in taking that view. I remember watching a game in 1995, just after my retirement, and hearing Keith Quinn, the most familiar of New Zealand commentators, say: 'Fitzpatrick to throw in. Probably the best thrower in the world . . . now Warren Gatland's no longer around.' Those words gave me a warm glow of satisfaction, although I'd have happily foregone the compliment in exchange for just one international cap.

Fitzy denied me that cap by delivering time and again in the Test environment and being so determined to stay on the field until the bitter end that it was almost a matter of religious conviction. For my part, I probably won more games against him than any hooker in the world. I felt we had a positive relationship, given the intensity of the Waikato–Auckland rivalry and the fact that we were fighting over the same international shirt, but there was the odd moment of strain. He had a mean streak, for sure, and while I was far from the most evil front-rower in history and went out of my way to play it fair, I wasn't fond of taking backward steps. There was a big provincial game at Eden Park when Fitzy ran straight at me and I picked him up clean off his feet and slammed him into the floor. It was a proper spear tackle – a cardinal sin in today's game but more or less legal back then. The following season, he waited for his chance and did the same to me. 'That's for last year,' he said, with one of his trademark wolfish grins. On another occasion, he almost removed my ear from my head with a handy bit of footwork at a ruck. I was so pumped up, I didn't realise the extent of the damage until I felt the sting of it in the shower. Agony. For the only time in my career, I thought to myself: 'If I ever get the opportunity, he's going to have some back.' As it happened, the chance never arose. Fitzy never seemed to be there on the floor, ripe for the picking, so to speak. And to be honest, I wasn't going out of my way to look for it. If you start head hunting, you're not concentrating on your game.

The 1989 trip, which began with a one-off game against British Colombia in Vancouver, was in essence a major tour of Wales and Ireland with all the front-line sides in those countries on the fixture list. It was a lively adventure, to say the very least, because various things happened on the field that would simply not be permitted in this day and age. I scored a try, my second and last in an All Black jersey, in the game against Swansea at St Helen's, but my recall is limited to the footage still hanging around on YouTube. Why? Because I was semi-conscious. Early in the match, I sprinted off the defensive line as the Welsh team tapped a penalty and as I tackled Billy James, my opposite number, there was the delightful cracking sound of knee on head.

His knee, my head. I was knocked out, clean as a whistle, and as there were no on-field medical assessments in those days, it was up to me to come round quickly and get on with it. Which I did, in a way. At one point, I saw the ball come into a scrum, apparently in slow motion, and took what seemed like an eternity to realise that it was my job to hook it back. And then there was the line-out incident. I thought I heard Buck Shelford call a throw to Alan Whetton, but when I looked up, Alan wasn't there. Andy Earl, a versatile South Islander who revelled in his image as a tough outdoorsman, was there instead, having come on as an early replacement. As I'd had my memory bank wiped clean by the James knee, I was just a little flummoxed. It was left to Richard Loe, my tight-head prop that day, to appraise Andy, or 'Worzel' as he was generally known on account of his wild hair, of the situation. 'Gats doesn't have the first idea of where he is,' I heard him say, his voice eerily faint. Andy nodded, turned to me and, in his gruff Canterbury tones, gave me the benefit of his wisdom. 'If you're not right, get off the field,' he said. My reply? 'Worzel, the only way I'm going off is on a f***ing stretcher.' He smiled and said: 'Gats, I like that.' It was a slow process, but I recovered my senses in time to track a high kick and score by the posts. We won 37–22.

Ten days later, I was on duty again. Newport were the opposition on this occasion and it was there, in front of a full house at Rodney Parade, that Buck Shelford's tooth-and-claw approach to rugby was laid bare. When they took the field, the Newport players headed straight for the far end of the field and stood deep in their own 22 – a clear indication that when it came to the haka, they wouldn't be anywhere near the halfway line to accept its implicit challenge. Buck considered this to be very bad form: if turning your back on the haka, as various Wallaby teams had done on occasion, was disrespectful, running away from it was beyond contemptible. He led us all the way down the pitch towards the Newport sticks and told us to perform the haka in front of their faces. That set the tone. We were pretty fierce that day and made a real mess of our hosts, putting more than fifty points past them. Their hooker was a guy called Keiron Gregory, who was bold enough to have a strike at our ball in every scrum and cheeky enough to ask me if I'd take it easy on the grounds that he was suffering from a sore neck. 'I'll take it a bit easier if you keep your bloody foot to yourself and stop striking on our put-in,' I responded. At the next scrum, he had another go and pinched the ball. I was so furious, I collapsed the scrum on him. It was dog eat dog – that was the spirit of the age – and as he'd broken an agreement, he had to accept the consequences. There again, I could have caused him a very serious injury by dragging down that set-piece, with all the human tonnage involved. How would I have felt then? It wasn't my finest moment on a rugby field.

We really hit our straps that day at Rodney Parade and turned in some accomplished performances from thereon in. Wales were beaten very comfortably in Cardiff, after which we crossed the Irish Sea for games against all four provinces, with a Test scheduled between the Connacht and Ulster fixtures. Grizz gave me a run against Leinster – we won 36–9 – and again against Connacht. I knew I wouldn't be starting the international at Lansdowne Road because Fitzy was showing no sign whatsoever of physical frailty, but I did assume I'd play in Belfast, not least because I absolutely worked my balls off in the Connacht match and felt I'd produced some of my best rugby. Bewilderingly, the coach had reached a different conclusion. All he said to me after our 40–6 win in Galway was: 'I don't think you played that well out there.' I disagreed with him, but disagreeing with Grizz was usually a waste of breath. So it turned out. He picked Fitzy for the Ulster match, even though it was being played just three days after the Test. I couldn't hide my disappointment, and it still rankles now.

In effect, it was the end of my tour. The only remaining piece of business was a weekend meeting with the Barbarians at Twickenham. At close of play, Grizz walked up to me as I was chatting to Ron Williams, our prop from North Harbour. Grizz had a habit of poking a fairly formidable finger into your chest when he engaged you in conversation, and he was in full prodding mode as he said: 'Warren, were you ready today?'

I wasn't quite on his wavelength. 'Eh?'

'Were you ready today?'

'Umm . . . why should I have been?' By now I had cottoned on and was keen to string him along.

'Because Fitzy got injured and we had to wrap a bandage round his head. So were you ready?'

'No, Grizz, I wasn't.'

'Whaddya mean, no? Why the hell not?'

'Because, Grizz, you didn't pick me on the bench.'

There was a pause as Grizz weighed things up, followed by an embarrassed squirm, a bark of disgust and a rapid retreat. Ron, another front-rower declared surplus to requirements that day, was reduced to tears of laughter. He may still be laughing now.

I may have seen things a little differently to Grizz from time to time, especially on the subject of my own form, but I learned a hell of a lot from him. He had interesting, forward-thinking ideas about fitness and despite his reputation as a player – he had been an unapologetically aggressive member of the Canterbury pack who laid waste to the Lions in the spectacularly violent Battle of Christchurch in 1971 – his coaching was all about pace and intensity and heads-up decision-making. Even when he was at his most extreme, as in that training session in Perth ahead of my first All Blacks outing, there was usually a carefully thought-out strategy behind it. If I had to criticise his approach more than thirty years on, during which I've learned a fair bit about the art and science of coaching, it is that he could occasionally be tactically inflexible.

Our tour of France in 1990, during which we lost our first games in Europe for four years, was a case in point. I didn't play in the opener in Toulon, where a Provence–Côte d'Azur Invitation XV took us by surprise on a good track in front of 15,000 locals, winning 19–15. I *did* play in Bayonne thirteen days later when a Côte Basque–Landes selection led by the big-kicking Test outside-half Jean-Patrick Lescarboura beat us 18–12. We fielded a strong side that day – John Kirwan and Terry Wright were on the wings; Graeme Bachop was at half-back; Richard Loe and Murray Pierce were in the tight five; the back-row combination of Alan Whetton, Michael Jones and Mike Brewer was pretty stellar – yet we played the wrong game in slippery conditions. The situation was crying out for a forward-oriented driving approach, but that was anathema to Grizz. I remember thinking: 'Our rugby may be attractive to watch, but we're being robotic rather than smart if we aren't prepared to make adjustments on the basis of the evidence in front of us.' In short, it would have been better if Grizz had shown just a little more trust in his players and encouraged them to make decisions on the run.

There again, it's only a minor quibble. Those days with the All Blacks will always stay with me. On that visit to France, hundreds of people turned up just to watch us train, and I remember saying to myself: 'This is something precious. Don't take it for granted, because you're one injury away from never experiencing it again.' I had the same feeling a year later in Argentina, where I played games in Cordoba, Buenos Aires and Mar del Plata. The rugby was hard, even though we went back to service as usual with nine straight wins, but the food was right up my street – steak, steak, more steak, added steak and extra steak, all topped off with steak. We had some very late nights in a late-night country and enjoyed ourselves immensely. Even Andy Earl, for whom Buenos Aires must have come as a serious shock to his South Island system. We were both picked on the bench for the second of the two Tests against the Pumas and while I had almost given up waiting for Sean Fitzpatrick to present me with an even break in the form of an international cap, Andy certainly felt he'd be playing an active role for the very good reason that Alan Whetton, our first-choice No 6, had been struggling with a hamstring all week. Ten minutes or so into the game, off limped Alan. Andy didn't move an inch. 'Worzel, you're on – get yourself out there!' I shouted, the other replacements joining in the chorus. Still he stayed put. Eventually, he dragged himself to his feet with all the speed of an elderly giraffe and growled, to everyone within earshot: 'I should have been on that bloody field in the first place!!!'

How many Tests did I spend manacled to the bench, waiting for Fitzy to break down and walk off the field in an act of front-row solidarity? I honestly don't know, because I never kept count. There were quite a few of them, for sure. Do I hold a grudge? Not at all. When you go away on a tour as the number two, how will you get to be number one? There are only two ways. Either the senior team plays poorly and the selectors make changes, or a guy gets himself injured. Personally speaking, I never wished injury on anyone and I always considered the ultimate success of the group to be massively important. I'd have liked to have had my chance, but a big part of touring for me was to be a positive influence on the group. You don't do that by wandering around with your head down or throwing your toys out of the pram. My job in those times was to help the team prepare, and as a coach today, I make it clear to my players that they should behave in exactly the same way. Yes, I expect them to believe that they're good enough to be in the run-on team and to be disappointed if and when they miss out. But I also expect them to rise above that disappointment and contribute.

This is a crucial aspect of the team dynamic and when the Lions go on tour to the southern hemisphere and have to become more than the sum of their disparate parts in a few horribly short weeks, it is absolutely make or break. The best example? Brian O'Driscoll in Australia in 2013. We dropped Brian for the final Test against the Wallabies in Sydney and it was quite a call: I don't suppose he'd ever been dropped by anyone, so it must have rocked him to be over-looked by the very coach who had given him his first Test cap. Yet he took it on the chin and made sure he gave everything of himself in helping those picked ahead of him to prepare for the big night. Rhys Long, our analyst on that tour, recounted that after the team announcement, he found himself sharing the hotel lift with the great Irish centre. 'I've talked the talk,' Brian said to him. 'Now I have to walk the walk.' It was his way of saying that he understood how vital it was that he did his bit. He'd spent a good part of his career as a captain, telling people 'yes, you've missed out, but you still have big responsibilities and we need you.' This was the moment for him to demonstrate at first hand how it should be done. Which is what he did. For that, along with so many other things, he has my respect.

Little did I imagine that when I took the field for the Mar del Plata game at the Estadio José María Minella, I was bidding farewell to All Black rugby. With the 1991 World Cup within touching distance, I felt I was in a good place to push for a place in the squad. I was wrong. When the team was announced for the Bledisloe Cup Test with Australia in Auckland – a major World Cup staging post – I wasn't in it. Graham Dowd, a good player from North Harbour who could play prop as well as hooker, was there on the bench instead of me. John Mayhew, the long-serving All Blacks doctor, told me that the line-up had been changed late on, which suggested that I'd been in the original selection but lost out in a sudden rejig. What lay behind it? I never went out of my way to uncover the specific details, but I suspect it had plenty to do with the fact that ahead of the tournament, the coaching team had been expanded to include John Hart and selector Peter Thorburn. John was a very different man to Grizz in both personality and approach: he was a smooth operator, urbane and articulate, and a very deep thinker on the game. Peter, meanwhile, had been coaching North Harbour and knew Graham's strengths as a versatile front-rower who ticked plenty of boxes. The decision had an impact on me – to be absolutely frank, I was gutted – but after a while, the pain eased. To have been an All Black was, and remains, a good reason to count your blessings. I've been doing that for half my life.

There was a postscript, of a kind. The All Blacks were knocked out at the semi-final stage of that World Cup by an inspired Wallaby outfit, for whom David Campese had one of his golden days on the wing, and relinquished the title. What was more, there hadn't been much in the way of harmony behind the scenes, where Grizz and John Hart proved to be an ill-starred pairing. A change at the top was inevitable and it came in the form of Laurie Mains, a former Test full-back from Dunedin who was appointed national head coach in 1992. I was back doing my provincial thing with Waikato when he contacted me to ask if I was interested in playing in a forthcoming All Black trial in Napier. It would be run on the basis of a Test XV against The Rest, with Sean Fitzpatrick in his customary place and me in mine. I accepted. Terry Shaw, my father-in-law, gave me a lift to Napier and I proceeded to perform to my maximum. Jonah Lomu played for us that day and we duly beat the 'elite' side. More importantly from my perspective at the time, I took one against the head off Fitzy and we scored straight from the scrum. I heard later that Graham Dowd, who was sitting on the bench, said about himself: 'I've got as much chance of making the Test team as Donald Duck, the way Gats played today.' Yet when the team was picked for the first international of the year against the touring Irish, I wasn't in it.

I knew then that my time was up, even though I was quickly asked to lead a New Zealand A team against England

B, who were skippered by Stuart Barnes, now of Sky Sports fame, and were a good enough side to contribute a bunch of players to the Lions squad when they toured New Zealand the following year. Ironically enough, our side was coached by . . . Peter Thorburn. I'd like to think that by the end of that little adventure, he understood more about me than he had the previous year. It was also the first time he'd worked with Duane Monkley, our local flanker-hero in Mooloo land. Peter was taken aback by him. 'Crikey,' he said to me. 'Someone told me he was good, but I didn't know he was *that* good.' Even if we kept it to ourselves, the Waikato players in the squad felt vindicated. I felt like saying to Peter: 'This is what you see when you look outside of Auckland.'

At least there was plenty left for me to enjoy on the New Zealand scene. At club level, I'd moved to Taupiri, a tiny township on the eastern bank of the Waikato River. There was a chance to coach as well as play and there were a few dollars in it for me, together with a car. The money wasn't life-changing, far from it, but it was more than nothing. At provincial level, meanwhile, there were all sorts of challenges. We were one of the very best sides in New Zealand, and with Super 10 rugby kicking in, we were keen to make the cut and play against the leading sides from Australia and South Africa. And then there was the Lions game in '93.

I'm being entirely serious when I say that we'd have beaten pretty much any team in the world on that particular day in late June. We were that good, to the extent that the Lions barely touched the ball for twenty minutes. We kicked off inventively, a short little grubber as I remember, and they were immediately tackled into touch. I said to Richard Jerram: 'Right, we'll push this hard with a "Willie Away" around the back.' This was a line-out peel, named after the great All Black captain Wilson Whineray, and was a familiar tactic designed to generate quick go-forward ball. Did the Lions handle it? Not quite. Buck Anderson smashed upfield on the stampede and was stopped just short, I drove it on, we came back to the short side and Doug Wilson scored in the corner. We were only into the first ninety seconds . . . Bang, bang, bang! It set the tone and by the time Will Carling, the England captain, capped a valiant individual display in adversity with a consolation try, we were thirty points up and out of sight. It was hardly a vintage Lions performance, especially up front, but they could have been twice as good and still been hammered. I'd felt it in the changing shed before kick-off and that's the way it turned out.

Sadly, my Waikato career – 140 appearances, a record at the time and still in the top four – came to an abrupt end. I played the full season in 1994 and continued to train hard through the summer under our new coach John Boe, a long-serving midfielder who had made a couple of tour appearances for the All Blacks in the 1980s. It so happened that Richard Jerram was getting married on the very Friday that John had arranged some fitness testing. As a couple of us had been invited – Matthew Cooper, our full-back, was also on the guest list – I rang Bruce Hodder, who was back at the province as fitness coach, to tell him that we wouldn't be around for the test. So far, so straightforward.

On the following Monday, I picked up the *Waikato Times* and read an interview with John Boe, which quoted him as saying that while he was happy with the results of the fitness testing in general, he was disappointed that Matthew and I had 'failed to front'. I took exception to that, big time. I'd been involved with the province since 1985 and worked my butt off season after season. What was more, I'd played plenty of rugby with John at Hamilton Old Boys. I was straight on the phone to him. 'JB, what's going on?' I asked. 'I rang Bruce and told him what was happening.' John didn't offer much in the way of an answer, still less an apology. 'What concerns me,' I continued, 'is that anyone reading this newspaper will think that I couldn't be bothered – that I didn't have the courtesy to turn up.' It really mattered to me what the incredibly loyal Waikato supporters thought about rugby affairs, so I wasn't pretending. I was seriously annoyed. It would have been so easy for John to smooth things over, but he didn't even try. So I brought the conversation to a fairly definitive close by saying 'F*** you, I'm retiring' and slamming down the receiver. And being a stubborn sort, I meant it. Subsequently, I played a few club games for Taupiri and helped out a mate Willie Hetaraka who was coaching Thames Valley. But to all intents and purposes, my playing days in my home country were at an end. Had I stuck with it, who knows what direction my life would have taken? As it was, the sport was on the brink of professionalism and I was a young coach with a good background and a willingness to travel. There was a big wide world out there, waiting to be explored. In fact, my adventures were already underway. Since the end of 1989, I had been splitting my time between the North Island of New Zealand and the emerald island of Ireland.

3

EMOTION IN EMERALD GREEN

Ireland. The Emerald Isle. The land of priests and poets and politics and pubs and pints of the black stuff, of wit and wild roving and a brand of rugby that was both rugged and romantic. This was the image in my mind when I first set foot in the country as part of the New Zealand tour party in 1989, little knowing that I would become intimately wrapped up in its sporting affairs for the next decade. Many things happened during my time there: a good number of them were deeply rewarding, a few of them bordered on the joyous and some of them were bitterly disappointing. But the big thing, the overwhelming thing, that happened in Ireland put sport in its proper context. Far more than that, it put *everything* into perspective.

I cannot think of Ireland without thinking of Shauna. But then, I think about her every day, no matter what I might be doing or where I might be on the planet. Trudi and I have been blessed with a wonderful family – Gabby, our daughter, was born in 1993, and Bryn, our son, came along a couple of years later – but Shauna was our first child and while she passed away at the age of four months, she lives with us always.

By the time I took the plunge with the Galwegians club as a player-coach after the '89 tour, I was a married man. Within eighteen months, I was preparing myself for fatherhood and looking forward to taking on a new and exciting set of responsibilities a million miles away, and a million times more important, than those attached to rugby. Trudi had joined me out there on the west coast of Ireland and had done all the right things during her pregnancy. When she was admitted to University Hospital in Galway, there was no reason to think that anything was amiss. But when Shauna was born, in the early hours of 17 January 1992, our world changed. She was a good weight, seven and a half pounds, and whatever problems she had didn't register with me at the moment of birth. But there were tears in the eyes of the nursing staff. Shauna was suffering from spina bifida. The nurses knew deep down that her condition was serious and an immediate scan confirmed the worst. We were devastated.

Over the next few days, as we talked things through with the specialist staff, it became clear that we would be confronted with the most awful of dilemmas. Should we follow the road of surgical intervention – the longest of roads for poor Shauna – or let nature take its course? I spoke to the hospital's professor of paediatrics and asked him to give it to me straight. 'On a scale of one to ten, how bad is Shauna's condition?' I asked. 'She's a nine,' he replied. That was the hardest, most gut-wrenching conversation of my life. Shauna would face one major operation after another, and even if the medical side went entirely to plan – even if she fought like a lion to survive – what kind of life would be on offer to her? There would be ten years, eleven years . . . twelve, thirteen, fourteen years of unrelenting surgery. She would be wheelchair-bound and at constant risk of infection. With the full support of the hospital staff, including those at the most senior levels, we decided to take the other route. A heart-breaking one, yes, but also the kinder one. The four months we had with her were precious, full of love and tenderness, and we treasured every second of that time. When Shauna died, on 13 May, we were living back home in New Zealand. To my profound and lasting regret, I was in Australia, on a rugby tour with Waikato, when she left us. I flew straight back across the Tasman to say my goodbyes.

By this time, I was in the third year of my spell with Galwegians. They had never been anything other than brilliant with me and when I most needed them to be sympathetic and understanding, they exceeded all expectations. Even though they had made a significant financial investment in bringing me over – they had taken a hell of a risk in flying me from New Zealand in the first place and then doubled down on the gamble by sticking with me – they quickly decided that the best place for Shauna and Trudi and myself would be back in Waikato, where we could be supported by our extended family. But the club had set its heart on promotion to the All Ireland League, which had been set up in 1990, and the play-offs were looming large. We had to take on the other provincial league winners, and having beaten the Leinster side Clontarf, everything rested on our match with Old Crescent, the Munster champions, in Limerick. I felt under an obligation to play, so I flew back for the match, which we won. The job was done. The team bus dropped me off at my Shannon Airport hotel and after performing a haka outside by way of farewell, I caught the next flight home.

If my life situation was completely new – deeply traumatic, a massive shock to the system – the nuts and bolts of travelling long-distance at 35,000 feet were almost as familiar as packing down between two hulking great props and attempting to scrummage the opposition into the dirt. Not to put too fine a point on it, I was fast becoming a brontosaurus on the carbon footprint scale. During the business part of the northern hemisphere season, I was a resident of Galway. The Galwegians club – one of the three biggest clubs in the Connacht province, along with Athlone and Corinthians – was my sole focus, with All Ireland League status the number one target. As soon as the main campaign was done and dusted, I would head back to New Zealand for another tour of duty with Waikato. In fact, many of my most memorable moments in Mooloo country occurred during that hectic spell of full-time, twelve-months-a-year rugby. How had it come about? Completely by chance.

At the end of the All Black tour in '89, I was feeling a little frustrated. Not because I had yet to win an international cap, thanks to the freakishly durable Sean Fitzpatrick, but because I didn't believe the standard of rugby I'd produced on that trip had been fully recognised by the hierarchy. It just so happened that as the squad were gathered at Dublin Airport for the flight to England and the tour-closing match with the Barbarians at Twickenham, my fellow Waikato front-rower Graham Purvis was approached by a guy called Mickey Heaslip, who had recently been president of Galwegians. He told Graham he was looking for a prop to stiffen up the scrum and pass on a bit of know-how. 'I'm off to play some rugby in France but there's someone who might be interested,' Graham replied, giving Mickey my phone number. Almost immediately, I received a call. 'I hear you're a tight-head prop,' Mickey said. 'Yeah, I can play tight-head,' I responded. If I'd added the words 'in theory', it would have been less of a bare-faced lie. But only just. The truth of it was that I'd never played No 3 in my life, and while the phrase 'how hard can it be?' flashed through my mind, I knew I was taking a liberty. Still, nothing ventured, nothing gained. After the Baa-Baas game, I made my way to Luton Airport and boarded an Aer Aran flight that stopped off at Waterford on the way. I remember the pilot apologising for a short delay, adding: 'We're just waiting for a farmer to clear his cattle from the runway.' I sat there in my tiny seat, shaking my head and thinking: 'What the hell have I let myself in for here?'

On arrival in Galway, I heaved my luggage – four or five bags of All Black kit and sundry accessories – off the plane and was met by Peter Crowley, the manager of the team. This was on the Wednesday. On the way to my accommodation, he said: 'OK, we have training on Tuesday and Thursday nights. What will you need for tomorrow?'

'How many players are you expecting at the session?' I asked him.

'About thirty, I'd say.'

'Right. One ball between two players . . . that's fifteen balls. Plus some cones and some tackle bags.'

This caused a fair degree of panic. Peter later admitted that the only two balls available to him were in the boot of his car at the time of our conversation, that one of them was flat, and that he had to scour the entire Galway area in an effort to source additional supplies. There were one or two other things he didn't reveal until some considerable time after the event: firstly, that at the previous night's training session, the attendance had been . . . six; and secondly, that the board had discussed canning the whole idea of importing an All Black as player-coach after losing to a junior club St Mary's from Limerick the previous weekend. Galwegians were officially in dire straits, so what was the point? The decision to press ahead had been taken with great reluctance, by no means unanimously.

As it turned out, Peter had given the players a very hard sell and succeeded in drawing good numbers to my first coaching run on foreign soil. There may even have been a full thirty-strong turnout. Some arrived in what might be called their own time, but at least they turned up. So it was, that we prepared for that weekend's away fixture at Sligo, about ninety minutes away by bus. I wasn't available, even though I'd spent the back end of the All Black tour in a state of enforced inactivity and fancied a game. Some form of compulsory stand-down rule was in place for newcomers, so I was surplus to requirements once again. The only consolation was that I could devote myself body and soul to organisation and my first move was to ensure that we prepared properly. A 10.30 am meet-up, departing at 11 am for a 3 pm kick-off? That seemed reasonable to me. Apparently, most of my new charges thought it entirely unreasonable. By 10.30, there were no more than half a dozen of us in the clubhouse, one of whom – yours truly – wasn't actually playing. Come 11.00, the number had risen to thirteen. I was spitting feathers. 'Right, everyone on the coach,' I said. 'We're leaving on time.' When we drove out of the car park we were already down to twelve, having left one player sitting on the toilet. Brilliant. I found myself sitting next to a young player who blessed himself every few miles which left me confused as well as angry, and it took me some time to understand that devout Roman Catholics made the sign of the cross whenever they passed a church or a cemetery.

Not long after arriving at our destination, I had a full team at my disposal. The latecomers had travelled by car and one of them had hoovered up the poor bloke I'd left on the throne back in Galway. My mood lightened slowly, but I still felt the need to address the issue immediately and asked for quiet before beginning my public address. 'If I told the story of what's just happened back in New Zealand, I'd be a laughing stock,' I told the players. 'Either we take this seriously and do things right, or I might as well get on the next plane and go home.'

'We have a right one here,' some of the players said to each other after I had delivered my message. It was the best move I could have made. We won the game, for one thing. For another, I used the moment to introduce a fines system for latecomers (the proceeds of which would always be placed on the bar) and brought in a few more simple rules with a view to sharpening up our general attitude. It wasn't too challenging a regime: by the standards of Grizz Wyllie and Buck Shelford, it was the equivalent of an all-inclusive holiday in the Caribbean. All I required of those players who were likely to be late for training, or who couldn't make it at all, was that they had the good grace to let me know. I also introduced a dress code, on the basis that if we looked like a team, we might have an outside chance of playing like one. To coin a phrase, I was going back to basics. Why? Because basic was where we were at. In terms of adult rugby, this was the lowest level I'd ever encountered. Forget Waikato, let alone the All Blacks. Even when judged against Hamilton Old Boys, the Galwegians side I found on my arrival in Ireland were not up to much. There were some promising youngsters and a few old hands who knew their way round a rugby field, so talent, or lack of it, was not the primary concern. It was everything else: fitness, discipline, attitude . . . the very things I'd been drinking in like mother's milk for most of my life. If we wanted to establish ourselves as the cream of Connacht club rugby and make our way into the All Ireland League, things would have to change. And change they did. We won eleven games straight, starting with that victory over Sligo, and within a year we were provincial champions.

Throughout the process, we had more than our fair share of fun – which, I should add, is an essential ingredient of any team-building exercise. It began after that first training session, when the players gave me a 'Guinness welcome' in the clubhouse bar. I must have had ten pints, if not twelve, so I was grateful for the offer of a lift back to my accommodation from Mickey Heaslip. A mile or so into the journey, we were pulled over by the Garda. My chauffeur decided to play the openness and honesty card. 'If you put that bag on me, I'm bolloxed!' he said to the officer. 'And I have an All Black in the car. He's just arrived.' There was a moment's silence before judgement was handed down. 'Get back in the car and get yourself home,' said the policeman. It couldn't happen now and I don't suppose it should have happened then, but that was the way of it in the wilds of west Ireland in the late 1980s.

As the months unfolded, I fell in love with the Galwegians club and the lifestyle my fledgling coaching career afforded me. Once the right structures were in place, there was a real buzz in the squad – the kind of buzz that comes not just from being top dogs on the local scene, but from travelling down to Dublin and beating opponents who were far better equipped and had long been used to giving the country boys a whipping. There were definite parallels with the

Waikato–Auckland relationship, even if the rugby was a little less intense. Personally speaking, I was having a ball. Trudi came out to join me and we ended up living in a two-bedroom mews house on Mickey Heaslip's property. I was operating on a holiday permit and whatever money I received was generally concealed inside a brown envelope, but it never occurred to me to worry about the informality of it all. The locals could never quite understand why I was willing to interrupt a teaching career in New Zealand, especially as Irish interest rates were high at the time and unemployment was on the rise, but I came from a different culture. If the folk in Connacht had been raised with a job-for-life mindset, a lot of Kiwis in their twenties were keen to see the world and embrace it. And besides, it wasn't as if I was leaving New Zealand behind. I would stay for the league season and then head for the airport, leaving Galwegians to find their own way through the provincial cup competition, which was considered of secondary importance. As we kept on winning the league, and as the side I left behind invariably bombed out in the first or second round of the cup, my reputation among the supporters (and probably the committee) was greatly enhanced. It was reassuring to think that in the time it was taking me to fly halfway round the world, there was someone down there on the ground making me look like a genius!

Over the course of my four-year stretch with Galwegians, I made some fabulous lifelong friends. Some of them happened to be excellent players into the bargain. There was

Brian O'Donnell, who had made an impact in Gaelic Football before turning to rugby; and there was Jody Greene, who worked for the Bank of Ireland and had come up to us from Dublin. I'd describe Jody as a burly No 9: even burlier than Piri Weepu, the unusually spherical half-back who played such a crucial role in driving the All Blacks to a long-awaited world title on home territory in 2011. Jody may not have been the fastest thing on two legs, but under the laws of the time he gave us plenty of go-forward off the back of the scrum, and if he had a habit of going to ground quickly, that was OK. In those days, if you were going forward you'd retain the ball and be awarded the put-in. That's how it worked for us. Some of the weather conditions in the far west of Ireland were absolutely horrendous and when the westerlies were really blowing in off the Atlantic, it was almost impossible to play any differently.

One of Jody's performances remains fresh in my mind. We were playing Athlone with the Connacht league title on the line and it seemed to me that the wind was reaching hurricane levels. It was also bitterly cold, to the point of Arctic-ness, and whenever there was a break in play, we huddled together and rubbed each other's backs in an effort to keep the circulation flowing. We had the advantage of the conditions in the first half, but in a thrilling display of champagne rugby, we registered precisely three points. It was three more than Athlone managed, but basically we were there for the taking. Indeed, our opponents spent the half-time break celebrating their imminent victory. Jody was having none of it. Throughout the second forty minutes, he inched forward off every scrum, every ruck and every maul, enabling us to cling to possession. It was perfect rugby for the day and it won us the game. The guy was a 24-carat hero that day.

Joe Healy and his wife Geraldine also became great friends along with their children Rachael, Hannah and Jordan, to whom Trudi and I are godparents. Joe had played against me in the Connacht match and had been in awe of the chance to play against his rugby hero Buck Shelford.

Together with Jody, Brian and Joe, I sank my fair share of foaming stout. I remember playing up in Ulster, against Dungannon. Jody was driving us home, with Brian and me in the back and a crate of beer strapped in the front passenger seat. The seatbelt was on because we didn't want it going through the windscreen: when it came to evaluating precious cargo, human beings were a very distant second. Having talked all sorts of rubbish on the journey to Galway, we decided to continue our discussion at a bar in town. Being a responsible sort, Brian rang his wife to tell her we were somewhere near Sligo and might be a wee while yet. I didn't stay out too long, so things were fine with Trudi. The next day, we went to Brian's house for a spot of lunch. Unfortunately, we hadn't thought to get our story straight and Trudi spilled the beans the moment the door opened. 'Warren wasn't home too late,' she announced to Brian's wife – a remark that put O'Donnell squarely in the doghouse. By way of a coda to the story, Jody had to drive to Dublin on the Monday.

Travelling in thick fog he was stopped by the Garda almost immediately, and when he wound down the window, the lingering fumes from our crate of beer flooded out. Trouble brewing, you might say. Fortunately, the attention of the officer was distracted by a buzzing sound in the distance that grew louder by the second. It was a man on a moped driving straight towards the two parked cars. When the policeman stepped into the road and put up his hand, the rider stopped and fell sideways off the bike. He was absolutely blasted. 'Get going,' the officer said to Jody. 'It looks like I'll be dealing with something more serious.'

Of course, the really serious aspect of my association with Galwegians was winning promotion to the All Ireland League. That was the principal aim and it was front, back and centre in my mind. If, when the league was launched, selection had been based on current form, Galwegians would have been included among the elite clubs in the country. Unfortunately for us, the administrators decided to go back a little way and assess the claims of the candidates over a stretch of time rather than go for a snapshot. While no Connacht side made it into the first division of the AIL, two were granted entry into the second flight. We weren't one of them – Athlone and Corinthians were the anointed pair – so we would have to fight our way in.

We began the process immediately and made the play-offs at the first attempt. The crucial game was against Dolphin, the famous old Cork club who had once boasted players as legendary as Jimmy McCarthy and Tony O'Reilly among their number. Their big-name international at that stage was Michael Kiernan, the goal-kicking centre who would win dozens of caps for Ireland. We had qualification in our hands as the match unfolded, and near the end, we could taste and smell it as well as feel it. But we all know the story about the fat lady and her singing voice. In the final minute, our fly-half Eric Elwood took a quick tap, banged the ball out on the full and conceded a scrum on our 22-metre line, from which Kiernan dropped a match-winning goal. I was devastated. I'd suffered painful defeats with Waikato and even lost a game in an All Black jersey, but for some reason this particular disappointment ran unusually deep. That year, the flight home to New Zealand seemed to take for ever.

To my considerable relief and satisfaction, we put things to rights the following season and made the great leap forward. Not that my own rugby life was growing any more straightforward. Back home in Waikato, I was playing in a successful provincial side with legitimate designs on a first National Provincial Championship title: a crown worn by only three teams, Auckland, Wellington and Otago, since the tournament had been reshaped in the mid-1980s. We were up against Auckland, our most implacable rivals, in the semi-final, and while we were second favourites in the eyes of the press, we felt we could win. (Yes, we'd come that far.) What I wasn't confident about was being in New Zealand for the final if we happened to make it through. The rules in Ireland stated that I had to be there in the country, physically, by 1 October, if I wanted to register as an overseas player. In fact, George Spotswood, the Irish union's first technical director, had to see me with his own eyes before he could grant me permission to play for Galwegians in the 1992–3 season. Annoyingly, the dates clashed pretty much directly, hence my conversation with Kevin Greene, the outstanding Waikato coach, at this crucial point in the team's history. 'If we beat Auckland,' I said, 'I don't think I can be here for the final.' Kevin was a brilliant man-manager and he immediately told me that if I could conceivably be available on the date of the final, and if Waikato were in it, he would pick me.

Climate change campaigners will not want to hear this, but I somehow managed to do the necessary. Once we had seen off the Aucklanders, I caught the Monday long-haul flight to Heathrow, transferred to Dublin, grabbed a lift to the Irish Rugby Football Union headquarters in Lansdowne Road, stood in front of George, completed the appropriate paperwork, drove to Galway that night for a Galwegians training session and stayed the night there before being driven back to Dublin for the plane to Heathrow and the return flight to NZ. I arrived on the Friday morning, trained that night with Waikato, had Saturday off and then took the field in Hamilton for our final with Otago, the reigning champions. We absolutely hammered them 40–5, scoring the bulk of our points in the first half. This was a blessing, to say the least, for there was no way I had eighty minutes of full-on rugby inside me. I remember looking up at the scoreboard five minutes after the interval, by which point serious fatigue was kicking in. We were winning 30-zip. Immediately, the thought came into my head that I could walk for the rest of the contest, happy in the knowledge that we couldn't possibly lose from there. We celebrated our first NPC triumph in good style, after which I got back on the plane and returned to Ireland. Did I break some records as a rugby traveller in the course of that endless week? I must have done. Forget 'Around The World In 80 Days'. Try 'Around The World For 80 Minutes'. The only evidence I can give in my defence is that all of those flights were economy class. Every last one of them. There's dedication for you.

To this day, there is a place in my heart for Galwegians. It was a special time, during which I learned a lot about myself, not only as a coach, but as a human being. Prior to 1989, I had never set foot outside the southern hemisphere. By 1994, I knew I could make a fist of things in a very different part of the world. I had been reasonably successful in hitting my targets, but more than that, I felt I had demonstrated a degree of resilience that would serve me well in the future. Apart from anything else, I had braved eight winters in four years (half of them in Ireland, the other half in New Zealand) and maintained a sense of humour! All joking aside, the lack of sunshine was one of the factors behind my decision to call it a day in Galway. I also felt that a four-year stint in one place was just about enough. I was still in the thick of the rugby scene back home, I had ambitions to coach in my own country and, most importantly, I had Trudi to consider.

There were plenty of reasons to think that the North Island of New Zealand was the right place for me to be. If my long career with Waikato had ended rather abruptly, there was still my coaching work at club level with Taupiri and at provincial level with Thames Valley. In addition, there was the day job. I had landed a teaching position at Huntly College, a small state school situated about twenty-five miles from Hamilton. The intake was very diverse: there were a lot of Maori kids on the roll and a high proportion of students from tough socio-economic backgrounds. More challenging from my point of view was that for a majority of the school population, rugby league was the game of choice. All the same, it was a hugely rewarding place to teach: loud, boisterous, high-energy and a lot of fun. But for a phone call, completely out of the blue, from Steve Cole, the headmaster of St Paul's Collegiate School in Hamilton, I would not have thought about leaving, even for a second.

St Paul's was an independent Anglican school with a very different pupil population. It really couldn't have been more of a contrast to Huntly College and I wasn't sure it was my kind of place. But Steve, the son-in-law of the outstanding All Black flanker of the 1960s and renowned educationalist John Graham, persuaded me to take a look around and then offered me a job. I said I was happy where I was. He offered me a generous salary hike; I asked him when he'd like me to start. If that sounds as though I was a complete pushover, I can only say that as a family man and a working man, the extra money made life a whole lot easier. And it's also true to say that I was drawn by the school's determination to become a centre of sporting excellence. I took immediate charge of the senior cricket team and while Gary Henley-Smith, a Commonwealth Games sprinter and rugby league professional, was running the union side of things, I was fully involved there too. For a small private school to stack up against the likes of Hamilton Boys' was no mean achievement, but in the classroom, I experienced something of a culture shock. During one maths lesson, I was sitting at my desk while my students, sixteen or seventeen of them, scribbled away with their heads in their books. The silence was deafening. Huntly College it wasn't, and I couldn't handle it. 'Right, I've had enough of this,' I said, suddenly. 'Get down on the floor, the lot of you. We'll do some rucking practise.'

In 1996, Steve asked me if I fancied an upgrade to director of sport, which was a co-ordinating role across the range of activities, with rugby, cricket, athletics and rowing at the heart of it. It suited me perfectly and I was just hitting my stride when, at four in the morning, I received another life-changing phone call. It was a guy called Billy Glynn and he was phoning from Ireland. I knew him well from my Galwegians days – he was a big mover and shaker in Connacht rugby – and my first reaction was to wonder if one of my friends from Galwegians had run into trouble, or been taken ill, or worse. Billy put me straight in a matter of seconds.

'Our coach has just resigned. That's the Connacht coach I'm talking about. And we have a tour game against the Wallabies on the horizon, as well as the inter-provincial tournament. We need someone pretty urgently. Could you come over on a twelve-week contract to help us out?'

I didn't know if it was possible, but I thought I'd show willing. 'When do you need me?'

'By yesterday,' Billy replied. 'We have a training camp organised. In Sweden.'

'Sweden? Are you serious?'

'Absolutely.'

I was thinking on my feet now. 'Look,' I said, 'I have to go into school. In about three hours or so as it happens. I'll see what I can do.'

I went straight to Steve and told him that an opportunity had opened up for me. Being a generous spirit, he gave me his blessing. So off I went to Sweden the following day – more air miles – to fill the Connacht vacancy. A vacancy created thanks to a coach by the name of Eddie O'Sullivan, with whom I would have some interesting dealings in the coming years.

We had a practice match against a Scandinavian team of some description and then returned to Ireland to prepare for the inter-provincials. I wasn't in a position to take a radical approach. This was a time for clarity and simplicity, and given the constraints, things worked out OK. We beat Leinster, which seemed like a feat in itself as Connacht had finished on the right side of that fixture on only half a dozen occasions since the end of World War II. We also finished within five points of Ulster, whom we had beaten only once in twenty years. The Munster game was a rough one and we conceded more than forty points that day, but all things considered, we had good reason to look forward to the big meeting with the Wallabies in Galway.

In the days leading into the game, I wandered along to an Australian training run and joined a group of onlookers on the touchline. It wasn't that I was spying: all I wanted to do was crack their codes and learn their secrets. What could have been more innocent? Someone must have recognised me, maybe from one of my tours with Waikato or the All Blacks, because within minutes, an official-looking bloke materialised and asked if any of us might be Warren Gatland. 'That's me,' I said, grinning. 'In which case, would you mind leaving?' And off I went, the very picture of obedience. What did it matter? We weren't going to beat them anyway. They had George Gregan at scrum-half and someone by the name of Campese on the wing. These people were just a little beyond anything we were bringing to the party.

In the event, we played pretty well: indeed, we made such a mess of the young Stephen Larkham, who was making one of his early appearances in the green and gold No 10 shirt, that when the second half came around, he was relocated to full-back, out of the way. With Eric Elwood kicking goals at every opportunity, we actually led by eight points at one stage in the third quarter and were almost daring to dream. In the final analysis, however, the Wallabies ran in five tries to our one and headed out of town with a 37–20 victory. At least the main talking point of the occasion concerned us rather than them. The try we scored was unusual, to say the least, and it was the product of what might now be called 'blue-sky thinking'. I'd been toying with the idea of a thirteen-man line-out for a while and ran the team through the idea in training with a view to calling the move if the circumstances were right. Funnily enough, it was the kind of ruse most commonly associated with the Australians themselves: back in 1988, when I was over there with the All Blacks, we played a New South Wales Country XV in Singleton and found ourselves on the embarrassing end of a thirteen-man scrum! The lawmakers quickly brought an end to that little stunt, but there was nothing in the book to prevent mass line-outs. Against the Wallabies it worked a treat, with Shane Leahy, our lock, touching down to a chorus of Australian voices screaming 'you can't do that!!!' The most bemused man on the pitch was David Campese, the trickster par excellence. All these years on, I can still see the look on his face.

My three months were up; classes at St Paul's beckoned. But things were moving fast in Ireland – fast by Irish standards, at least – and within a few weeks, the committee types on the IRFU, many of whom had once seen any move towards professionalism as the work of the devil, agreed that full-time rugby at provincial level was the obvious way forward. I was offered the Connacht post and after a formal interview, the job was mine. Yes, it meant more upheaval, but proper money was being pumped into the sport in the northern hemisphere and the prospect of making a career out of coaching was highly attractive. The 1997–8 season was my first full campaign with Connacht, and with the European Challenge Cup adding a cross-border dimension to the fixture list, there was plenty to interest me.

To this day, there are clubs in England and France who see the Challenge Cup as a second-tier, after-the-lord-mayor's-show affair, unworthy of their full commitment. It wasn't the way we looked at it in Galway. This was the first tournament to be run on a home-and-away pool structure and we'd been drawn in the same group as Northampton, coached by Ian McGeechan no less, and a couple of French teams, Begles–Bordeaux (as they were then known) and Nice. No one thought we could conceivably find a route into the knockout stage, least of all a fellow New Zealander by the name of Linley MacKenzie, who was a journalist on the *Galway Advertiser*. When I met up with Linley before the start of the season, she was bluntly honest with her opinions. 'I'm really not sure where you're going to win a game,' she said. I wasn't quite sure myself about the road ahead, but I couldn't roll over and let the comment pass.

'I promise you this, Linley: we'll win a game.'

'Which one?'

'I don't know yet, but we'll win one.'

What else could I have said? I didn't think an admission along the lines of 'You're right, we're absolutely screwed' would do much for dressing-room morale.

First game up was Northampton at home. A tough start, for sure: they had quality players in most areas and an unnervingly large number of them had participated in the triumphant British and Irish Lions series in South Africa earlier that year. They were one of the big noises in the newly professionalised English club game. Us? We were the silent quarter of a four-team provincial set-up. I didn't know a fat lot about the internal politics of the sport in Ireland, but certain things were obvious when it came to Connacht. We were the poor relatives, to the extent that in the brave new world of full-time rugby, we were blessed with a grand total of three full-time players. The most renowned of them, Eric Elwood, had agonised for some time before giving up his job with Irish Distillers and throwing in his lot with us. He was not easy to convince, and I should know. I was the one doing the convincing.

The game was due to be played in Galway on the first Saturday in September, but the sudden death of Princess Diana changed all that. Given her family links with Northamptonshire, the tournament organisers felt it best to delay the fixture for seventy-two hours. It eventually went ahead on the following Tuesday, unattended by anyone even vaguely influential at IRFU level. The union had scheduled a committee meeting in Dublin for that day and the men in suits had no intention of missing it, especially as Northampton were certain to smash us to all parts, from Erris Head to the Aran Islands and back again. However, one of the high-and-mighty types was sufficiently interested to phone the clubhouse at the Sports Ground during the evening, just as we were enjoying a pint or two in the bar.

'Just checking on the score,' he said to the man who lifted the receiver.

'That would be 43–13,' came the reply.

'Well . . . that's not too bad, I suppose,' the committee man said. 'You'll be reasonably happy with that.'

'More than happy,' said our chap. 'It was 43–13 to us.'

That night was memorable. At least, it would be if I could remember it. In all conscience, I couldn't tell the players to keep a lid on their celebrations ahead of the trip to Nice the following weekend: by beating a side as strong as Northampton, and by such a margin, they had driven Connacht rugby into new territory. And they'd done it in the face of considerable handicaps. Far from training all day every day, there were two evening sessions in Athlone, a night in a hotel on the Friday and a recovery session on the Sunday. That was it. It was little wonder that the boys felt they had achieved something significant. Little wonder also that they stayed up until 5 am, squeezing every last drop of enjoyment from their astonishing effort. It certainly gave a new meaning to the term 'recovery session'.

As it turned out, we lost narrowly in Nice, largely because the referee saw fit to award the Frenchmen a last-minute penalty try so outrageous in its injustice that our hosts were even more embarrassed than we were exasperated. But we beat the men from Bordeaux home and away and won the return fixture against Nice, all of which left us needing victory over Northampton at Franklin's Gardens to win the pool and proceed to the quarter-finals.

This was no small ask: when the Saints named their side, players as good as Gregor Townsend, Matt Dawson, Martin Bayfield and Nick Beal were in the starting line-up. Yet the momentum was with us. The players had developed a sense of togetherness far deeper than anything they had experienced previously – partly, perhaps, because they saw the 5 am celebration as a blueprint for all future success – and they drew additional strength from their status as rank outsiders. It was said that Oliver Cromwell had coined the phrase 'to hell or to Connaught' as a threat to Irish Catholics during his rampage through the country in the 1640s. Three and a half centuries on, we emblazoned those words on our match-day T-shirts as an expression of resistance. We also had a lovely team song, 'Red Is The Rose'. I asked Michael Cosgrove, a passionate man of Connacht and assistant coach against whom I'd played back in 1989, to sing it, and he had the lot of us in tears. Michael and I have become great friends over the years and I think we really built a strong coaching team during that period. Billy Glynn made sure the wives and partners were given free travel and tickets, so we had vocal support from the first whistle. By the final whistle, the scoreboard read 20–15. Even though we scored a couple of great tries the moment of brilliance came from Nicky Barry, our wing. In the final few minutes with Northampton having a four-man overlap, Nicky sprinted off his line to tackle Gregor Townsend ball and all to save the day. It was what the team was all about, someone who wasn't known as a great defender putting his body on the line for the team. Just in case anyone from the IRFU was wondering, the twenty points belonged to us.

We were through and it was a magical moment, but there was a slight sting in the tail. Wandering casually through the airport the next morning with Trudi and a couple of backroom staff, we discovered we had been too casual for our own good. The gate had shut and as we argued in vain to be let through, the plane headed for the runway with a bunch of highly amused players watching events from the window seats. The result? A heavy fine for me!

A whole bunch of pool winners finished with five wins and one defeat that year and we missed out on a home quarter-final because our points difference was lower than everyone else's. Looking back, the nonsense in Nice cost us dear. We went back to France to face Agen, who were terribly difficult to beat in front of their own kind at Stade Armandie, and with the mighty Abdel Benazzi in their pack, they were just that little bit too strong for us. Had Benazzi, one of the very best forwards of his generation, not been there; had we not messed up a big overlap bang on half-time and conceded an intercept try as a result . . . who knows? I felt we'd played well enough to be in the game when it came to the business end, but it didn't quite happen that way. Still, our 40–27 defeat was a long way short of a hiding. All in all, I was incredibly proud of our achievements in Europe. I felt we were going places.

As it turned out, I was the one going places. Trudi had joined me in Galway with the kids and we were nicely settled;

Bryn was coming up to two years old and was speaking with a strong Irish accent! I had no reason to believe that my life would not carry on along the Connacht track for the foreseeable future. But as I'd already discovered, there was always the chance of an upheaval just around the corner. And this time, it was an upheaval on a grand scale.

The man at the centre of it was an Englishman. Not that Brian Ashton was your typical Englishman in the rugby sense. By the standards of the world's biggest union-playing country at that time, he was something of a visionary. I prided myself on thinking outside the box, to use the modern phrase, but the way Brian saw the game in terms of its attacking possibilities, the box didn't exist.

Quite how easy he would find applying that vision to the Irish international team in the mid-1990s was not entirely clear when he succeeded my countryman, Murray Kidd, as head coach in the first days of 1997, but the IRFU decided action was urgently required after a painful Test loss to Italy at Lansdowne Road. It was quite a change. Murray, a fellow North Islander who hailed from King Country (an easy drive from Hamilton), had been appointed after coaching a couple of club teams down in Munster. Brian had been one of the main men at Bath, the best team in the whole of Europe for well over a decade, and had worked with some of the finest talent to be found anywhere in the sport: Jeremy Guscott, Stuart Barnes, Richard Hill, John Hall, Ben Clarke, the rugby league cross-coders Jason Robinson and Henry Paul . . . the list went on and on. Perhaps unsurprisingly, given the number of tournament triumphs with which he had been associated, he felt he might be on to something when it came to building a winning side, and I assume he believed his new employers would back him in his methods: after all, they were the ones who had brought him in. It didn't work out that way. After eight games, six of which were lost, he was gone.

How much attention was I paying to all the shenanigans in Dublin? I was interested, of course, but Ireland Test affairs were not in the forefront of my mind. However, I was definitely intrigued by Brian's ideas and he invited me to watch some of his training sessions. On one occasion, I took Connacht across the water for a camp at a swanky school in Gloucestershire – so swanky, it had facilities for Real Tennis, Racquets and other games largely reserved for the children of squillionaires – and Brian made the short trip from his home just outside of Bath to cast an educated eye over my techniques. But as the newspapers say a hundred times a day, professional sport is a results-driven business. When Brian's relations with the governing body began to go south, it was not a complete surprise.

What would the Ireland hierarchy do now? I didn't have much of an idea until the Ireland team manager Pat Whelan phoned me, the day after a particularly uncomfortable press conference at which he and Brian had sat side by side and effectively severed their relations in public. Pat went straight to the point. How would I feel about coaching the Irish side for the remaining three games of the Five Nations

Championship (Ireland having just lost the first of them, to Scotland)? I didn't quite know what to say. On the one hand, I was a young coach, still only thirty-four, and while I was rolling along quite nicely with Connacht, an international role was a whole different ball game with very little security attached to it, as had just been demonstrated. On the other hand, I knew that each and every one of the teams I had coached to date – Taupiri, Thames Valley, Galwegians, Connacht, even assisting at St Paul's Collegiate back home in Hamilton – had over-achieved, and that I must therefore have been doing something right. And yes, I had ambitions to work at Test level. Add in a touch of the young man's 'no fear' attitude and there was something in the back of my mind saying: 'Warren, this is an opportunity. It's a three-game, make-do-and-mend proposition, which means you can't really fail; and anyway, the Connacht job will still be yours at the end of it. Why not give it a go?' And that was the decision I reached. My friends, Joe and Ger Healy, reminded me recently that the setting of that life-changing phone call was in a Westport hotel the morning after Joe's sister Ruth's wedding (in Ireland weddings go into the wee small hours). We were all sitting around having coffee when I took the call. My face must have given away my initial shock because when I'd hung up they all knew something was up. 'I've just been offered the Irish job.' Then the shock registered on their faces.

My first game in charge would be in Paris against a French side who had already beaten Clive Woodward's England side on home turf and then put Scotland through the mincer by clocking up a half-century of points at Murrayfield. They already had the look of Grand Slammers about them with Philippe Bernat-Salles and Christophe Dominici on the wings, Thomas Castaignede at No 10 and a sprinkling of world-class forwards, from Christian Califano and Raphael Ibanez in the front row to Fabien Pelous and Olivier Magne in the back five. Therefore, the overwhelming question – the *only* question – facing me was this: how could I piece things together convincingly enough to give us a puncher's chance of restoring some dignity? The one-word answer? Pragmatism. I wouldn't dream of criticising Brian Ashton because I've long considered him a rugby philosopher of the first rank, but the Irish side of the time simply wasn't capable of putting his ideas into practice. He wanted all fifteen of his players to be able to catch and pass. I knew for a fact that such skills were beyond at least half of them, particularly under pressure. I completely understood what he was aiming at, but if you don't have the tools, you're in 'Mission: Impossible' territory. Trying to teach people to do things in the international environment that they should have been doing a decade earlier but weren't . . . well, good luck with that.

The way I saw it, this was another 'back to basics' moment. If we had something going for us, it was the lack of expectation from the Irish rugby public. No one gave us a snowball's chance of returning from Paris with a win, so it was open for me to play on the negativity surrounding us and create a siege mentality. Morale among the players was

Even All Black hookers were innocent once. This is me at six months and again at the grand old age of four. A year later, I was attending Bankwood Primary School in Hamilton. I'm on the far left of the middle row.

Haircuts United! Scrummaging with Graham Purvis (*left*) and Craig Stevenson for Waikato against the Lions in 1993.

My try in that momentous game was watched, if not admired, by Richard Webster and Will Carling.

Pride in the jersey. Smiling sweetly for my All Blacks tour mug shot.

Helping out my team-mate Bernie McCahill against Newport in 1989.

Finding Steve Gordon, my great friend and fellow 'Mooloo' All Black, on a beautiful day in La Rochelle during the 1990 tour of France.

My Connacht days were an inspiration. *Above:* laughing with assistant coach Michael Cosgrove. *Below:* getting serious with half-back Conor McGuinness, Michael Cosgrove, manager Seamus King and skills coach Tommy Conneely.

Making a firm point about the scrum to the Ireland front row of Nick Popplewell, Ross Nesdale and Paul Wallace. The fiery Trevor Brennan is listening in.

Our agony, their ecstasy. Losing to Argentina at the 1999 World Cup.

Coaching is about watching and talking. *Above:* I am flanked by my Ireland colleagues Eddie O'Sullivan (*left*) and Donal Lenihan, one of whom I knew was entirely on my side. *Below:* the players listen to my take on events.

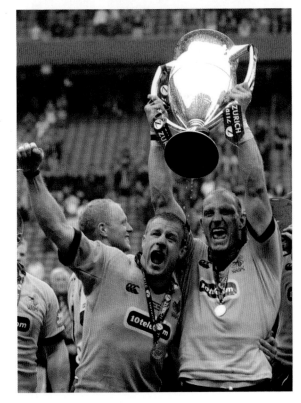

Nobody was throwing the term 'Warrenball' at me when Wasps were winning trophies with some brilliant attacking rugby. After Stuart Abbott scored the winning try against Bath in the 2004 Premiership final at Twickenham (*top*), the back-rowers Paul Volley and Lawrence Dallaglio celebrated with a passion.

Mark van Gisbergen's try against Toulouse in the 2004 Heineken Cup final helped us to a famous victory (*top*), and he was at it again a year later, scoring against Leicester in the Premiership final (*left*).

If Lawrence made a big statement on the field before lifting the trophy, I made a bigger one with my tie . . .

far from good: they were afraid to take 50–50 chances, let alone genuine risks, because as a collective, they believed that if they didn't make any mistakes, there was an even-money chance that they wouldn't find themselves out of the side for the next game. Yes, they wanted the satisfaction and the profile of being international players. What they didn't want was all the pain and criticism and baggage attached to failure. Fear was outweighing desire. It was a bad mindset, and it was deep-rooted.

When we arrived in France, we found ourselves checking into very grand accommodation in Versailles. (One thing you could say about the decision-making class on the IRFU in the 1990s was that they knew how to make themselves comfortable.) Almost immediately, the first of my little plans started to work. Before departure, I mentioned in an interview that if the public really wanted to back us in our hour of need, they should send messages of support to the hotel fax number. By the Friday evening, we'd received more than 5,000 faxes from every corner of the country. We pinned them all up in the team room. 'Don't read the papers or listen to the radio or watch television,' I said to the players. 'Just read these faxes.' I was also working on a second ruse, which involved a change of defensive system. Defence back then was not quite a science in the way it is now, but I felt if we could shut down the French space as fast as possible, we'd upset their rhythm. I'd watched an All Blacks game in which that magnificent wing Jeff Wilson had flown up on his opponent at high speed, trusting his colleagues on the inside to ensure the line didn't fracture. Analysis was still in its infancy back then, so I'm not sure if the Wilson approach was a plan or an accident. Either way, it was effective, and I believed it could work for us.

Plan number three was to convince the players that if they believed deep down in their capabilities, they could win the game. To do this, I needed a narrative. The story I chose concerned four American soldiers in the heart of the Vietnam jungle. They were in a jeep on a narrow track and when they came under sniper fire, the captain told his men they had three choices. 'We can try to make our way back to the safety of the camp on foot,' he said. 'Alternatively, we can attempt to drive through the gunfire. Or we can turn the jeep around and head back the way we came. That's the best option, provided we can lift the jeep. Can we lift it?' 'Yeah, we can do this,' came the reply. The soldiers grabbed a corner each, turned it round and made it back unhurt. When they told their story in camp, their mates didn't believe them. Bets were laid, money changed hands and eventually, the jeep was driven into the middle of the parade ring. On the captain's command, the soldiers attempted to repeat the feat . . . and failed. 'That's what I mean,' I said to the players. 'When they really believed, they made it happen. When the negative vibes kicked in, they couldn't.' As a mind game, I felt it had worked. Until, that is, the Munster loose-head Peter Clohessy sought me out later in the day. 'Gats, can you answer me something?' he said. 'I've been thinking about that story. Why didn't they just put the jeep in reverse?' Bloody props. They're more trouble than they're worth.

The bookies were giving us no chance, even in a two-horse race: some of them had the French winning by thirty-five points minimum. Yet with the rain falling and our new-fangled defensive system knocking our hosts out of their stride, we were 16–13 up after seventy-five minutes. Then, at a line-out a few metres from our line, our Lions hooker Keith Wood undercooked his throw to Mick Galwey at the front, which led to a scruffy tap-down and a winning try in the corner for Keith's opposite number, Ibanez. I was gutted, completely and utterly. We'd been in touching distance of one of the great Five Nations upsets and we'd chucked it away. When the sharpest pangs of disappointment eased, however, I felt we'd achieved something worthwhile. The mental shackles were off, the joy of the game was back, there was a road ahead. Against terrible odds, we'd made a start.

4

THE END OF THE BEGINNING

When you are spending every waking hour dreaming up ways of setting a new project in motion and giving it a sense of direction, the last thing you think about is the dead end ahead. I was perfectly aware from the start that my role with the Ireland team would be time-limited, and the fact that I was awarded a bare-minimum, one-year contract after my initial Five Nations adventure underlined the inherent instability of life as an international coach. But equally, I was certain that if I made the right moves in selection and organisation, delivered something positive on the results front and provided evidence of solid progress over successive tournaments, I would be treated with fairness and understanding. Which just goes to show where certainty gets you.

Not for one second have I ever regretted my sojourn in Ireland: a good number of the friendships I made there are still an important part of my life, and in pure coaching terms, the experience was formative. In fact, I would even go so far as to say that when it came to an end in a fashion so bewilderingly unexpected that I spent the following days lost in a fog of confusion, the timing worked in my favour. But that last benefit took a while to register. When I look back on my final days and weeks with the Irish Rugby Football Union, there is always a lingering sense of disappointment at the way things were handled, not to mention confusion over what happened and why. It wasn't as if I'd inherited a winning side and found myself in a 'steady as she goes' situation. Ireland had been going through coaches the way a hungry dog goes through a sirloin steak, and when it came to Five Nations performances, their record was dire. Only once in a decade had they won more than a single match in the tournament, and over that stretch of time they had never finished outside the bottom two. This was not easy street by any means. For the long-suffering supporters, it was the highway to hell.

There was so much to do, both technical – our scrum and line-out needed serious attention; our defensive structure was in desperate need of modernisation – and more generally, not least in the fitness department. Having identified the things we couldn't do, I had no choice but to focus on the things we could do. If I'm honest, there weren't that many of them at the start of the process. Therefore, I had to lay some foundations. That began with conditioning, an area where we simply weren't at the races in terms of competing fully for eighty minutes at Test match intensity. If we could just find ways of winning a tight game or two, we would send out a signal to our opponents that they would have to work far harder than expected if they were to beat us. There was no way of doing this unless we were fit enough to go deep into the final stages of our matches. Once we were doing that on a regular basis, other things would follow: not least a growth in confidence and trust in each other, which was sadly lacking throughout the group. This was where Craig White came in.

At that time, our conditioning programme was run by Andy Clarke, who certainly knew his stuff. You don't get to work in high-end professional football with the likes of Liverpool and Manchester United if you're not on top of your job. But with a seven-match, two-Test tour of South Africa following hard on the heels of my initial dabblings in the Five Nations, I felt we needed to up our game in this area. When Andy said he wanted to join us in mid-trip so he could fulfil other commitments – he wasn't being held under lock and key by the IRFU – I made a stand by insisting that we needed a specialist fitness man for the whole mission. Andy was perfectly reasonable about it. He knew Craig and recommended him. It was the start of something good, because Craig came in with fresh ideas, a high level of commitment and the precious ability to make the players feel better about themselves. Quite quickly, they stopped being scared of their own shadows and hiding when the going got tough. It wasn't purely a physical thing: there is more to rugby than the ability to lift heavy weights and run for ever. But Craig's contribution was important because he helped drag Irish rugby into the modern age.

When we arrived in South Africa, one thing was

abundantly clear: from top to bottom, the Springbok rugby community had zero respect for us. As the reigning world champions, they were almost contemptuous: they didn't rate us and as a result, they couldn't imagine any circumstances in which we might give them a hard time, still less beat them. When I'd visited the country as a Super Rugby-playing Kiwi, the mood had been very different. New Zealanders were held in reverence the length and breadth of the country. Why? Because we'd earned the respect of the South Africans over generations: for most of the twentieth century, the Test series between our two countries had been the high water-marks of international rugby union. As for Ireland . . . who the hell were Ireland? You could almost see them looking down their noses at us. Certain members of the Springbok establishment were particularly dismissive, but the feeling that we were nothing more than an irrelevance was hardly confined to the committee men. It seemed the whole rugby nation thought we were easy meat. Our hosts were only a few years out of apartheid and for a certain class of rugby man, the superiority complex of old was still alive and kicking. That was my take on it, at least.

Some of the things that went on were almost laughable. On one occasion, we arrived at our designated training ground to find the place in lockdown and were forced to hang around outside for what seemed like ages until someone found somebody somewhere who happened to have a key to the gate. At other points during the trip, we were made to feel like second-class citizens during after-match functions. And when, after a difficult warm-up programme, we showed enough grit and determination to stay competitive in two unusually physical and bad-tempered Tests, we were widely condemned by the locals for 'crossing the line of acceptability'. My response? It takes two to tango. The first of those meetings with the Boks was in Bloemfontein and we went down 37–13 – which was probably closer than the locals had anticipated. There was a lot of off-the-ball stuff in that match and our hosts were responsible for more than their fair share of it, but we had some people who could look after themselves: Kevin Maggs, the Bristol centre, was far from a shrinking violet, and with forwards like Paddy Johns and Trevor Brennan on the field, we were always going to give some back.

We were certainly in no mood to be bullied come the second Test in Pretoria, and even though we were beaten more comprehensively that day, no one accused us of laying down. Trevor was a real handful by nature and, being at the start of his international career, he was understandably pumped to high heaven and desperate to get stuck in. 'Whatever you do, don't get yourself sent off,' I said as he took the field from the replacements' bench in front of a big crowd at the mighty Loftus Versfeld. If I'm honest, it was a plea rather than an instruction, one made more in hope than expectation. Yet somehow, despite the pandemonium all over the pitch, he was still out there at the final whistle.

It may sound strange, given the nature of the 'hospitality' and the disappointments on the scoreboard, but I look back on my first tour as an international coach with a sense of fondness. Three incidents stand out in my memory, all of them funny in their different ways. My first attempt at psychological one-upmanship was a complete disaster, for which I'm not sure Paddy Johns, the toughest of Ulstermen, has yet forgiven me. I got it into my mind that as a team, we looked soft and unhealthy, particularly when compared to the heavily muscled, ultra-athletic Springboks, and that this had something to do with the fact that so many members of the squad were pale of complexion. I knew that serious competitive body-builders routinely bronzed themselves up as a way of accentuating their musculature, so why not us? 'How about getting yourselves a fake tan?' I said to the players, thinking it would send out the right kind of message to our opponents. Some followed my advice, some didn't. One of those who went for it was Paddy. Come match day, his face was bright orange. When he ran onto the field in Bloemfontein, it was like witnessing a second sunrise. It wasn't the greatest of brainwaves, if I'm honest, but it seemed like a good idea at the time.

Then there was the stag do we held for our fly-half David Humphreys, who was getting married straight after the tour. I wouldn't dream of going into too much detail, but it was quite a night. And then there was the incident with Wales, who were playing the Springboks at Loftus Versfeld precisely one week after our match there. As luck would have it, they had booked into the same hotel in Pretoria and were checking in just as we were heading out. They were pretty condescending to us, I have to say: more than one of their tour party suggested that if we extended our stay for a few days and bought tickets for the game, we might learn a thing or two about taking on the might of the southern hemisphere. We decided against acting on this generous advice, but I soon wished I'd done so. Wales lost 96–13. Did I allow myself a quiet chuckle when I heard the result? Hand on heart, I cannot deny it.

Not that this little moment of schadenfreude added up to much: five matches into my international coaching career, I had yet to taste victory. It still felt that way when we resumed hostilities with the Springboks in late November, despite having scored well over 100 points in beating Georgia and Romania in a pair of qualifying matches for the 1999 World Cup. There again, I believed there were signs of progress on the field and was confident that with continuing improvements on the fitness front and greater familiarity with the style of rugby I had introduced, results would come our way. We certainly had the forwards in our squad: Keith Wood, Paul Wallace, Jeremy Davidson and Eric Miller were all recent Test Lions; Paddy Johns and Peter Clohessy were not the types to take backward steps; Victor Costello was making strides as a No 8 of quality. The South Africans won that autumn international 27–13 – with Nick Mallett as coach and Gary Teichmann as captain, they were a very strong side on a record run of high-end victories stretching back well over a year. We then lost again, by a point to France, in the opening round of the 1999 Six Nations. But our victory over

Wales at Wembley a fortnight later was no more than we deserved and when we toured Australia that summer, during which a certain Brian O'Driscoll took his first steps on the big stage, we gave an encouraging account of ourselves against the Wallabies in Perth.

Away from the pitch, things were a little more testing. Some issues were above my pay grade as a young coach: I'm thinking here of an image rights row between Keith Wood and his paymasters at the IRFU. Keith, massively popular among the Irish rugby public and a man who knew his own mind, was playing his club rugby across the water at Harlequins. As a result, there was a complicated dispute over who owned what part of him when it came to sponsorship and advertising. I kept well out of it: my only comment at the time was on selection policy, to the effect that if there was a 50–50 call between an Ireland-based candidate and a rival playing overseas, I'd give the nod to the local bloke. But it wasn't a huge concern at the time. The real fun and games on this subject would begin some years down the track, after my move to Wales.

More worrying from my point of view was the governing committee's inability to recognise that professional rugby on the cusp of a new century had less and less in common with the game they had played, with varying degrees of success, in the dim and distant past. Things were changing fast before their very eyes, but if they were looking, they weren't seeing. And I hadn't been in place long enough, and wasn't experienced enough in the ways of northern hemisphere rugby politics, to enter into an arm wrestle with the establishment. Apart from anything else, I wasn't even sure of their opinion of me. They must surely have recognised what I'd achieved at Connacht on limited resources – why else would they have asked me to succeed Brian Ashton? – and I had reasons to hope that some of the national team's recent performances had left them encouraged, if not elated. But the power in Irish rugby was in the hands of a very small group of people, the most prominent of whom were a couple of Lions from ages past in Syd Millar and Noel Murphy, together with a couple of Eddies, Messrs Coleman and Wigglesworth. Coleman chaired the all-important election sub-committee, while Wigglesworth had been appointed director of rugby development. Not much moved without their say-so, and while I may have been coaching the shop-window side, I felt a long way from the head office.

I did, however, have an ally in Pat Whelan, another signif-icant figure in the Ireland set-up. Pat was the team manager when I was appointed, and together with the backs coach Phil Danaher, he joined me on selection. Relations between the three of us were good for the most part, although I was more than a little alarmed when, having picked an Ireland A side for a second-string international, the line-up was changed at the last minute without any input from Phil or myself. It didn't require the services of an ace detective to work out that Pat must have been responsible for the deci-sion, because two of the three-man panel knew nothing about it and he was the last man standing. I had no hesitation in making my views known and it never happened again. What was Pat's rationale? I failed to get to the bottom of it. Perhaps he thought that as I was a recent arrival with no background in international coaching, there was an opportunity to exert a little additional control. Perhaps he wanted to establish just how far he could push me before getting a reaction. It was a peculiar incident, for sure, but in general terms he was supportive of me. When he suddenly resigned from the job after an ugly bust-up with journalist Tom English in the rest room of a Limerick sports bar, I wasn't sure what the ramifications would be. As it turned out, Donal Lenihan filled the vacancy. And Donal was brilliant from start to last.

Yet not even Donal, one of the most recognisable figures in the Irish game and a man who had earned maximum respect after spending more than a decade in the engine room of his country's scrum and captaining the midweekers on the 1989 Lions tour of Australia, could persuade the committee men to embrace modernity. For me and my colleagues at the sharp end to get anything past them was an effort of will. Take the Great Scrummaging Machine Pantomime as an example. Put simply, there came a point when our existing scrum machine had outlived its usefulness. It was ancient and knackered and completely out of date: nothing more than a bit of wood on sleds that cracked and splintered every time the Ireland forwards walked past it, let alone packed down against it. There were some excellent new models on the market with all sorts of funky techno-gadgets, the best of them developed by the former England lock Nigel Horton. The price? Five thousand pounds.

To secure this money from a union with £30 million in the bank and a portfolio of expensive property in some of the swankiest corners of Dublin, I had to fly to England for discussions with Nigel, and then make a full presentation to John Lyons, the treasurer. After which, I was asked to make a similar argument to the full board. I was gobsmacked. I assumed I would simply mention it to the chief executive, Philip Browne, and wake up one morning to find the machine in the middle of the training pitch, ready for use. Instead, I found myself up to my neck in negotiations more long-winded than Brexit. Imagine my amusement when, a short while later, we travelled to Italy for a Six Nations game and the committee, the ex-presidents and their wives booked themselves into the Cavalieri Hotel in Rome at a cost of £150,000 for the weekend! I remember three buses waiting for us at the airport: one for the players, coaches and staff; two for the travelling IRFU officials. One way or another, I learned a thing or two about the way the establishment works during those years in the Irish capital.

What I didn't learn nearly quickly enough was the importance of having a support base. I simply didn't know how to play the committee game, or understand how important that game was in the years following the collapse of amateurism. The Connacht element on the IRFU had my back to a significant degree – at least, they always talked to me at after-match functions, regardless of the result – but they were hardly in the majority. There was always a lot of politics going on in the background, and the higher up you went, the more raw the politics seemed to be. Looking back, it was a difficult time for everyone involved in Irish rugby: there were fears that the clubs in England and Wales would form a British League; there were fears over the primacy of the international game. In short, there was fear everywhere. It was a time of wheels within wheels, and I didn't always have a clear idea as to which way those wheels were spinning.

What I did understand was the importance of the 1999 World Cup, which was nominally based in Wales but was in reality played at venues across the Five Nations. One of those venues was Dublin, and the way I saw it, we had a very strong chance of playing a quarter-final in front of our home crowd if the pool stage went to plan. Yes, we were in a group with the Wallabies, who had players of the highest quality in John Eales, Joe Roff, Tim Horan, Stephen Larkham, George Gregan and a bunch of others. But the top two would be going through and I had no reason to think that we would struggle unduly against Romania or the United States, the other contenders. A runners-up finish would land us with an extra game in the form of a quarter-final play-off – the result of the tournament's unwieldy five-pool format – but the draw was kind. There was a distinct possibility that Argentina would be our opponents, and I knew we could beat them. Why? Because we'd done so in a warm-up game just before the start of the competition, scoring four tries in the process.

That Puma side was coached by none other than . . . Grizz Wyllie. Talk about a blast from the past. Eight years previously, it had been Grizz (among others) who had left me out of the All Blacks squad for a World Cup and that memory still rankled. I replayed the whole saga in my mind. Why had it happened? I hadn't challenged Grizz about it at the time – challenges to his authority were not seen as a great career move – and in the years since, I'd sometimes allowed myself to wonder whether my awkward history with Richard Loe in the Waikato team had been a factor, in light of Grizz being Richard's uncle. I don't think I ever fully believed there was any such link, but the fact that it even occurred to me exposed the true depth of my disappointment.

Sure enough – it must have been written in the stars – we came up against Argentina in the play-off, which was played in the northern French city of Lens. I remember that night vividly, in all its gory detail. We had the individuals to win the game: the Pumas were no pushovers, but the players who would drive them to a podium finish at the 2007 World Cup, from Agustin Pichot at scrum-half to Mario Ledesma and Gonzalo Longo up front, were still works in progress in '99. We, on the other hand, had a bunch of players who had been around a bit and grown familiar with each other. We had the tools to do the job, without question, and took the field knowing that victory would secure us a quarter-final against a struggling France in front of our home crowd at Lansdowne Road. So much for the theory. We were all over the Pumas for a large part of the match, but we made enough unforced errors to fritter away a healthy twelve-point lead. Gonzalo Quesada, a dead-eyed marksman in the No 10 shirt, banged over penalty after penalty to tighten up the contest and then, seven minutes from time, the Pumas opened up from a strong attacking position to create a try for their wing, Diego Albanese, who was a pretty good player, to be fair. Suddenly, as if from nowhere, we were a point down. Make that four points down, for within a couple of minutes, Quesada had kicked his seventh and final penalty.

I was struggling to believe what I was seeing, but there was still a chance for us at the death in the form of a line-out bang on the Puma line. We went for a version of the old Connacht trick: a thirteen-man line-out featuring everyone except Keith Wood, the thrower, and Tom Tierney, the scrum-half. It was the start of a siege that took the game clock towards ninety minutes, with the Pumas inventing new ways of stopping us short, none of which were remotely legal. Under today's laws, their bench would have been overflowing with sin-binned players and we would have won the game with a penalty try. Under the laws of 1999, as interpreted by the Australian referee Stuart Dickinson, they got clean away with it and dumped us out of the tournament. I was completely beaten up by the result: I'd never felt as low after a game of rugby. At the final whistle, a team from RTÉ, the Irish broadcasters, marched up the steps of the stand and set about interviewing me where I sat. It was completely unacceptable, but I wasn't in a state of mind to argue with them. What did I say? I don't have the faintest memory of my comments. What I do remember is feeling like a pariah as I arrived at the airport the next day and checked in for the flight home. I knew there was already a lot of talk about the union getting rid of me, which didn't make me feel any better about life, and my spirits would have been even lower but for Donal, who told me that if I went, he'd follow me out of the door. He must have swayed some opinions at a high level because there was no immediate move to sack me, but it still took me a good while to drag myself out of the emotional pit. With the media on my back, I was under a weight of pressure completely outside my experience. I'd never come close to feeling anything like it.

According to Trudi, who was worried about me, I went to bed as soon as we returned to Galway and barely got up for a couple of days. The house was full of people: her parents were staying with us, along with a couple of old friends. I wasn't much company, coming down for dinner and then disappearing again. As for Trudi's dad, he was literally burning the newspapers the moment he laid hands on them. On the third day, I walked into the kitchen while everyone was having breakfast. Our friend Alan Steel saw me in the doorway and said: 'Jesus, put the knives away, quick.' That joke broke the ice and we all laughed together for the first time since the defeat. Immediately after the meal, we piled into a couple of cars and headed down to Cork for a short break. We went to Kinsale, visited the Blarney Stone, did some fun things. And all the while we were down there, people were coming up and expressing sympathy and support I hadn't known existed. Certainly, it hadn't been reflected in the press.

Even though I wasn't reading the papers, I knew what was being written. The bad stuff went on for some time and there was no escaping it: friends would mention it and I had a press officer briefing me on the latest commentary. Why wasn't I reading it myself? It was a deliberate decision. The year before the World Cup I'd gone to the shops to pick up some things and bought a paper. It was following some defeat or other – the precise details escape me – and the resident critic was slaughtering me, even though we'd actually performed quite well. Bryn was sitting in the back seat of the car and asked for an ice cream. I turned around and snapped at him. Immediately, I regretted my outburst and thought: 'My God. These media people are f***wits. What kind of idiot am I to let this affect me and my family?' I screwed up the paper, threw it on the floor and that was it. I haven't opened any such publication since. Ever.

There was a gap of something like fourteen weeks between the calamity in Lens and the not insignificant challenge of playing England at Twickenham in the first round of the newly-expanded Six Nations. I would be taking the side across the water and fronting up at a venue where Ireland had won only three times in a quarter of a century. Needless to say, I'd have had plenty on my mind without a change to the backroom team. But there *had* been a change. A significant one. Phil Danaher had walked away after the World

Cup failure and Eddie O'Sullivan had joined the staff as assistant coach. He was not a man I knew personally, even though he had been my predecessor at both Galwegians and Connacht. But I knew *of* him. Eddie had been in the IRFU set-up for some considerable time, as a development officer and a fitness advisor as well as in a coaching capacity at provincial level. He had also been at the 1999 World Cup as assistant coach of the United States – the very USA on which we'd stuck fifty-odd points in the pool stage. He was said to be an ambitious type, very strong technically but not quite so hot when it came to the man-management side of the job. Still, I was happy to meet him for a coffee and talk about a possible role. A lot has been said and written about this subject down the years, but it was my decision to bring Eddie on board. He wasn't forced on me, by any stretch of the imagination. The other Eddies in the equation, Wigglesworth and Coleman, were in the loop. In fact, it was Wigglesworth who suggested the meeting in the first place. But it was my call. No one else's.

England did not go well for us: we lost 50–18. When I reviewed the match, it seemed to me that the scoreboard had done us no favours whatsoever. Yes, England played some terrific stuff and their attacking game, shaped by Brian Ashton and executed by such highly-skilled players as Jonny Wilkinson, Mike Catt, Austin Healey and Matt Perry, was of a very high quality indeed. Even so, I felt we had made a better fist of it than the critics made out. Unfortunately, this was an argument I couldn't win. Fifty points conceded and a big loss off the back of Lens? I was a sitting duck. If the pressure had been intense in late October, it was off the scale in early February.

Trudi tells a story about sitting at Twickenham with all the wives and girlfriends. As it was all going wrong, she says she felt herself growing increasingly emotional. Why? Because she knew I was going to be crucified. At the final whistle, she went straight to the loo, had a cry and took some deep breaths in an effort to calm herself. Keith Wood's wife – maybe she was his girlfriend at the time – came in. She was always such a nice person. She took one look at Trudi and asked her if she was OK. When Trudi retreated into one of the cubicles and began to cry again, she refused to leave.

The next day, a newspaper came out with a picture of my face behind bars, under a headline talking about 'crimes against rugby'. We both saw it. We couldn't avoid seeing it. I wondered whether we might be misreading the message – that the intention was to show me standing outside, looking into a cell full of convicted committee men. That seemed unlikely, however. Phil Danaher's wife, Eimear, phoned Trudi from Limerick and said: 'How are you doing?' 'Not good,' my wife replied. 'This is horrible.' They met for lunch on the Monday, during which Trudi was still in tears. She said she was concerned for my health – that I had bags under my eyes and looked shocking. The thought that struck her most forcefully was that when people talked about rugby being only a game, they didn't know the half of it. 'This is more than a game,' she thought. 'This is our life.'

Our next game was Scotland at home a fortnight later and it came down to this: if we lost, I would tender my resignation. It goes without saying that I wrestled with this decision for hours on end, not least during the hours of darkness, but a few days before the game I arrived at my grave conclusion. What other choice did I have? Once a big-selling newspaper has put you behind bars and accused you of crimes against the sport you love, you need the skin of a rhinoceros to shrug your shoulders and carry on regardless. My skin wasn't that thick. Not at that point, at least – and to be frank, I'm not sure it is now, two decades on. It wasn't that I didn't think we could beat the Scots – I had some very clear ideas about how we should approach the game, based on a radical approach in selection – but I simply couldn't see a way through for me in the event of another defeat. It was a difficult couple of weeks, to say the least.

I changed more than half the team, including some significant figures: Conor O'Shea and David Humphreys went from the starting back division; Paul Wallace and Dion O'Cuinneagain went from the pack. I turned to the likes of Girvan Dempsey and Denis Hickie in the outside backs and restored Mick Galwey to the second row of the scrum. I also handed out some debuts: to Shane Horgan on the wing, Simon Easterby on the flank, John Hayes at tight-head prop and, most high-profile of all, to a pair of Munster half-backs by the names of Ronan O'Gara and Peter Stringer. And after a quarter of an hour or so, we were ten points down. I remember sitting high up in the gods, concocting my resignation speech, which I would deliver at the press conference. It was over for me. Done and dusted. Finished.

At which juncture, we proceeded to score the next forty-four points. Yes, forty-four. It was only at the very dog-end of the game that the Scots ran in a couple of consolation tries. Had they not done so, 44–10 would have been the final margin of victory. The turnaround started with a try from Malcolm O'Kelly, the lock I'd decided to stick with rather than drop, and continued with eight points from the O'Gara boot. That gave us a half-time lead, albeit a narrow one. After the break, it was joy unconfined. There was a freshman's try for Horgan within two minutes of the restart, a score for Brian O'Driscoll, a five-pointer for Humphreys off the bench and a crossing of the Scottish line by Keith Wood to take us beyond forty points – a record for Ireland in championship rugby. Did I feel vindicated? Yes, to a degree. But it was also the case that the situation had demanded a bold approach. For the England game, I'd stood by a number of players who had been so tormented by the World Cup experience and offered them a shot at redemption. The half-century of points conceded at Twickenham had changed the picture completely. There was now no argument against introducing a new generation of talent to the Test arena and offering them an opportunity to state their credentials as potential World Cup candidates in 2003.

Italy were next up, another home game for us, and my selection for that one was a little less interesting. I made precisely no changes and we duly ran in half a dozen tries. Then we won in Paris, for the first time since 1972 (Ireland hadn't beaten the French anywhere since 1983). That was some victory and it should be one of my fondest memories. In many ways, it is. It was the day Brian O'Driscoll scored a blinding hat-trick of tries and confirmed to the worldwide rugby public what many of us in Ireland had known for some time: that he was a centre of the rarest gifts, a midfielder for the ages, and the kind of player who expands the range of his position. There was mention in the press of French injuries, but they were hardly short of class: their starting pack included Christian Califano, Marc Dal Maso, Franck Tournaire, Fabien Pelous and Abdel Benazzi. As far as I was concerned, this was a serious marker for the Ireland team and a big moment on the personal front.

Yet when I look back on it today, in the light of subsequent events, some of the shine has gone. I remember quite a few of us, players and staff, piling into one of the Irish bars in Paris – is there a great city in the world, or indeed a city of any description, without an Irish bar? – and running into a sea of green-shirted supporters celebrating the moment in time-honoured fashion. As we headed upstairs in search of some space, the throng at the bar started singing my name. For me, being a shy sort, it was an 'oh shit' moment. I sheepishly acknowledged them with a gentle wave and ducked into the crowd of players. It seems Eddie O'Sullivan saw the incident differently. In his book *Never Die Wondering*, he claimed to have seen me at the top of the stairs 'waving to the crowd like the Pope in St Peter's Square', adding that 'he loved them and they loved him'. What a joke. Anyone who knows me would struggle to take a single word of this nonsense seriously. It's a ridiculous reading of events. But as we're on the subject of Eddie and that trip to Paris, I should report that a very senior member of the party told me a long time after the event that Eddie hadn't celebrated the victory at all. In fact, he was heard to say: 'This means Gatland will be in the job for another two years.' Sums it up, really.

A self-inflicted loss to Wales in the last round of the tournament left me feeling a little flat, but we'd finished third in the table, which was as clear a statement of progress as anyone could have wanted, even the committee types in Dublin. But things were darkening. Donal Lenihan, such a supportive manager, was lured away by the British and Irish Lions ahead of their 2001 series in Australia. His departure hurt me. So too did the continuing commentary in some parts of the press, where my 'rivalry' with Eddie O'Sullivan was part of the daily back-page routine. I'm not sure I saw our relationship in quite those terms, but there was a fair bit of suspicion in the air. There was also something of a breakdown in relations with Keith Wood, a totemic figure in Irish rugby and captain of the team. This is how things unfolded.

We were good enough to win the title in 2001, despite England gathering momentum and playing at somewhere near the height of their powers. Sure enough, we won our opening games against Italy and France, but the outbreak of foot and mouth disease in the United Kingdom meant the tournament – or rather, our role in the tournament – was interrupted. We did not play our third-round match, against Scotland at Murrayfield, until September. The game went wrong in a big way and we were outscored four tries to one in a 32–10 defeat. As I reviewed the game, I noticed that Keith had made a tackle on the halfway line and then walked back towards our posts while the Scots were going through ten or twelve phases before scoring. I was splutteringly angry. My whole rugby background had taught me that win or lose, the one area where you don't compromise is commitment. I showed the footage in a team meeting and said: 'I don't care who you are, this is unacceptable.' It was a blunt way of dealing with the situation and I'm perfectly happy to accept now that there may have been better methods available to me, but I was determined to make a point. From that moment on, things were frosty between me and Keith.

I took a fair bit of hammer from the committee after Edinburgh, which annoyed me even more. These were people who had last played serious rugby in the 1970s and had seen the game once, live. And they were ripping into the coaching team who had been through every second of footage a dozen times over and understood exactly what had happened and why. Even when we finished the tournament with two excellent victories, over Wales and then the Grand Slam-chasing English, my dealings with the blazered classes were strained. Still, there were interesting challenges ahead, not least a chance to coach a Test team against the All Blacks for the first time. New Zealand were our last opponents of the calendar year and my old Waikato teammate and first flat-mate John Mitchell had taken charge of them. Here was a proper event. My contract with the IRFU would be up after the match, but I was confident of staying through to the World Cup in 2003. If we could just put up a show against Jonah Lomu, Tana Umaga, Doug Howlett and the rest of them – the rest including a promising debutant flanker by the name of Richie McCaw – I'd be a shoo-in for an extension. That much was obvious.

Put up a show we did. After a hell of a first forty minutes, we were 16–7 ahead. When Denis Hickie touched down early in the second half, the score was 21–7. That was the high point, sadly: a first green-shirted victory over the silver fern was quickly blown away on the wind. Jonah went to work on us in that third quarter and the All Blacks went bang, bang, bang. Three tries in eleven minutes. We lost 40–29. Was I disappointed? Bitterly. It had been a massive game, not just for me but for the whole of Irish rugby. Yet while we'd clearly lacked belief and had a good way to go before we could match the best over a full eighty minutes, we'd still won six of our eight games in 2001 and finished level with England at the top of the championship. When I travelled to Dublin for my contract talks, I was absolutely certain that Philip Browne, CEO of the IRFU, would offer me new terms.

It was the end of November. The meeting was at the

Berkeley Court Hotel, close to Lansdowne Road, and there were three people present: me, Philip and Eddie Coleman. Philip came straight out with it. 'We'd like to thank you for what you've done for Irish rugby, but we're not going to offer you a new contract,' he said. I was completely taken aback. I mumbled something about being disappointed, that I'd set my sights on taking the side through to the World Cup, that I felt we'd made some big strides . . . and that was it. No more words came out. Philip asked me if there was anyone I'd like to call straight away, so I rang Trudi and told her they were letting me go. Her response? Something along the lines of 'What???!!!' I asked her for Billy Glynn's phone number. Billy was our solicitor. He was also on the IRFU committee and was one of the members of that august body with whom I got along. He was gobsmacked when I told him the news and did not hesitate in agreeing to represent me – *against* the IRFU, in which he was a significant figure! Only in Ireland. He ended up playing a blinder on my behalf, securing me a more generous financial settlement than some of his senior colleagues on the union had been anticipating. The downside? I had to sign the usual bit of paper, promising not to talk about things in public.

A less than perfect end to a less than perfect day awaited me. I walked out of the Berkeley Court just as Eddie O'Sullivan was driving in. 'Now *there's* a funny thing,' I thought to myself as I made my way down the road to another hotel, Jury's, to meet up with my old Connacht friend Joe Healy. Trudi had contacted Joe's wife, told her the news and said that if Joe was in town, I might be grateful for a shoulder to cry on. At this point, I bumped into John Hussey, an IRFU committee man, who wished me all the best with the contract talks. He didn't have a clue, clearly. But then, no one had a clue, apart from the very small handful of people in the thick of it. When I walked in the door of our home in Galway a few hours later, I had remarkably recovered enough to greet Trudi with a smile and the words 'a great weight has been lifted off my shoulders'. She was relieved to see me and realise I was OK about it all.

Two weeks later – a fortnight during which I really didn't feel good about Ireland or rugby or myself – I was named Phillips Coach of the Year and caught the train down to Dublin, where I received a standing ovation as I accepted the award. How ironic is *that*? By the time I arrived back home, something inside me had changed for the better. In fact, I felt great, as light as air. And since that day, I've looked back on my years in Ireland as formative, a period of accelerated experience in which I learned an enormous amount about a huge number of things. I don't have any traumas about it because I think I came out on the right side of the ledger. What happened back then led me to the here and now, so from that perspective, I'm grateful.

Only once, when Ireland were playing England in 2004 and I found myself in hospitality at Twickenham in the company of the visiting committee men, did I allow my lingering negative emotions to rise to the surface. Don Crowley, a Connacht man to his bones, had assumed the presidency of the IRFU and when he saw me, he greeted me like a long-lost brother. 'Gatty, Gatty . . .' he said, almost running towards me with his arms spread wide. My reply? 'F*** off.' It wasn't like me and I shouldn't have said it, but had Don contacted me after my sacking and showed some support? No. I told him: 'Don, you're a Galwegian and I'm a Galwegian. You didn't have the courtesy to give me a call, despite our association.' There were other Connacht men present and all of them raised their eyebrows, but I think they understood.

Yet to this day, I have the deepest respect for Irish rugby. Even if Munster and Leinster had not won half a dozen European titles between them; even if Declan Kidney and Joe Schmidt, two of my successors in the head coach role, had not delivered Grand Slams . . . if none of those things had happened, rugby union in the Emerald Isle would still be a sporting miracle. To have an all-Ireland team playing at the very top level of a major sport, despite all the history and politics and tension between the communities in those four great union-playing provinces, is an extraordinary thing. When I started with Galwegians, I already had some under-standing of the sensitivities at work in the country because I'd made a study of the events surrounding the 1916 Easter Rising and associated matters during my time at university. I think it helped me avoid saying daft things or making dumb mistakes. Not that there weren't times when I was just a little irreverent: for instance, I remember sprinkling holy water on boots belonging to David Humphreys, very much a man of the Protestant persuasion who was known in the squad as 'First Minister'. Did I feel guilty? Not when he kicked five out of five the following day. That was the wicked side of me. It came about as our bag man Patrick O'Reilly (Rala) always used to clean David's boots and had holy water from Lourdes as part of his kit. Rala was a brilliant bag man and was loved by the entire squad and that is why he has been used in that role in the last three Lions tours.

There was a flipside, however, as I knew there would be: after all, I'd seen the soldiers on the streets when I toured Ireland with the All Blacks. This flipside took the form of a letter addressed to 'Gatland, Lenihan and Danaher' after the three of us picked our squad for the South Africa trip in 1998. It read as follows: 'You biased bastards from the south . . . we understand from our rugby friends that you haven't picked enough players from the north. Enjoy your trip to South Africa. We know where you live.' The purported sender? 'The Red Hand of Ulster.' We gave it straight to Special Branch. That was the only time I had personal experience of a threat, although some time later, a senior member of our group was directly affected when his son was badly beaten up and thrown in a skip one Christmas Eve. The IRA made contact with him, saying they knew the identities of those responsible and asking if he wanted them to 'deal with it'. He declined.

5

BUILDING THE BLACK WALL

Trevor Leota was different. An Aucklander of Samoan descent, he was only 5 ft 9 in tall, a statistic that would have done him no favours at all as a professional rugby player but for the fact that he also gave the impression of being 5 ft 9 in wide. Trevor was not spherical, like so many of the game's most celebrated front-row folk heroes. He was square. A square with hair. 'Like an omelette served on two tree-trunks,' wrote one journalist, referring to the bright yellow crop of curls up top – very much a Trevor trademark – and the unusually large circumference of the legs down below. In the tale of the tape, this bloke's story was unique.

After leaving the Ireland post, I had been working in the English Premiership with Wasps for eighteen months or so when I had a numbers discussion with Craig White – the same Craig White who had made such a contribution on the strength and conditioning front during my time with Ireland and was now spending his time ensuring that Wasps, already the fittest club side in the land when I joined, would stay well ahead of the field. Between us, we had decided that

Trevor's true fighting weight was 123 kg, or just over 19 st in old money. Whenever we put him on the pitch at 123, we felt the balance of close-quarter power and open-field mobility was just about perfect. The problem? Let's just say that Trevor's readings were a little on the inconsistent side, largely as a consequence of his fast-food intake. What struck me was that his weight was so different almost from one week to the next. Something odd was going on and I had to get to the bottom of it.

The scales in the spit-and-sawdust gym at our training ground in Acton were situated inside an old cupboard, where there was barely enough room to swing a cat.

'Can you weigh Trevor now,' I said to Craig on this particular day.

'He was weighed yesterday,' came the reply. 'He was 123 kg.'

'I know. Do it again . . . and this time, pull the scales out of the cupboard.'

Trevor duly hopped on and the needle went into orbit, stopping, a little reluctantly, at the 129 mark. The man was nearly a stone heavier than we'd thought, which confirmed my suspicions. Trevor was so wide, he'd been jamming his shoulders into the sides of the cupboard and easing the pressure on the scales. I wasn't the happiest man on the planet when I called him into my office. 'Go home, Trevor,' I said, 'and do not dream of returning to this club until you're down to 123 kg.' I was thinking it would take him a week to remove most of the excess, so plenty of time to reflect on the error of his ways and learn his lesson. Three weeks later, I hadn't heard from him. So I rang him and said: 'Trevor, I think you'd better come back in tomorrow.' He turns up, we put him on the scales . . . and he's 132 kg. Oh well, so much for my man-management.

The following season, while his wife Ruth was back home in New Zealand and we were fast approaching the Heineken Cup semi-finals, the problem reared its head again. Trevor was consuming buckets of KFC the way a serious drinker sinks pints of beer and was not exactly getting himself to bed before the watershed, so I offered Paul 'Bobby' Stridgeon, fitness coach extraordinaire and the proud owner of a PhD in positive thinking, an extra £500 to act as a round-the-clock, live-in chaperone. It was a naked bribe, but we needed Trevor at his best for the big challenges ahead. Paul has a bigger energy supply than the national grid, but after three days, he returned to the club defeated. 'I can't do it, Gats,' he said, a broken man. 'Trevor comes home from training, hits the PlayStation and then, late at night, tells me he has to go to the airport to pick up his cousin and gets back at two in the morning. And that's leaving aside the food and drink he puts away in front of my face. It's the cycle from hell and I can't keep up.'

Yet Trevor, as difficult to keep in check as he was brilliant when fit, played a very significant part in our many and varied triumphs between 2002 and 2005: three straight Premiership titles, a Heineken Cup title, a European Challenge Cup title. The supporters loved him in the way he loved a

Jack Daniel's and Coke on a night out, revelling in his bravery and commitment, his devotion to the club, his individuality. Why do I talk about him at this length, when so many other Wasps of that time – Lawrence Dallaglio, Josh Lewsey, Simon Shaw, Rob Howley, Matt Dawson, Craig Dowd, Joe Worsley – were far bigger names at international level, some of them nothing short of stellar? Because in his way, Trevor the one-off Samoan hooker summed up the club as a collective. We had a habit of providing a home for players who found it difficult to settle elsewhere. Just as there was no one quite like Trevor, there was nowhere quite like Wasps.

If it hadn't been for the fact that Gabby and Bryn were both in school and needed some continuity, it's perfectly possible that we would all have headed back to New Zealand the moment my spell with Ireland reached its premature conclusion in 2001. I knew I wanted to stay in coaching, partly because I felt I had a point to prove but mostly because I sensed that I'd developed a hell of a lot in a short space of time and was better placed to make a success of myself. You don't come into rugby coaching fully formed. You grow into the job not just by refining the tactical ideas that work and rethinking or abandoning those that don't, but also by improving your human skills: working on your communication; building relationships with your paymasters to create the best environment within budgetary constraints (and breaking through those constraints when the situation demands it); establishing codes of conduct and chains of command; understanding your own responsibilities and living up to them. I'd merely scratched the surface in Ireland. Wherever I worked next, I wouldn't repeat the mistakes I'd made in Dublin.

I had no clue as to where that 'wherever' would turn out to be. There were expressions of interest from Wales and France, but it was not until Nigel Melville phoned that something lit up in my mind. Nigel was in charge at Wasps, who at that point were involved in a struggle to protect their status as a top-flight English club, and told me he was in need of an assistant coach with some expertise in the forward department. Two things occurred to me. Firstly, the chance to work in London was incredibly enticing and might not come again. It would be a phenomenal experience for the whole family. Secondly, it was blindingly obvious that Wasps were a better club than their parlous position in the Premiership made out. They had good players, top-end players, some of them, and a recent history of success. Yes, they'd found the transition to professionalism challenging off the field, but they were hardly alone in that. There were real possibilities for me there if I could make things fit together. I immediately expressed an interest and when Nigel wondered how much money I might be looking for, I gave him a figure higher than I had been paid at Ireland and his response was: 'I thought it would be about that.'

My first job was to cast an eye over the team, so I ventured across the water and watched them play up at Newcastle. Kenny Logan won the game late on with a kick from the touchline – good value though he was, you couldn't always bank on Kenny hitting the spot – and I hooked up with the squad the following week. Nigel was also running England Under-21s and within a fortnight or so, he was off with them, leaving me to run most of the coaching operation, if not quite all of it. I was also picking up some rumours that he might be moving to Gloucester and that if he went, it would be before the end of the season. Those rumours turned out to be spot on. Quite quickly, Nigel sat me down in his office and told me he had informed Chris Wright, the music industry magnate who had bought a controlling share in the club some six years previously, that he was indeed heading for Kingsholm. It turned out that Nigel had always seen me as more than a forwards coach. Uncomfortably aware that his decision to move clubs might leave Wasps in an awkward position, he wanted to recruit someone capable of being top dog. One of those who recommended me was Rob Henderson, the Lions Test centre who I had capped during my time with Ireland and had made fifty-odd league appearances for Wasps before moving to Munster.

As far as the existing personnel were concerned, Wasps were in a good place. Certainly, there was no reason under the sun why they should have been routinely leaking forty points against beatable opposition and scrabbling around for crumbs at the foot of the Premiership table. There were more than enough high-class players in the squad to front up at the very top level of club rugby, together with some quality coaches. Rob Smith, a former head coach, was busily engaged in the process of establishing our academy as a market leader.

More importantly, given the situation, a certain Shaun Edwards was in place when I arrived and was already showing signs of developing into one of the great defensive strategists in the history of the game. Almost immediately, we kicked around some ideas on changing our defensive system – on painting the black wall, as the players liked to call it, an even darker and more impenetrable shade of . . . well, black. 'Why are we sticking with a push defence?' I asked him. 'Maybe we should start upping our line speed and blitzing the opposition.' Shaun said he'd been thinking about it for ages and was desperate to give it a go. Apart from London Irish, who were coached by the World Cup-winning Springbok centre Brendan Venter (the first qualified GP to create his own patients, as one joker put it), no one was using the blitz. From thereon in, we won six on the bounce – it would have been seven but for injuries at Sale, which forced us to ask our hooker Phil Greening to kick goals as well as perform his front-row duties – and almost qualified for the following season's Heineken Cup. Which, I firmly believe, we would have won. As it was, we won the second-tier Challenge Cup instead.

What the club didn't have was an infrastructure worthy of a professional sporting set-up. The set of scales in the cupboard at the Twyford Avenue training ground was the least of the issues. The gym was crammed into one of two old squash courts – the physiotherapy 'department' was shoehorned into the other one – and the analysis facilities were rudimentary at best. We had an elderly television screen, an ancient video recorder and a remote control blessed with a mind of its own. Shaun would fast-forward the footage, then rewind. Forward, back, forward, back. It took for ever. One day, the television went kaput and Shaun punched it. Hard. Needless to say, it stayed kaput. 'I think we have to do something about this,' I said, with an air of understatement. It was time to gamble.

We were still stuck in the bottom half of the league at this point, and at the next board meeting, Chris Wright was worried.

'I've done my numbers and we need thirty-two,' he said.

'Thirty-two what?' I asked.

'Points. If we get to thirty-two, we'll avoid relegation.'

'Chris, I can promise you this: we won't be relegated,' I replied.

It was then that I rolled the dice. 'The thing is, Joe Worsley's contract is up at the end of the season. He's a great player for us, one of our biggest assets, but I'll be happy to let him go elsewhere if you give me the money to improve the infrastructure. We need some up-to-date analysis equipment, a new gym, more strength and conditioning staff. To be honest, we're not even feeding the players properly.'

The response from the boss was all I could have hoped. Chris said he didn't want to see Joe go, but I could have the money anyway. Result. I should have bought myself a lottery ticket the same day. Speaking seriously, I was proud of the outcome. Chris owned Queen's Park Rangers as well as Wasps and when it came to sport, he looked at things through the football lens. The way he saw it, big-name players were a central plank of his investment strategy. As far as I was concerned, environment was more important. I believed I could afford to lose one player, however good he might be, if it meant improving things for twenty or thirty others. As a result of this episode, I was able to bring in Craig White to run the conditioning and my countryman Tony Hanks on analysis – two genuine experts who would make a massive contribution to our success over the coming seasons.

We did all sorts of trendy things, keeping ourselves ahead of the field in the process, and it was based around a recognition that the dynamics of the club game were changing. On the one hand, age-old European traditions were still in place. On the other, elements of the southern hemisphere game were being introduced. Back home, rugby people tended to concentrate on events at the top of the table rather than the bottom, and we were well used to play-offs – semi-finals and finals, big must-win matches, championship games with everything on the line. These things were now starting to feature at Premiership level, but as promotion and relegation were still in place, I felt we needed a bespoke approach. Essentially, I wanted my players to be at their peak for the decisive business at the end of a campaign, not the building-block business at the start and in the middle. Yes, we had to perform well enough in early season to put ourselves in a position to challenge later on, but there was no point finishing top of the table in such a knackered state that we couldn't close out the deal.

The Rob Howley story illustrates the change in culture. One of my first significant decisions as head coach was to sign the brilliant Wales and Lions scrum-half from Cardiff, pretty much from under the noses of Bath, who had been on his trail for a while. Rob was nearing the end of his career, but Martyn Wood, our existing first-choice No 9, said he thought he would improve his all-round game if he felt under more pressure for his place. Martyn was one of the best passers of a ball I'd ever come across, but to his credit, he was worried about being stuck in his comfort zone. When Kenny Logan, a terrific servant of the club, heard that Rob might be on the move out of Wales and mentioned it to me, I invited Rob up to London and completed the formalities in double-quick time. As for Martyn, his face fell a mile when he heard the news. 'I know what I said, Warren,' he remarked, 'but I didn't mean Rob bloody Howley!' Rob made his debut at the start of the 2002–3 campaign. The following week, I stuck him on the bench. Rob came to see me the moment he saw the team list.

'What have I done wrong?' he asked. 'Why am I dropped?' Here was a world-class player in a serious panic.

'Rob, it's September,' I explained. 'The Premiership final is in May and I intend us to be in it. I want you to play twenty-two or twenty-three games tops and a lot of those will be off the bench until I really need you to start a bunch of matches in a row.'

The penny began to drop, but only slowly. 'Oh. I'm used to playing every week,' he said.

'At this club, Rob, you will definitely *not* be playing every week.'

There were fresh initiatives – for instance, we travelled to Poland well ahead of the common herd, for cryotherapy sessions, not least because it was a relatively cheap trip in the early 2000s – but perhaps the biggest part of our revolution, if you want to call it that, was based around the idea of days off. When it came to down-time, our players were given more than any of their Premiership rivals. We guaranteed them eight weeks away from the club in the summer, while making strength and conditioning staff available to them if they found themselves climbing the walls through boredom. When they returned, there were carefully constructed individual plans for the entire season: six-week cycles of intense activity, followed by non-negotiable breaks of four days. Whether you were Lawrence Dallaglio or an unknown wing on a rookie contract, you could plan ahead and book trips away with the family. It was as much about mental freshness as it was about physical wellbeing. There was a lot being said and written about the number of matches we were cramming into the northern hemisphere season, as there is now, but the games weren't the problem. Everyone wanted to play games – that was why they were professional sportsmen in the first place. It was the training that took its toll. The endless week-in, week-out trudge of life in the gym and on the practise pitch. If the players knew there was the prospect of a proper breather every six weeks, there was a reasonable chance of them retaining their enthusiasm for the day job. In essence, it was an All Black thing: train hard, train well . . . but don't train yourself into the dirt.

This radical idea of treating players as human beings really came into its own when Clive Woodward was stepping up his World Cup preparations with England in 2003. Not all of the Premiership coaches and rugby directors were head-over-heels happy at the prospect of England get-togethers for the wider squad on Mondays and Tuesdays throughout the season, and some of them were a whole lot less impressed when Clive started requesting additional days here and there. I sat in a number of meetings where high-profile bosses flatly refused to give another inch in helping out the national team and had to be dragged kicking and screaming into agreeing by their more generous-spirited colleagues. My view was simple, partly because I'd been on both sides of the fence and understood the delicate nature of the issue. I wanted my players to achieve international status and told them to their faces, with my hand on my heart, that I'd do everything conceivably possible to help them get there. It wasn't an entirely selfless gesture. I knew how much my All Black shirt had meant to me, and how being an All Black had helped me raise my standards at provincial level with Waikato. If Lawrence, or Simon Shaw or any of the others could raise Wasps up a notch as a result of their exposure to Test rugby, what wasn't to like? I went further. Because we shared the QPR stadium at Loftus Road and played most of our Premiership games on Sunday after-noons, the squad were almost always given Thursdays off.

But if the internationals had been flogging themselves raw on Mondays and Tuesdays with England, it seemed just a little harsh to make them train on the Wednesday. I told them to report back on the Friday, do the captain's run on the Saturday, play on the Sunday and shoot off back to Clive once they'd had a shower and a cup of tea. Very soon, we had a reputation as the most enlightened club around – a club who really cared about their players.

'When are you back in with Wasps?' one of the Leicester boys would ask one of ours after England training.

'Friday.'

'Jesus! They want me in at 7 o'clock tomorrow morning.'

It was a fascinating experience, building that Wasps environment, and it left a mark on me: during my long spell with the Wales team, I used many of the same ideas and techniques to create a sense of togetherness where the players were happy to give everything of themselves because they knew the feeling was reciprocal. There were times at Wasps when some of our bigger names were offered tens of thousands of pounds to switch clubs. Pretty much without exception, they found the extra money easy to resist. I remember Phil Greening, who was earning a lot less with us than he had been in a previous life up at Sale, saying to the squad one day: 'Listen, boys, money isn't everything. No matter how much you're being paid, if you're not happy going to work in the morning, it isn't worth it.' It seems to me now that Saracens, so wildly successful in recent years, have followed the Wasps model. Not in the fine detail, perhaps, but certainly in the creation of a value system that brings them together as a community. Funnily enough, two of their outstanding backroom staff, Mark McCall and Phil Morrow, were together at Ulster when I was in London and they came over for the day to find out how we were going about things. I took Phil, a strength and conditioning specialist, on the Lions tour of New Zealand in 2017. One night, he said to me: 'Gats, do you remember that day we spent with you at Wasps? The moment we got home, we implemented everything we saw.'

Of course, we could have developed a culture richer than that of Ancient Greece and still drawn a blank with our results had we not been blessed with players of unusual ability and astonishing depths of competitive spirit. Call it attitude, call it balls, call it bloody-mindedness, give it any name of your choice – people like Lawrence Dallaglio, Joe Worsley, Paul Volley, Josh Lewsey, Simon Shaw, Fraser Waters (or 'Farquhar', as he was popularly known, on account of his privileged public-school education and no obvious need for a salary) and, in the second half of my time at the club, Matt Dawson, had what it took to bring it all home. I always had a huge amount of time for Lawrence. In fact, I believe him to be the best captain I've ever seen in the game. That's quite a statement from someone who played under the likes of Buck Shelford and has had close working relationships with such major international figures as Keith Wood, Paul O'Connell, Sam Warburton and Alun Wyn Jones. But it's not just me. Ask Rob Howley, a Wales legend who loved nothing better than to stick one on England. Ask Craig

Dowd, who won sixty caps as an All Black front-rower. They'll tell you the same thing. Lawrence was the man.

I saw him in the bad times as well as the good ones – times when he had personal problems that would have blunted the edge and crippled the spirit of 99.9 per cent of rugby players worldwide. Yet never once did I feel the need to question his value or commitment to Wasps. Indeed, I can recall him addressing the squad during one of his down periods and telling them: 'Do you know why I love coming through these gates every morning? Because I know that here, in this room and out there on that pitch, there are people who will always have my back.' He repaid that faith and support week after week, month after month, season after season. Such was his sense of pride – not just as a Wasp, but as an Englishman, despite his Irish–Italian parentage – there never seemed to be an opponent who could subdue him. Naked courage? A sense of responsibility? The willingness to drain himself of every last drop of energy? All of these things were prominent parts of his make-up. So was honesty. If he could be hard on colleagues when he felt they had slipped below the accepted standards, he always gave himself the hardest time of all. After a poor perform-ance, he would stand in front of the mirror – literally, not metaphorically – and curse himself to high heaven. He hated losing, with a capital 'H'. I don't think I've ever seen a player more driven.

Matt Dawson wasn't too far behind on the attitude scale. When Rob Howley retired in 2004 – he was struggling with injury and more importantly, his father had fallen seriously ill – we had a hole to fill in the scrum-half department. So we went for Matt, who had just lifted the World Cup with Lawrence and the rest of our England contingent and felt his career-long spell at Northampton had reached its natural conclusion, not least because he was beginning to build a media career for himself and was drawn by the potential of playing what remained of his rugby in London. I had always admired his spirit and on one memorable occasion, I ran into him personally during a Premiership match between Wasps and Northampton; or rather, he ran into me. Deliberately. I was on the touchline the moment the half-time whistle sounded, bitterly complaining to the referee that our opponents were gaming the replacement system. Noticing our conversation and almost certainly being aware of its content, Matt changed direction on his way to the tunnel and treated me to a full-force shoulder-barge. 'My sort of bloke,' I thought.

When Matt joined us, I knew there would be the odd complication around his interests outside of rugby: most obviously, some clashes between our training sessions and his broadcasting commitments. Was it ideal? Of course not. Was it beyond the wit of man to compromise? Same answer. I told him we would work around it with a little judicious juggling. When he had a similar conversation with Andy Robinson, who by then had succeeded Clive Woodward as England coach, the outcome was different. Andy told him that if he couldn't make himself available for every squad session without fail, he wouldn't be considered for selection. Frankly, I think we handled it better, and as a result, Matt gave us some excellent service. I think we were good for him, too. When he turned up at Twyford Avenue for his first training session and started flicking out his passes, I could hear his new clubmates giving him a hard time, along the lines of 'Who's this bloke? Fifty England caps? He's useless.' It was true that Matt's pass was not the strongest part of his game, a fact not lost on Alex King, our outside-half. Alex stopped the session and chucked the ball back at Matt, together with a message. 'I am NOT taking any more of that shit,' he growled. Matt's reaction? Silence. Not a word. No hint of a 'show me *your* caps and I'll let you count mine' response. Instead, he spent time after every training run at the back of the pitch, improving his core skills. He could have said: 'I'm an England man and a World Cup winner, so stuff you all.' Instead, he bought into what we stood for, heart and soul. I take my hat off to him.

That level of dedication was probably the principal factor in our winning run, which began in 2002–3 with a Premiership–Challenge Cup double. With the World Cup in Australia looming large in the thoughts of our international brigade, the likes of Lawrence and Joe Worsley were playing out of their skins. Such were their levels of fitness and drive, they would play a league game or a European pool match and then join the substitutes for an extra half-hour of conditioning work, just to burn off their unused energy. In the Challenge Cup, we drew Stade Français in the quarter-finals, to be played over two legs. The Parisians were a class act and even though we won our home match by thirteen points, I knew we would be pushed hard in the return fixture across the Channel. Our victory that day, by a fifteen-point margin, was nothing short of magnificent and a decisive statement of our potential. In the semis, we overcame a tough Pontypridd side with a little to spare. In the high-scoring final against Bath at the Madejski Stadium in Reading, we were always in control and ran in half a dozen tries to win 48–30.

A week later, we were at Twickenham for the first winner-takes-all Premiership final. Gloucester had won the league by more points than they knew what to do with. Their reward? A three-week break. We finished second and played two more games before Twickers – a Premiership semi-final with third-placed Northampton and that Euro final with Bath. The prevailing view among the pundits was that in our knackered state, we would struggle to beat a well-rested Gloucester. Which just showed what the pundits knew. The West Country club's inactivity played straight into our hands, especially as we had looked at the long-range weather forecast and spent six weeks training in bin liners as a means of replicating the heat of early May. It was a beautiful day in southwest London and when Tony Spreadbury, the referee, poked his head around our dressing-room door, he was full of the joys. 'Hello, lads,' he said in his usual jovial manner. 'Great day for it.' I did not enter into the spirit of it. 'Tony, we're here for a game of rugby,' I replied. 'We expect to win and win well. I really don't give a shit about the weather.' That told him. And on the field, we told Gloucester a thing or two. They accumulated the grand total of three points that afternoon, the small matter of thirty-six fewer than us.

Watching our England internationals go about their work that season, I reached the conclusion quite early on that Clive Woodward's team had the winning of the Webb Ellis Cup within them. Martin Johnson, Neil Back, Phil Vickery, Richard Hill, Jason Leonard . . . like Lawrence and his fellow Wasps, these were tough men in mind and body. With Trudi and the kids, I watched the final with some London friends who had laid on a champagne breakfast. Gabby and Bryn were both in England jerseys – not simply because the Wallabies were the other team, although that was undoubt- edly a part of it, but because they really wanted the Wasps boys to win the big one. So did I, for the same reasons, but things happened during that compelling contest in Sydney that defied both logic and belief. Not least some of the South African referee Andre Watson's decision-making, particu- larly at the scrum. With twenty minutes left, I knew there would be extra time and said as much over yet another glass of mid-morning bubbly. Happily, it turned out for the best. It did the club no harm on the business front when our England contingent put an extra few thousand on the gate.

This was the beginning of our golden run, the realisation of the potential I'd recognised on joining the club in early 2002. Right from the start, I'd immersed myself in Wasp's history, of which there was rather a lot. Some 135 years' worth, as a matter of fact. The thing that had struck me most was an article in a programme from the tough depression years of the 1930s, written by a second-teamer – he may even have been a regular in the third XV – who had left England for a new life somewhere in Africa. The gist of it was that he 'missed the boys', and he included a line that is still used today. 'Once a Wasp, always a Wasp.' As a summing-up of the ethos of the club, it was perfect. What was more, it was something I recognised from my own rugby background. Back home in Hamilton, I had grown up playing alongside people from all walks of life and all sections of the community. Perhaps more than any other major club in and around London, the social melting pot was the defining characteristic of Wasps. They had their fair share of well-to-do types, led by Harrow-educated 'Farquhar' and a couple of others, but overall there was something of the blue-collar spirit about them. Far more so than Harlequins, to cite an obvious example. As a sporting family, we trained hard, played hard, partied hard and supported each other every step of the way. It was healthy, it was good . . . and as the records show, it was hugely successful.

When Lawrence and the rest returned from World Cup duty, we gave them some time to rest, recuperate and reunite themselves with their loved ones. Then it was down to work. There was a Premiership title to defend and a Heineken Cup to win – a far bigger European title than the Challenge Cup version we still held. Having convinced myself that we would have won the Heineken tournament the previous season had we qualified for it in the first place, I was not in the mood to let it slip this time. But slip away it almost did, thanks to a small administrative cock-up that could easily have turned into an error of major proportions.

We'd based our campaign around two squads: one to cover the immediate aftermath of the World Cup, without our international contingent, and a much stronger one aimed at the business end of the tournament. The organisers had set a clear date for the change of personnel. And yes, we missed it. I wouldn't have known until it was too late but for a chance conversation with one of our management team, who was responsible for player registration. We were playing Newcastle in the Premiership one Saturday afternoon. Deadline day for the confirmation of the new squad had been the Friday. 'Everything OK with the European stuff?' I asked him. He'd forgotten. Talk about hitting the panic button. All sorts of things went through my mind, not least the prospect of resignation. It wasn't a foregone conclusion that the Heineken Cup staffers would insist on their elite competition going ahead without a bunch of World Cup-winning mega-names, but rules are rules and the people who frame them generally like to enforce them. If they did so, I'd have no choice but to hold up my hands and walk. There was one chance of getting out of jail. As quickly as we were able, we sent a fax through to the tournament headquarters, checking that our non-existent communication of the previous day had been received. 'Just trying to be helpful,' we wrote. 'We haven't received a response from you.' They swallowed our story and allowed us to 're-file' the squad. Phew. There *is* a god.

Even then, there was no guarantee we would make it into the knockout stage. We were in one of the toughest of the six pools and had already lost at home to the now defunct Celtic Warriors, then one of five teams representing the newly regionalised Welsh club system and no one's idea of a soft touch given the presence of Test Lions past in Neil Jenkins and Dafydd James, together with three Test Lions of the future in Gareth Thomas, Gethin Jenkins and Matthew Rees. It left us needing a result in our last pool game against Perpignan, down there in the rugby badlands of the French–Spanish border . . . and Perpignan never lost at home. For one thing, they were very well coached by Jacques Brunel, who would go on to build a career at Test level. For another, they were brutally physical. When Jacques declared in the local press the day before the match that 'to beat Wasps tomorrow we have to be mad', it was not a message that required any reading between the lines. True to expectation, the game was both blood-curdling and blood-spilling, played out in an atmosphere as hostile as I've ever encountered. The off-the-ball stuff had to be seen to be believed, and if memory serves, there were nine citings for foul play. The outcome? We stuck thirty points on them, running away with it in the second half. It was a great performance and it started in the dressing room, where the mood was so intense that players were in tears. It left a mark on the coaching staff too. Paul Stridgeon said to me as the passionate words of

Lawrence and his lieutenants continued to ring in our ears, 'There's no way we'll be losing after those team talks.'

After that, there was little reason to think that we'd struggle to beat Gloucester in the last eight, especially as we were at home. We duly won 34–3. The semi-final was a very different proposition, however: Munster away, in front of a full house at Lansdowne Road in Dublin. It was the first time I'd been back there since my sacking as Ireland coach, and in his infinite wisdom, Lawrence used this fact as the basis for a tub-thumping address shortly before kick-off. 'Warren was shafted by these people, so it's payback time.' That sort of thing. Part of me wanted to scream 'aaarrrgghh . . . don't go there.' Another part of me understood Lawrence's reasoning. It turned out to be one of the great games in the annals of European rugby, high-paced and high-scoring. We based our plan around going after Ronan O'Gara, the Munster fly-half, and making his life a misery. Unfortunately, he picked up a hamstring injury early in the game and was replaced by Jason Holland, a very different kind of operator. Holland performed out of his skin and it wasn't until the death that Trevor Leota, our geometrically unique hooker, scored the close-range try that took us through 37–32. It was one of the most exhausting, exhilarating days I'd ever spent as a coach. I had only two regrets. The first was that of the near 50,000 audience, only 2,000 were Wasps followers. The second was that as a club we didn't cash in on our lack of travelling support. 'What did you do with the rest of the tickets,' I asked one of the girls in the office during the week of the match. 'We didn't need them so I sent them back.' 'You did what? Are you kidding me?' We could have sold those tickets back to the local clubs in Munster, like Stade Français did in the quarters, and made an absolute killing for the club. At least Trudi and the kids were there to help boost the numbers, along with four families of friends from London, all of them freshly paid-up members of Wasps. They had an amazing weekend, a traditional singalong in the bar of the Jury's Hotel setting the tone. On match day, they all kitted themselves out in Wasps gear and waved their flags with gusto. It was another example of the loyal Gatlands sticking together.

Poorer than we should have been but rich in confidence and momentum, Wasps were now at the point where things really mattered. Our training was focused wholly on knockout rugby, and as a result, we ended our regular season league campaign with a couple of defeats, the second of which, against Leicester at home, was unusually heavy. But we already knew we'd be in the shake-up for a place in the Premiership final, while Leicester were going full tilt just to qualify for the following season's Heineken Cup. We duly won our semi-final against Northampton and set about preparing for the seven days that would define us.

First up were Toulouse in the final of the Heineken Cup – a Sunday match in front of more than 73,000 at Twickenham. Two-time winners of the tournament, the Frenchmen had an offloading game to die for and so many top players in every department that just looking at the team sheet made my eyes water. Clément Poitrenaud, Émile Ntamack and Cédric Heymans among the outside backs; Yannick Jauzion at centre; Freddy Michalak and Yann Delaigue at 9 and 10; a scary front row of Patrice Collazo, William Servat and Jean-Baptiste Poux; Fabien Pelous and my old hot-headed friend Trevor Brennan in the engine room; the super-powerful Maka brothers, Finau and Isitolo, in the back row. Someone, somewhere would have to do a major job for us. That someone was Joe Worsley, who made forty-odd tackles in the game, chopping down opponents at the knees like some record-breaking lumberjack. If you used Joe properly, which England conspicuously failed to do for years, he could win games on his own with his defensive prowess. If he was not a one-man black wall, he was the biggest brick in it. I didn't make a single move off the bench – not one substitution, not one injury replacement. It was a first in Heineken Cup finals and there has been no repeat. Toulouse were so good, there was no option but to keep the best men on the field for the duration. Yet we were the ones who made the most of the final minute, Rob Howley playing the ultimate opportunist card to capitalise on Poitrenaud's fatal hesitation and score the winning try.

We partied as though our lives depended on it that Sunday night and kept partying for a very long time. Nobody surfaced until the Wednesday and while we deserved to let our hair down, it was also true that we were playing Bath in the Premiership final on the Saturday. I can't pretend we were at our very best in that game and poor old Trevor Leota had a worse time of it than anyone. His line-out throwing, never the most reliable part of his game, went seriously wonky and as a result, the Bath lock Steve Borthwick stripped us bare. There came a point in the second half when, with Trevor preparing for another throw, our centre Stuart Abbott could be heard yelling to Alex King: 'Kingy, what's the call? I don't know the call. What's the call?' Alex's reply? 'Get up and defend!' Yet with twenty minutes to go, the score as tight as a drum and Bath all over us, I knew we'd win. I just couldn't see Bath scoring. The black wall was doing its job once again and when Ben Gotting came on at hooker – I'd had enough of Trevor's darts for one day – we started to secure our own ball and saw it out by four points.

All the way through this extraordinary adventure Shaun Edwards had been a crucial figure. It wasn't simply that he knew how to organise a defence, although his depth of knowledge in that department was off the scale. Equally important was his contribution to the culture. A rugby league great, he had been a professional sportsman since the age of seventeen and understood the things that made players tick. He talked constantly to the squad, from the highest to the lowest, always choosing the right anecdote for the occasion and tailoring his message to suit the situation. Not that he always pressed the correct button as far as I was concerned. The day after a Premiership game up at Sale in 2005, he called me to one side and said we had a problem with a member of our pack, most of whom were fully-fledged internationals.

'What about him?'

'He wasn't trying yesterday. My mum watched the match and told me. She's dead right.'

I looked at the stats sheet and sure enough, the individual concerned had hit only one ruck in the whole contest.

'You have to sack him,' Shaun continued.

'Eh?'

'You have to sack him. Get rid of him.'

This was no small thing. We were talking about a top player who had rarely let us down. Shaun appeared to have a point, nevertheless, and on the basis that it's sometimes necessary to fire a shot across the bows, I suggested that the two of us speak to the 'condemned man' in my office.

'That wasn't good enough and we can't have it,' I told the poor bloke. 'We're going to let you go. We'll pay you out to the end of the season, but that's it.'

The player went white. 'You can't do that to me. I love this club.'

'Sorry, it's the way it is.'

He started sobbing. And what did Shaun say?

'All right. We'll give you one more chance.'

I looked a proper fool. Afterwards, I gave it to Shaun with both barrels. 'You bastard,' I said. 'If that had been the other way round and I'd done that to you, God knows how you'd have reacted.' Still, it worked out for the best. The following week, the 'reprieved man' hit forty-six rucks. One to forty-six: there's a differential for you. The threat of being moved on tends to keep players on their toes.

That 2004–5 campaign could easily have seen us retain our European title, but we messed things up in the Basque country against Biarritz, who were a high-calibre side, and failed to make the cut for the quarter-finals. This was a body blow, not least because I'd decided to move on at season's end. It wasn't that I had a problem with coaching at Wasps or living in Ealing: I subscribe fully to the old saying that if you're bored with London, you're bored with life. I loved going to the West End shows with Trudi; the kids were perfectly happy in school, with Gabby at St Augustine's and Bryn at St Benedict's, both situated near home. If the traffic was a little more challenging than it had been in Hamilton or Taupiri or Galway, our house was handy for the motorways and close to Heathrow. But Gabby and Bryn had spent next to no time in New Zealand and it preyed on my mind a little.

Bryn had a really strong Irish accent because he had learned to talk there; Gabby had lost her Irish accent and picked up a rather posh English one. Trudi took them out for a bite to eat one day and a woman at the next table said: 'Sorry, I don't mean to be rude, but I have to ask: how do you have a daughter with an English accent, a son with an Irish accent, and you speak with a New Zealand accent?' That was the life we were living. The thought occurred to me that with good experience as a coach in Europe safely in the bank, I could go back to Waikato and make some big moves there, secure in the knowledge that if it didn't work out, I'd have a good shot at another front-line job in the

British Isles. Trudi readily agreed, so just after Christmas, I told Chris Wright that I'd be moving on in the summer.

My final weeks were dominated by Leicester, the other major force in the English game. First up was a league game at Welford Road in the last round of the regular season. The Tigers were highly charged emotionally, with Martin Johnson and Neil Back, two all-time greats, saying their farewells to the home crowd after long and distinguished careers. The scoreboard wasn't pretty from our point of view: it's hard to put a shine on a 45–10 defeat. But when I looked back at the footage, territory and possession had been reasonably even and we hadn't enjoyed much in the way of good fortune, conceding an intercept try and finding ourselves on the rough end of some tight refereeing calls. It also struck me that Leicester would find it very hard to light those fires again in a hurry and that turned out to be the case. When we met them in the final at Twickenham a fortnight later, we overran them 39–14 to win the title for the third year in succession. It may have been billed as the 'Johnson and Back Retirement Show', but we were the ones who dominated the stage. Something similar would happen when I coached the Lions in Australia, but that was still eight years away.

After the match, Peter Wheeler popped into our dressing room to congratulate us. Peter, a fellow ex-hooker, had been an influential figure at Leicester for decades: as a player, a captain, a coach, a chief executive, a rugby director, a committee man . . . as pretty much everything. He was also in the thick of English rugby politics. I shook his hand and thanked him for the Welford Road experience two weeks previously. 'That game got us ready for this one,' I said, adding that we'd also had the advantage of an extra match, our semi-final against Sale, while his lot had spent a fortnight kicking their heels. What happened the following season? There were two semi-finals rather than one. As I say, Peter was a man of influence!

Those Twickenham finals were fantastic occasions not only for the team, but also for the Wasps supporters. Trudi would turn up at the office a week out from the game and order 100-plus tickets for the many families we had met during our time in Ealing. They had become passionate rugby followers and revelled in the match-day picnics, which would be in full swing three hours before kick-off. Together with our friends, we would celebrate with the trophy deep into the evening and be the last to leave the west car park. Another highlight was watching Bryn and Gabby run out onto Twickenham as mascots. Gabby's biggest fear was tripping over while holding Lawrence Dallaglio's hand and embarrassing herself in front of a 75,000 full house and a television audience in the millions. I assured her that Lawrence would be so pumped-up for the contest, her feet would barely touch the ground. I was right.

6

WELCOME TO THE GOLDFISH BOWL

Wales looks good from the air, especially when the sun is shining and you've just been head-hunted for one of the prime jobs in rugby. It was late 2007. I had just been asked to take on the head coaching role with the Red Dragons, and Roger Lewis, the chief executive of the Welsh Rugby Union, was giving me a guided tour of perhaps the most fabled stretch of oval-ball territory in the world. By helicopter. We flew over Cardiff and Newport, over Swansea and Llanelli and Neath, over the coast and the valleys, over the old pit towns and the tiny villages that had produced some of the finest talent ever to grace the game. Roger had even organised the weather. A beautiful day here, in the dark depths of the Welsh winter? I knew he was a man of power and influence, but this was stretching a point.

Things would look a whole lot different at ground level, but the view from above was tantalising. So it was that I found myself, less than a week later, sitting in a hotel in West London – right on the Chiswick roundabout, a stone's throw from where the Gatland family had lived during my spell with Wasps – in the company of Justin Page, my trusted advisor. On the table in front of us was a WRU contract and a pen. The question? Should I commit myself to another tour of duty far away from home, or should I leave the document unsigned and board the next flight back to New Zealand. It wasn't as if I was feeling professionally unfulfilled. After returning home from the Wasps job in 2005, I'd coached Waikato to a provincial title and I was also working at Super Rugby level with the Chiefs. Wales, on the other hand, had just bombed out of the 2007 World Cup at the pool stage and were ranked tenth in the world, just ahead of Italy. Should I stick, or should I twist?

I remembered a conversation I'd had with Trudi just after Ireland had dispensed with my services. One of the first teams to contact me was the Celtic Warriors, a merger of the Bridgend and Pontypridd clubs and one of the five teams launched when the WRU decided to abandon its elite league structure in favour of regionalisation. I wasn't interested and told them so over the phone, as politely as I knew how. 'There's no way I'm coaching in Wales,' I told my wife. 'The place is a goldfish bowl. We'd never have a moment's peace.' And yet . . . here I found myself, wrestling with the implications of taking on a job far more high-profile than anything the Warriors had been offering.

Justin could not help me with the decision, because it wasn't about terms and conditions, about dollars and cents. He had done his job in that regard and done it well. This was about me and my family, my ambition as a coach and the effect that ambition would have on them. And I was wrestling like hell with it when my phone rang. It was Gabby, my daughter, now in her teens. 'Dad, don't do it,' she said. Four tough words. Really tough. My thoughts were all over the place, my heart absolutely pounding through my chest. I spent the next few minutes wondering, really seriously, whether I shouldn't just get out of my chair and walk towards the door of the hotel, waving to Justin over my shoulder and saying 'I just can't do this' on my way out. Twenty minutes later, the phone rang again. It was Gabby, again. 'Dad, if you really want this, go for it,' she said. 'We'll support you.' So I signed.

Why did I put pen to paper when I'd spent so much emotional energy thinking of reasons why I should do precisely the opposite? Because in the end, I felt the scale of the challenge justified the sacrifice and believed that with the right people around me, the national team could be successful. Far more successful, certainly, than they had been for much of the professional era. When I looked at the standard of the top-level players, I had the same feeling I'd experienced before moving to Wasps. Namely, there was no good reason why these people should be struggling for results. I also felt I had a basic understanding of the nature of the rugby culture in Wales, because when all was said and done, it had more in common with New Zealand than with anywhere else. It was like home, only more pressurised and confrontational.

I was right about that. There is certainly a goldfish bowl

element to life in New Zealand, but it doesn't extend much beyond the All Blacks because of geography. Rugby politics in Dunedin doesn't count for much in Wellington. In Wales, where all the major rugby is played along a sixty-mile stretch of the M4, the rivalries are more concentrated and the fires of tribalism burn hotter. New Zealand would be exactly the same if the whole of rugby life was crammed into the few dozen kilometres separating Auckland from Hamilton.

But it was still a big call, for a number of reasons. Most importantly, Trudi and the children were happy back in Waikato after the years in Galway and London. We'd bought some land twenty minutes outside Hamilton and had built our dream house. Bryn, my son, was getting stuck into his age-group rugby and was improving all the time. Gabby was enjoying a sporting life of her own – she had developed a talent for rowing – and was completely comfortable with her academic work. Both kids were in Anglican schools, having attended Roman Catholic schools during my spell with Wasps, but this was not a problem, even though Catholicism runs through our family. I simply wanted them to have the best education available. Trudi's background is primarily Catholic; my maternal grandmother was also of that religious persuasion, although it was not entirely straightforward from her point of view. My grandfather was a divorcee and when they decided to marry, the church wouldn't hear of it. When my mum was born, the priest said she should be baptised into the faith, but my grandmother said: 'You wouldn't marry us, so you're not baptising her.'

She performed the ceremony herself, with the aid of a bathtub and some holy water! My own baptism was in New Zealand, on the same day as Gabby's. Some mates came along for the occasion and claimed they could see steam rising from my head as Father Daly went about his business. A fortnight after my baptism and confession, Father Daly died of a stroke. My mates accused me of killing him with my first confession.

As well as revelling in our family life in NZ, I was enjoying things from a professional point of view. Towards the end of my time at Wasps, I had felt there were opportunities for me back home. It had also occurred to me that if things didn't work out, I'd pieced together enough of a track record to stand a chance of returning to Europe and working at a high level. When the Waikato role opened up, Wasps were good enough to waive the final year of my contract – a generous act that allowed me to throw myself straight into the job in Hamilton. We struggled at first and there was some criticism of me. 'So Gatland's come back. He may have been successful in Europe, but he's not finding it so easy now he's up against New Zealand coaches.' That kind of thing. I'd had no break and no input into the shape of the Waikato team, but that was no excuse. In the end, we weren't good enough. I had tried to implement a style of rugby that the players struggled to deliver, partly because our tight forwards hadn't been fit enough, and we'd paid the price. That setback made me more determined to take Waikato to the top of the domestic rankings and I set about improving the side, especially up front. I spotted two relatively young props playing on the local club scene – Craig West from Hamilton Old Boys, my old stamping ground, and Nathan White from Te Awamutu – and asked some questions about them, only to be told: 'Nah, they've been in the system and blown it. They're not good enough.' Which set me thinking. 'They're twenty-three and twenty-four,' I said to myself. 'I don't expect them to be any good until they're twenty-eight or twenty-nine.' I decided they had the capacity to play at the tempo needed to execute a brand of rugby that could win us a title and brought them on board. Sure enough, they were in our starting front row when we beat Wellington in the 2006 grand final.

The Waikato set-up still had a special spirit about it – the spirit I'd encountered during my own time playing alongside John Mitchell, Duane Monkley, Steve Gordon and the rest. That year, we sold out the stadium for big games and were the only provincial side in the country to turn a profit. Once we started bringing in the results, the rugby public responded just as they had in the good old days. And those results came thick and fast because the side we had that season was very strong indeed. Keith Robinson and Jono Gibbes were our locks, both of them All Blacks. Jono was very talented, Keith absolutely terrific – as tough as you like. In the back row we had Steven Bates, our captain, and Marty Holah and Liam Messam on the flanks, with Sione Lauaki at No 8. Sione never really showed his full potential as an All Black, but after we brought him in from Auckland he was incredible for us: a great character, incredibly skilful and ultra-powerful. He was the type who could leave Hamilton on a Friday, enjoy a big weekend with his mates in Auckland and come back 5 kg heavier than when he left. There were times when I thought: 'Jeez, another Trevor Leota on my hands! That's all I need.' But he was worth the hassle. It was the saddest of days when he died at thirty-five, having struggled with kidney problems.

Outside the scrum, we had top internationals in Mils Muliaina at full-back and Byron Kelleher at scrum-half, not to mention a No 10 by the name of Stephen Donald, who would go on to kick the all-important World Cup-winning goal in 2011. As for our wings, Sosene Anesi was the quickest and Sitiveni Sivivatu the most astonishing. In fact, the word I associate with him is 'WOW!' I would describe Sitiveni as the most talented rugby player I've ever coached – and I've had the good fortune to coach some pretty good ones. He was a typical Fijian in some ways. He always had this relaxed, casual manner about him and was uniquely gifted when it came to making a difference in the biggest games. Very intelligent, he could make up moves on the pitch, completely out of thin air. He could also sidestep defenders at full pace with no drop-off in speed. That's hard to do, as you'll discover when you try it yourself and hit the floor with a bump. I remember him playing left wing against Northland and pulling his hamstring. The physios ran up to him as a scrum was being set and told him that was it for the day – that there was no way he could continue, even if we wanted him to, which we didn't. His reply? 'No, no, no . . . I want to score this try first.' So we had the scrum, the ball came out to our 10, there was a straightforward switch with Sitiveni off his wing and he limped over the line, put the ball down under the posts and walked off the field. Incredible.

The final against Wellington was a major event, for they too had big names coming out of their ears. Jerry Collins on the flank, Rodney So'oialo at No 8, Piri Weepu at scrum-half and a back line full of stellar talents: Tana Umaga and Conrad Smith at centre, Cory Jane and Ma'a Nonu on the wings. Not bad, all things considered. This was the very best New Zealand provincial rugby had to offer and it was a real feather in our cap when we came through 37–31, despite conceding a couple of late tries and subjecting ourselves to a traumatic last sixty seconds – to this day, one of the most nerve-jangling minutes of rugby I've experienced. Our loose forwards ruled the roost that afternoon and Kelleher scored a couple of tries. A lot of people felt Byron wasn't the brightest spark on the electricity grid, but he was an intelligent reader of the game and was the best defensive half-back I'd worked with at that point in my career.

It was a satisfying moment, winning that title: Waikato's first since 1992, when I had been in the middle of the front row, and only the second in our history. I was also the first man to win a domestic championship as both a player and a head coach. But I was looking for more and felt I was on my way at Super Rugby level, having been taken on as a consultant with the Chiefs. Quite quickly, I was given a more formal role as assistant coach to Ian Foster, my old provincial playing mate who had worn the No 10 shirt the day we spanked the Lions in front of our home crowd. I felt I had a good chance of succeeding Ian in the top job, but when he signed a contract extension in 2007, I informed him that I wouldn't be staying on. It was around this time that Wales signalled an interest in my services, and things moved rapidly in that direction. In fact, I met with Roger Lewis and two other big hitters from the WRU hierarchy, Gerald Davies and David Pickering, during that year's global tournament – shortly after an unusually miserable few hours during which we relinquished our provincial title by conceding more late tries, this time to Hawke's Bay in a quarter-final in Napier, and the All Blacks lost a last-eight tie of their own to France and found themselves dumped out of a World Cup they had been favourites to win. If it was a considerable shock to the system, seeing my national team fail on the big stage for the fifth time in succession, Roger's phone call came as an equally big surprise.

Not that it was the first time I'd had an approach from Europe. In 2006, in the middle of our title-winning season in Waikato, I took a call from someone representing the London arm of Odgers Berndtson, the executive search and recruitment specialists. Would I be prepared to fly to Sydney for discussions over a head of rugby position at Twickenham? Working on the 'nothing ventured, nothing gained' theory of life, I booked myself a flight and grabbed a cab to the Hilton Hotel down on the bay. As the head-hunter outlined the job spec, it became clear that this was about executive planning – lots of meetings, presentations, pen-pushing

– rather than coaching. This really wasn't my idea of fun. A couple of days later, Odgers phoned to say they wanted to talk some more. I told them I was a hands-on coach and wanted to stay that way. The next week, I received a third call. The message? I could turn the job into anything I wanted: if I wanted to coach the England team, fine. I couldn't see myself walking into Twickenham with a long list of people to be sacked, so I pulled out of the discussions. I also forgot to claim expenses for the flight from New Zealand to Sydney, so I emerged from the episode a poorer man.

Wales were in a different place, with a different set of issues. Out of the World Cup running at an early stage and with Gareth Jenkins already removed as coach, Roger and his colleagues were flying to New Zealand on a recruiting mission. Would I meet them for a chat? I knew this wouldn't go down terribly well with Trudi and the children, but there was no harm in hearing what the visitors had to say. I wasn't the only individual on their 'possible' list: they spoke with Robbie Deans down in Christchurch and had one or two others in their sights. Roger subsequently told me that his opposite number at the New Zealand union, Steve Tew, was less than impressed that a Welsh delegation should have flown into the country while a World Cup was in progress on the far side of the Equator, but as Roger put it: 'My father once told me that if you're going to burgle a house, it's sensible to do it while the occupants are out.' We met at Auckland Airport and it was a relaxed affair. I wasn't giving anyone the hard sell. I just chatted about my experiences with Ireland and Wasps and offered a few thoughts on how I saw the international game developing over the coming years. I didn't know it at the time, but this was the interview. A week later, Roger phoned and offered me the job.

As I had suspected, Trudi didn't perform cartwheels of joy at the thought of me heading back to Europe. But the financial offer was good and that had to be taken into consideration. Money has never been the overriding factor in my career planning, but I hadn't come from an especially privileged background and security and opportunity for the kids was important to me. Not that Roger was a pushover when it came to discussing remuneration. He was a good negotiator, a good businessman: in his previous life, he had held very senior positions in the music business and in broadcasting, and he knew what he was doing when it came down to the numbers. I have a huge amount of respect for him, but was he always easy to deal with? No. For instance, he wouldn't budge an inch when it came to buying me out of my Waikato contract. He agreed to pay them a certain amount of compensation and no more, so I ended up buying myself out.

Roger understood that the national team was Welsh rugby's cash cow and recognised the need for investment, but as he was also trying to find a way through a web of financial difficulties relating to the Millennium Stadium, it was important for me and our team manager Alan Phillips to box clever in budgetary discussions. He would always start out by telling us how tough things were financially, pulling out his pockets to prove he had no money (before declaring a £5 million profit at the end of the year, needless to say). So when it came to the team, we would go significantly over the top in our financial demands, knowing that when he knocked us back, it would only be to the figure we actually needed.

My first job was to piece together the coaching team. This was not as easy as it might have been. Nigel Davies, a former international centre who had been one of Gareth Jenkins' assistants in the failed World Cup campaign, had been performing a caretaker role, but had no clear idea – still less any guarantees from the union – as to what the future might hold. So when Roger arranged for me to meet the existing staff before the last match of the year, a one-off Test against the newly-crowned world champions South Africa, my immediate thought was 'how awkward is this?' If I didn't want to be there for obvious reasons, they didn't want to be there for the same reasons. They also had a match to think about. Along with Nigel and his coaching panel, Alan Phillips was in the room. He had been team manager for five years and I was being told by some people that this was long enough and he should be moved on. At the same time, others were telling me he was at the heart of the environment, a key figure in the set-up. I was keen to make my own decision and I decided to give it a go with him. As we shook hands on it, I said: 'I'll be honest with you, and if you're honest with me, things will work out. But I'll tell you this right now: I'm shitting myself.'

'Why's that?' he asked.

'Well, you've been through six coaches already. I don't want to be the seventh.'

Having met the coaches and pondered the options, I saw no reason not to stick with Neil Jenkins as kicking specialist and Robin McBryde in the forwards department. I saw great potential in Robin. I also learned that he had once held the title of 'Wales' Strongest Man' and had been appointed Grand Sword Bearer of the National Eisteddfod, so there was more than one powerful argument for keeping him on board. As for Nigel . . . that was a different matter. I wanted to bring in Rob Howley as attack coach: the time we spent together at Wasps had been highly productive for each of us and I knew that Rob was blessed with the sharpest of rugby minds. So I rang Nigel to give him the news – a decision that earned me a rap over the knuckles from Roger, who told me I had acted above my pay grade by sacking someone without the union's permission. Believe me, I hadn't made the call because I thought it would be a fun thing to do: it's by far the toughest and most unpleasant part of the job. But I felt it was my responsibility and looking back, I'm glad I did it. I wouldn't have wanted Nigel to hear it from anyone else.

As for the position of defence coach, Shaun Edwards was my go-to man. He was still at Wasps and there was interest in him from England, but they were offering him something less than the world: namely, a role with the second-string Saxons team. I felt there was a chance of pinching him from under their noses if an international job was on the table and asked him if he'd be interested in joining me in Wales, just for the 2008 Six Nations. 'I've been watching the Ospreys train down in Swansea,' I told him. 'Mike Phillips, Alun Wyn Jones, Jonathan Thomas, Adam Jones, Duncan Jones . . . these blokes are big and physical, and they can all catch and pass. There's something to work with here.' I gave him the salesman's patter and he bought it. My front-line coaching panel was complete.

We were, however, right up against the clock, our opening Six Nations game being against England at Twickenham in a matter of weeks. And having just reached a World Cup final, Brian Ashton's team would be hot favourites. There was no time to be inventive in selection: there was a reasonable number of players with fifty-plus international caps available to me – Shane Williams, Stephen Jones and Dwayne Peel outside the scrum; Gethin Jenkins and Adam Jones among the front-rowers – and I picked them all in my squad for the competition. I also made it my business to talk the open-side flanker Martyn Williams out of Test retirement. I needed his experience, his skills, his rugby brain. It was one of my better ideas, although Martyn quickly told me that if he'd known how hard the training would be, he'd have made a different decision. The most significant newcomer was Jamie Roberts. We picked him as a wing with potential to play full-back, although it quickly became apparent that he possessed all the qualities of a Test-class inside centre.

And then there was Gavin Henson. It did not occur to me for a second that he shouldn't be involved, but there was baggage that came with him. Gavin was the most talked-about, written-about rugby player in the country, partly because his rugby-playing career had long had a touch of the soap opera about it and partly because he was in the midst of the celebrity whirl through his relationship with singer Charlotte Church. He had been through the emotional wringer on the Lions tour of New Zealand in 2005, spent part of his time struggling with injury and another part apologising to his colleagues for comments he made in a book, and been left out of the World Cup squad in 2007. But I believed he would add value to the squad and never had reason to regret that call. I had no issues with him or his work-rate. Yes, he was one of those players you wanted to be right on the day: if he wasn't 100 per cent, if he had a niggle, he wouldn't really be up for it. But he trained really hard and I found him to be a good professional.

I think Gavin had a bad rap during his career, largely from the press. There was no doubt that with a few drinks under his belt, he had the capacity to put himself in difficult, confrontational situations. There again, he wasn't alone in that regard. That's the way things were back then. He was actually very introverted, shy, quiet – the whole thing with the tan, the hair, the boots, all that was a shield. People thought they were looking at a show pony, but it was completely the opposite of what he was. He was such a skilful player, such a talent, and while there were occasions when he was messed around and times when he messed himself up, he always responded positively when people were honest with him – black and white, straight up, to the point. I don't suppose the frenzy around his relationship with Charlotte helped. I would chat with her after games and there was one point where I came away thinking the two of them wouldn't be together for too long. So it proved. Professional sports people living their lives in the celebrity space? It can be challenging, for sure.

I picked thirteen Ospreys to start the England game and Gavin was one of them. Ryan Jones, another player who had missed the World Cup, was another. He was skipper too. I had talked to various people in and around the squad about the captaincy question and one or two names cropped up, including that of another Ospreys back-row forward, Jonathan Thomas. But I wasn't completely sure Jonathan was a nailed-on starter, so Ryan, another of those mentioned, seemed a better choice. I asked him if he'd be prepared to do the job, he accepted, and the news was announced. It was only after completing those formalities that I put together an exercise aimed at forming a leadership group among the players. We had a big collective brainstorming session, with two questions up for debate. What are the ingredients that make up a champion team? What are the virtues that make up a champion player? I wrote some obvious buzzwords on the board – unselfish, hard-working, never gives up, that sort of thing – and asked the players to pick out five key qualities before writing down their own views on which five people among those in the room best represented those qualities. My theory was that the captain was certain to be among them. So much for theory. When I sat down to collate the results, Ryan was well down the list. 'Shit, I've made a huge mistake here,' I said to myself. 'I've picked the wrong captain.' The problem needed addressing, clearly, but I had to be really subtle about it: I couldn't just chuck him in the senior leadership group and allow the others to start talking among themselves and asking each other if they'd voted for Ryan. 'Did you choose him?' 'No. Did you?' 'No. So what's he doing here?' That would have been disastrous. They'd feel I hadn't been straight with them, that I'd manipulated the process and rigged the vote.

So I met with Ryan and said: 'We have a bit of an issue.'

'I know what it is,' he replied.

'OK, tell me.'

'I didn't get many votes, did I?'

'No, you didn't. What are you going to do about it?'

'What do you mean?'

'You'll have to address the players,' I said.

In fairness to him, he stood up in front of the squad and said openly that he'd have to take their views on board. 'The next time we do this exercise, I'm going to make sure I'm in that top five or six,' he told them. It was a powerful moment and a significant one, because it underlined the value of honesty and humility in the group. Later, I was told that he'd done quite a lot of media work during the World Cup, commenting on the Wales matches, and that a breakdown between him and his fellow players happened as a result of some of his criticisms. The problem wasn't that his colleagues didn't respect him as a person and a player, but was directly related to what happened around that tournament, which had been a painful one for everyone directly involved and was still a sensitive topic.

The moral of the story? It shows, once again, that when you're actively engaged in top-level sport, you need to choose your words carefully. As it turned out, I had been as guilty as the next man of speaking out of turn. Before settling into the Wales job, I had stopped over in Dubai to watch the annual international seven-a-side tournament. While there, I gave an interview about my new role and happened to mention that whatever happened, the players would be made to work hard in training. 'I might break a few of them,' I said. It wasn't the brightest comment or the most justified, because I had no reason to believe there was a serious problem with fitness and conditioning. I felt the weakness in Welsh rugby was one of mental toughness and application, not physical capability. I thought no more about the remark at the time, but it quickly came back to bite me.

We did put the players through it ahead of the England match. The mantra from the coaches was always the same: 'More. Give us more. Do you think England are working this hard? Of course not. No one else is training this hard. Give us more.' When we went to Twickenham, we were confident of our staying power. What wasn't quite so encouraging was the Welsh record on that particular patch of grass. It had been twenty years since the last victory there and the desperation to end two decades of misery was obvious in the minutes before kick-off, when Robin McBryde gave one of the most pumped-up team talks I had ever heard. He out-Bucked Buck Shelford, by a distance, and as the 'effs' were flying around the changing room, I thought to myself: 'Oh my God, what's going on here? Are the Welsh always like this?' Robin has calmed down a fair bit in the intervening years, but he was really flying that day. Not that it had the required impact. Having planned to play smart in the right areas of the field, we took the territory thing too literally and kicked away a lot of possession. As a consequence, we were 16–6 down at half-time and on our way out of the contest. Had we not manned the barricades and resisted some heavy pressure just before the break, it would have been over before the oranges had been peeled.

It wasn't a comfortable situation for any of us: all I could hear were renditions of 'Swing Low Sweet Chariot' and I could feel Shaun's eyes on me, the unspoken message being something along the lines of 'why the hell did I let Gats talk me into coming here?' But the interval arrived at the right moment. England had picked up some injuries, losing two open-side flankers in Lewis Moody and Tom Rees – a double whammy that forced them into a major back-row rethink. As for us, we started trusting ourselves more with ball in hand and slowly rediscovered the best of our game. James Hook reduced the deficit with a couple of penalties and, growing into the contest, beat three defenders to create a try for Lee Byrne, our full-back. Minutes later, Mike Phillips scored from a chargedown. Against considerable odds, it was 26–19 and we were home and dry. Shaun's eyes were bright and cheery, all of a sudden. As for me, I was approached by a Welsh journalist as I made my way down the steps of the West Stand, a broad grin on my face. 'When Graham Henry came to Wales from New Zealand, we called him The Great Redeemer,' he said. 'What are you going to be known as, Warren?' I thought for a second before replying. 'I'll be known as The Lucky Bastard,' I said, and disappeared down the tunnel.

After the game, we enjoyed a few beers on the bus home and another few in the bar at The Vale Resort (known by everyone as the 'Vale of Glamorgan'), our team base. It was there that Shane Williams, not the first rugby player to be a little lively in drink and assuredly not the last, asked me outside for a fight! It transpired that my remarks in that interview in Dubai had gone down badly with him and he saw this as an opportunity to make his point. Happily, I thought better of taking him up on his kind offer. The following morning, Shane could barely remember a thing. He was sheepish, he apologised, I told him not to worry about it and that was it. My first game as head coach of Wales had been quite an adventure. 'What happens when we lose?' I thought to myself as I reflected on events.

On the subject of rugby teams and booze, I take a fairly straightforward view. If the players are keen on a late night after a big victory, it's not unreasonable to give them some time and space to enjoy themselves. If they've lost, I'm not so keen. Some of my initial calls in this area were not wildly popular, but these decisions were soon being made by the players themselves, which is how it should be. The question is how and where any celebrations should take place. Fifteen or twenty years ago, people could go out and let their hair down without worrying too much about the consequences, provided they weren't stupid about it. Not now. There is so much scrutiny, so many wind-up merchants out there looking to make a name for themselves in front of the camera-phones. I'm happy to let the players set their own rules and today's generation are more on-message about potential pitfalls than any of their predecessors. But as head coach, you still need to have a hand on the brake. It's a fact of sporting life at the professional level.

Take the events at the 2011 World Cup in New Zealand as an example. We had a reputation of being whiter than white during that tournament, with a lot written about the Welsh players' self-imposed drink ban. It wasn't quite like that, to be absolutely truthful, but we were a lot better than the England players, whose behaviour in Queenstown after their opening game quickly became the stuff of scandal. However, I also heard on the grapevine that the Irish team had been just a little on the liquid side down there in the South Island before the England incident. We had a couple of Irish girls staying with us who had been out with the Irish players in Queenstown. They said they had a great time with them but when one of them added 'Just how serious are Ireland about this World Cup? They were out until four in the morning . . .' it was a lightbulb moment for me. Four in the morning? During a World Cup? Even if you're drinking orange juice, four in the morning is not a good look. As a result we put a curfew on the team after matches to be back in the hotel at 1 am. That gave them a couple of hours to go out after arriving back at the hotel after the evening matches. The hotel bar was open and they could have a few more drinks there if they wanted but most didn't.

After beating England, we shut out Scotland in Cardiff, denying them a try while scoring three of our own in a 30–15 victory. Shane Williams was responsible for two of those touchdowns and he claimed two more against the Italians in round three. Which left us as the only unbeaten side in the competition ahead of our meeting with Ireland at Croke Park in Dublin – a big game from my perspective, for obvious reasons. There was a lot riding on it from every point of view and it was as tough as hell, so it was good to have a match-winner like Shane in such outstanding form. He claimed the only try of a tight contest midway through the third quarter, drawing level with Gareth Thomas as the leading try-scorer in Welsh rugby history in the process, and we scraped through 16–12. All things considered, Shane was probably the best player I coached during my long spell in Wales. Yes, he was small in stature, but pound for pound he was the equal of almost anyone in the international game. Yes, he was a mercurial type, but mercurial can take you to the next level. As a coach, you have to understand that and recognise that talents like Shane don't come along every day. Such talent is the difference between good Test teams and the very best.

In the professional era, there is next to no difference between the northern and southern hemispheres in size and fitness and strategy. The gap has been in the X-factor department, with the likes of New Zealand having four or five special performers capable of changing the course of a close game. Shane was our point of difference, and in 2008, he was in full bloom.

Did the victory over Ireland bring a smile to my face? Yes, it cheered me up a little: I confess to pumping my fist at the final whistle. There was a black-tie dinner at the Shelbourne Hotel afterwards, during which my opposite number, none other than Eddie O'Sullivan, approached me and asked if we could talk. We chatted away, pints of Guinness in hand, and he tried to assure me that he hadn't stabbed me between the shoulder blades back in 2001. Rightly or wrongly, I was a bit 'ah yeah, whatever' about it and the conversation petered out. Also among the dinner guests were Billy Glynn, very much a supporter of mine during my days in Ireland, and his wife Margaret. So much had happened since that initial dead-of-night phone call from Billy, asking me if I'd be interested in helping out at Connacht. As I went over to speak to the Glynns, I could feel plenty of eyes burning into my back. There were a lot of people in that room who I liked and respected, but there were pockets of hostility too. Did it upset me? No. Not with a Triple Crown in the bank.

Four from four, we headed home for our Grand Slam match with the French. They had a new coach in Marc Lièvremont and there was a different look to them: since losing to England in front of their own supporters in Paris five months previously, only three forwards remained in their starting pack and there were changes across the back division. But the likes of Yannick Jauzion, Julien Bonnaire and the magnificent Thierry Dusautoir were still there and I expected a hard game. As it turned out we played really well, particularly in the second half. Shane Williams scored the try that took him to the top of the scoring chart and there was another for Martyn Williams to set a crown on his return to the international scene. What impressed me the most was our level of confidence, of belief – qualities that allowed us to absorb the blow of losing Gavin Henson to the sin bin after he hit Fulgence Ouedraogo with a high tackle. It would be an early sign of the team's best characteristic: an ability to build on each victory and become ever harder to beat. When Wales have momentum behind them, they seem to grow an extra arm and leg. It explains my widely reported comment in front of a room full of journalists before the start of the 2019 tournament. 'If we beat France in the first game, I think we can win the Six Nations,' I said then. Which was what happened.

A clean sweep at the first attempt? I was feeling good about life. Yet I was still in the foothills with Wales, still learning about the players and the broader rugby community, still in the early stages of learning how things worked and why. That summer, we travelled to South Africa for a two-Test series with the world champions. The first was in Bloemfontein and we landed in a heap. Having conceded only two tries in the whole of the Six Nations, a new record for the tournament, we leaked double that number in a chastening eighty minutes on the highveld and went down 43–17. I make no excuses: we were well and truly thumped. Yet one odd thing did occur to me. The Boks seemed to know all of our plans in advance – our moves, our defensive patterns, everything. Had anything funny gone on before the game? Were there spies at work, filming us on the quiet and poring over the footage in the analysis room? I can't deny that it crossed my mind. There again, we fronted up far better a week later in Pretoria, when, in theory, they should have known even more about us. The major change was our decision to move Jamie Roberts from full-back, his position in the opening match, to inside centre, where he would develop into a performer of the highest class. Jamie couldn't prevent us losing 37–21, but he did enough to convince me that his future lay in midfield.

If our defeats in South Africa taught me anything, it was that success at international level is about prioritising the right things. The mistake I made on that tour was assuming we could just pick up from where we had left off against France. Rugby doesn't work that way. After a break, you have to revisit your basics, reassert and refresh your core values, remind yourselves of who and what you're trying to be. Ahead of our four-match autumn series, I concentrated all my efforts on doing just that. The result? We got within five points of a fully-loaded Springbok side – Bryan Habana, Jean de Villiers, Fourie du Preez, John Smit, Bakkies Botha, Victor

Matfield, Juan Smith and Schalk Burger were all there at the heart of their operation – and we then beat both Canada, which we expected to do, and Australia, who were a different proposition entirely. Wales had beaten the Wallabies just once since the third-place play-off match at the inaugural World Cup in 1987, so it was a big deal to match them on the try-count and close it out 21–18.

The one bad result of the autumn, on the face of it at least, was a 29–9 defeat at the hand of the All Blacks. Yet even then, I wasn't ready to hang my head in shame. We led at half-time and while my countrymen pulled away in the second-half, it was more through the genius goal-kicking of Daniel Carter than a trademark flurry of long-range tries. They were a class apart at that point, if I'm honest. They'd come up short at the World Cup and were hurting. Graham Henry and his coaching team had kept their jobs, against most expectations, and they had a point to prove. You could sense they were looking hard at themselves and were completely committed to driving themselves onwards and upwards. Certainly, the team they fielded against us was almost scary, with the likes of Mils Muliaina, Joe Rokocoko, Ma'a Nonu and my old Waikato superstar Sitiveni Sivivatu alongside Carter outside the scrum and Richie McCaw, Jerome Kaino and Brad Thorn in the pack. The least I wanted from us was to look them in the eye and give them a scrap. This we did, from the moment we took the field.

The All Blacks had played Ireland at Croke Park a week previously and along with Rob Howley and Neil Jenkins, I had been in the crowd. I made the point that while the great New Zealand teams always carried a man-mountain reputation with them, they were not that big in reality. Great athletes with amazing footwork? Yes. Supersized in the weights and measures department? Not so much. I convinced Rob and Neil that there was no reason for our players to feel inferior in the physical sense and they agreed. So it was that we began to talk about the haka and our best response to it. In Dublin, there had been a passionate rendition and at the end, the All Blacks stared at the Irish until they turned their backs and lined up for the kick-off. I thought we could do better than that. I wondered whether the Welsh players should perform a haka equivalent, some form of cultural expression that would prevent the New Zealanders owning the final minutes before kick-off. In the end, I simply said to Ryan Jones: 'Look, when the ABs do the haka, it's about the battle ahead. Basically, they're questioning your manhood. Your job is to accept the challenge and give them an answer to that question. When they've finished, let's stand there for two or three seconds and wait for them to turn. When they turn, we'll turn.' I didn't know there would be a stand-off, and I didn't expect it to last ninety seconds. Ryan and the players stood motionless in a line, eyes fixed on their opponents. The All Blacks stared back. After twenty seconds, the crowd picked up on what was happening and a great swell of noise began to envelop the stadium. After forty seconds or so, the South African referee Jonathan Kaplan blew his whistle. He blew it to himself, for no Welshman moved an inch. Kaplan then spoke to the New Zealanders, who appeared not to listen, before approaching Ryan, who told him in no uncertain terms that he wouldn't move until they did. 'We're not going anywhere,' he said. And he was true to his word. When the stand-off eventually became a stand-down, it was the All Blacks who cracked first. I'd been involved in my fair share of hakas back in the day and I understood its meaning. I may be a New Zealander, but I couldn't have been prouder of the Wales team at that moment.

Ryan was a strong captain for us, but there were other big individuals in the team around that time. Martyn Williams was very influential, as were Shane Williams, Tom Shanklin and Jonathan Thomas. Matthew Rees, the Scarlets hooker, was another. Matthew was not a fifty-cap veteran, but it was obvious to me that he was a senior figure in the making. It is widely assumed that in rugby, stature in the dressing room is directly related to experience. The more caps you have, the louder your voice. It's not true. Adam Jones had spent a lot of time as an international tight-head prop by this stage and was very important to the team, but he was not a member of the leadership group. That had surprised me. Remember, that leadership group was put together not on the basis of my intuition, but through a ballot of the players themselves. They were spending a lot of time with each other and their perceptions had to count for something.

Sometimes, a player comes in and shows leadership qualities within a few months. Sometimes, long-serving players don't reflect the views or gain the respect of younger people in the party. And it's not all about the senior playing group. It's important, but as a coach you don't automatically take their views on board without thinking about it. There can be an element of self-preservation at work: often, players are the last group to put up their hands and take responsibility. They will often seek out targets for blame before they dream of blaming themselves. 'The coaches, the training facilities, the chef . . . anyone and anything except us.' I remember experimenting with lighter training weeks because that was what the players wanted. What happened? Performance levels dropped off. Hard work suited this particular group of players, and when I pointed out that fact, I met some resistance. But the results were supporting me, not them, and the more the team evolved, the less time I had to spend fighting my corner. Team-building is a process and it didn't start and end in 2008. We had, however, taken some big strides up the hill.

7

A DIFFERENT SHADE OF RED – PART ONE

The Lions. One of the miracles of twenty-first century professional sport, just as they were one of the glories of twentieth
century amateur rugby. Every four years, the critics and the
sceptics write them off as a relic, a museum piece – a buried
artefact from a distant age, unearthed by some giant metal
detector operating on a time loop. And every four years, for
better or for worse, they make time their own. Everyone
with the slightest feeling for the union game, and many who
would never dream of watching a club match in Llanelli or
Limerick or Leicester, drops everything on Test match day
and heads for the nearest television screen. The best of the
British and Irish against the finest the southern hemisphere
has to offer? It is, and always has been, unique.

If the full force of the Lions experience hadn't really
struck me back in 1977, when Phil Bennett's team came to
my corner of New Zealand, I was certainly aware of it a little
over a decade and a half later when, on the same patch of
Hamilton grass, I helped Waikato to one of the great victories
in their history. And who was this on the phone to me now,

towards the back end of 2008? That would be Ian McGeechan, who had already earned himself a place at the heart of Lions lore as a player and a coach, and was putting together a coaching team for his latest tour of duty – to South Africa a few months hence. Three mighty meetings with the reigning world champions in Durban, Pretoria and Johannesburg. It was a fabulous opportunity and there wasn't the slightest chance I would turn it down.

Geech and I were on good terms. He had succeeded me at Wasps and had been wise enough, and sufficiently comfortable in his own skin, to recognise that there wasn't much in need of fixing. We had kept in touch, off and on, running into each other at functions and after big matches, and he was kind enough to say, in print, that the Lions' defeat in Hamilton in 1993 had influenced many of the ideas he was in the process of forming at the time. It had been a big moment for me on the field, that 38–10 win. Having readily agreed to take on the role of Lions forwards coach for the 2009 trip, more big moments were ready and waiting to be experienced.

After the initial thrill of receiving Ian's offer of a role on the staff, there was the less exhilarating task of negotiating my own terms and conditions with John Feehan, the chief executive of the Lions and a man of some power, given that he was also running the Six Nations at that point. The financial deal on the table was not terribly flattering and as all the coaches were negotiating as individuals, it was a matter of fighting my own corner as best I could. Frankly, the situation was ridiculous, even though I understood that John was simply doing his job as he saw it on behalf of the people paying him his salary. It is of course true to say that a Lions invitation is a precious thing and that any coach worthy of the name would jump at the chance of being involved. Equally, it is true to say that rugby coaches are no different to anyone else in the professional world in wanting to feel valued. They certainly don't want to discover, midway through a Test series, that there are serious monetary disparities among the group, simply because Coach A has negotiated harder and more successfully than Coach B. On subsequent tours, over which I wielded far greater influence as top dog, I did my best to address this issue, and I'm still trying to address it now. Before the 2017 tour of New Zealand, some of the staff I'd appointed weren't happy with the proposed contract. I told them to dig in their heels, adding that they should threaten to pull out if there was no movement from the management and that I would support them all the way, to the point of resigning if there was no satisfactory solution. That did the trick. In the Lions context, I see nothing wrong with a little old-fashioned collective bargaining.

There was plenty of work to be done between reaching my agreement with the Lions and flying out for the tour. Wales started the 2009 Six Nations as reigning Grand Slam champions, and with England and Ireland at home, I had a good feeling about the tournament. There was an issue around the scrum-half position, where injuries to Gareth Cooper and Dwayne Peel left us exposed, but we had eight players in the fifty-plus cap bracket and some encouraging newcomers in the contrasting shapes of Leigh Halfpenny, selected as a wing, and Bradley Davies, who joined Alun Wyn Jones, Ian Gough and Luke Charteris in the lock department. We opened up with a decent win over the Scots at Murrayfield, scoring four tries to one, and then beat England 23–15, thanks in large part to their indiscipline and some fine goal-kicking from Stephen Jones. England were in a transition stage – Brian Ashton had been pushed out as head coach in favour of the World Cup-winning captain Martin Johnson – and came to Cardiff as distant outsiders. But they showed themselves capable of thinking outside the box by positioning Joe Worsley, an automatic back-row choice for me during my time at Wasps, in the defensive back-line as a means of stopping Jamie Roberts in his tracks. This was right up Joe's street: used correctly, as opposed to the way some England coaches used him, he was a difference-maker. He showed this during the contest in Cardiff and by the end of it, I was more than happy to take the win.

We should also have beaten France in Paris, which would have put us in prime position for another Slam challenge, but we were not at our most accurate and despite opportunities to pinch a tight one at the death, we lost 21–16. It was my first experience of a Six Nations defeat with Wales. A win in Rome left us hosting the Irish, who arrived with four victories from four outings and a shot at a first clean sweep in more than sixty years. Unsurprisingly, they were up for it. So were we. It was an edge-of-the-seat game, bitterly fought and extremely physical, and when Stephen Jones dropped a goal after a break from a seriously pumped-up Mike Phillips to put us 15–14 up in the closing minutes, the victory was almost ours. But Stephen kicked out on the full from the restart – a stone-cold error under the white heat of pressure – and that gave Ronan O'Gara the field position to respond with a drop of his own. There would be one last chance for us to wreck the Irish dream, but Stephen narrowly failed to land a long-range penalty with the clock in the red. If I was disappointed, I was also happy to take my hat off to Declan Kidney, the Ireland coach. I had a lot of time for Declan, who, during my spell with Waikato, had been kind enough to offer me a role under him at Munster. Given the circumstances of my departure from Ireland, I was grateful to him for thinking of me.

When we turned our attention to the Lions agenda, I found myself in familiar company: Shaun Edwards, Rob Howley and Neil Jenkins were all on the coaching ticket under Geech, along with Graham Rowntree from the England set-up. Additionally, there were plenty of Welsh players in the original selection, from every row of the scrum and every area of the back division. As a result, we were able to introduce and implement some of the ideas behind our upturn as a national team since the 2007 World Cup, including a properly functioning team room. This would be a focal point for the whole party where all communal business would be conducted – a hub, an inner sanctum, a place where everyone could do a bit of everything, from analysis to physio, from playing snooker and table tennis to shooting the breeze with colleagues over a cup of coffee. There had been a good deal of criticism of the way Clive Woodward had run the previous Lions tour, the 'blackwash' trip to New Zealand in 2005. Clive's radical approach, based on an unusually large playing squad and a separate coaching team for the midweek 'dirt-trackers', had not gone down well with the traditionalists, who felt there was something disjointed and divisive about the entire venture. We were all under the strong impression that we were on a rescue mission – that we were charged with the task of saving the Lions from a slow death, of justi-fying the team's continuing place in the game. They had won only two series since 1974 and had lost five Tests on the bounce, the most recent of them badly. Another misfire would leave the Lions hierarchy with some very difficult questions to answer, and we knew it.

There were some early knockbacks for us, even before we flew south. Three players withdrew through injury – the centre Tom Shanklin, the scrum-half Tomas O'Leary, the hooker Jerry Flannery – and there were continuing concerns over the fitness of Leigh Halfpenny that delayed his depart-ure. To add to our problems, the Irish flanker Alan Quinlan picked up a suspension for gouging in a Heineken Cup semi-final and never appeared on the flight manifest. Quinlan was replaced by a very different kind of back-rower in Tom Croft of England, who had been close to selection anyway and would feature strongly in the Test series, while the versatile James Hook and a couple of Scots, the half-back Mike Blair and the hooker Ross Ford, came in at short notice. There again, such disruption is part and parcel of top-level sport. When we finally boarded the plane to Johannesburg, we did so in a spirit of optimism.

We felt we knew what to expect from the Springboks. Geech had overseen the Lions' victory over them in 1997 and understood the specific nature of the challenge in South Africa, and while he expected the opposition to be significantly stronger than they had been a dozen years previously, he also believed that this was a Lions squad with potential. There were some strange experiences, not least when we opened our programme with an up-country game against an invitation side in the thin air of Rustenburg, where the Royal Bafokeng Stadium had been upgraded ahead of the 2010 football World Cup. It was an eerie spectacle: despite the massive publicity surrounding the tour, the 12,000 spectators were virtually lost inside a venue with a capacity of almost 50,000. Why the mass stay-away? There were a couple of reasons. For one thing, the Bulls were playing my beloved Chiefs in a Super 14 final just a few dozen miles down the road in Pretoria. For another, the tickets for our game were very expensive indeed. Arguments over pricing would become a theme of the tour, but of more concern to us was the inability of our Saturday selections to match the midweekers when it came to performance levels. The opening game was too close for comfort – but for seventeen points in the last ten minutes, we would have suffered a big embarrassment – and the next two weekend games, against the

Cheetahs in Bloemfontein and Western Province in Cape Town, were won by margins of two and three points respectively. By contrast, we ran in a total of fifteen tries in scoring seventy-odd points against the Golden Lions in Johannesburg and putting almost forty on the Sharks in Durban. After a slow start we were beginning to find our rhythm.

Despite the scares, we headed into the Test series unbeaten. With the unerring value of hindsight, I am now of the opinion that we went into that game, again in Durban, with an inflated opinion of ourselves. The South African management had held back all the Springboks from those early games and left us with a false sense of where we were as an international-standard unit. When we ran out at King's Park, what hit us was completely different. It was another of those 'wow' moments. The weather, the intensity, the physicality . . . South Africa is a hard place to play at the best of times, and these particular South Africans were on a mission. Our front row took a real hammering, with Phil Vickery having a horrible time of it against Tendai Mtawarira, otherwise known as 'The Beast'. As early as thirty minutes, I was suggesting a change on the tight-head side of the scrum. We had Adam Jones on the bench and I felt he had the technical capacity as a pure scrummager to shore things up and give us a chance to play some front-foot rugby rather than be repeatedly shunted back into penalty-concession territory. Graham Rowntree saw it differently. He wanted to give it until half-time and won the argument. It is my view that by giving Phil that extra fifteen minutes, we subjected ourselves to unnecessary extra hassle. Which is not to throw Phil to the wolves. There was just something about our set-piece that day, something about the physics of it, that simply failed to stack up. When we needed Phil to redeem himself in the final Test in Johannesburg, he did so magnificently. Nothing on the tour gave me greater pleasure than his performance at Ellis Park that afternoon.

As a matter of fact, we outscored the Boks by three tries to two in the opener, but our second-half scores (after making changes upfront) through Tom Croft and Mike Phillips came just a little too late to tip things our way and we found ourselves in the place where the Lions never want to be in a three-match series: one down, with the prospect of being dead seven days later. There was a long discussion in selection for the second Test in Pretoria, and not just about the scrummaging. There was a feeling among some of the coaches that Ugo Monye, the England wing, had bombed a couple of opportunities and that he should make way for Luke Fitzgerald of Ireland. I took a different view, arguing that Ugo had at least put himself in a position to score tries, and that on any other day he might take his chances and make a real impact on the scoreboard. I lost the argument and was disappointed about it. I still feel to this day that it was the wrong call, and that we missed a trick.

The other debate – a rather ironic one, given what would happen at Loftus Versfeld – surrounded our outside-half options. In the midweek game separating the first two Tests, against the Emerging Springboks in Cape Town, we'd started with Ronan O'Gara at 10. It was a wet day and conditions suited Ronan's kicking ability and his skills as a tactician. As we ran out for the second half, O'Gara was missing. James Hook, more of a running 10, was on instead. I was heard to ask what the hell was happening as I took my seat in the coaches' box, at which point Geech turned to me and said he'd promised Ronan that he'd be off at the break. It transpired that Ronan had gone to Geech early in the week and asked if he was under consideration for the second Test. Geech had told him he was and by way of reassurance, said he would play only forty minutes in midweek. There are two points to make about this. Firstly, Hook was nowhere near as suited as Ronan to the conditions in Cape Town and when he attempted to play some rugby from deep with the rain hammering down, he put us under pressure. Had O'Gara still been on the field, we would have won. In the event, we drew. Secondly – and again, this is with the benefit of hindsight – we should have named James on the bench for the Pretoria Test, ahead of Ronan. It was bone dry in Pretoria, and the going was fast – perfect conditions for Hook. Had he been on the field in the closing seconds, would he have played it the way Ronan played it and conceded the penalty that gave Morne Steyn the chance to win the match, and the series, for the Springboks with the very last kick? It's impossible to say for sure, but I doubt it somehow.

We're talking here about one of the hardest, most unforgiving Tests ever seen in rugby union. It was brutal. Off-the-scale tough. I wince when I look back on it, even now. There usually comes a point on a tour of South Africa when things get a little tasty and it had already happened on this trip, down in Port Elizabeth against the Southern Kings in the final game before the Durban Test. That had been one of those cheap-shot affairs, with the locals scoring more points in the he-man department than they were capable of managing through tries or kicks at goal. Pretoria was something different. Yes, there were some deeply questionable incidents involving two of the Springbok forwards, Schalk Burger and Bakkies Botha, but beyond that it was a match of perfectly legitimate physicality, raised to a level rarely witnessed. I cannot remember feeling more completely gutted at the end of a game, so totally crushed, than when Steyn hit the spot with that long-range penalty to put the South Africans two up with one to play.

Would it have turned out differently had Burger been sent off for gouging Luke Fitzgerald in the opening seconds of the match? Probably. Given the transformation in scrummaging fortunes – our all-Welsh front row of Gethin Jenkins, Matthew Rees and Adam Jones, with Paul O'Connell and the outstanding Simon Shaw stoking the fires in the engine room, were too strong for the Boks at the set-piece – it is difficult to believe that we would not have prevailed over fourteen men. And Burger certainly should have been off the field for the duration rather than for a mere ten minutes. A yellow card? For scratching away at an opponent's eyes? Please. Bryce Lawrence, my fellow New Zealander, was running the touchline that day and was the closest official to the incident. Whenever I've spoken to him about it, he has insisted that he really didn't see what happened. Yet he was the one who recommended the yellow-card sanction.

Even then, we were in full control when Botha, who revelled in his reputation as a hard man and went out of his way to knock his opponents around, clattered Adam Jones at a second-half ruck – a horizontal missile smashing into a static object. There could be only one winner of that little match-up, and it wasn't Adam. He ended up in hospital; we ended up with uncontested scrums. Suddenly, the likes of Pierre Spies, that most athletically gifted of No 8s, were fully in the game and causing us grief. If the gods of rugby exist, they were against us that day. There could be no arguing with the decision at the end, when O'Gara challenged Fourie du Preez in the air and brought him crashing to earth. But across the eighty minutes, we were on the rough end of it. I still consider that defeat as one of the most painful I've ever had the misfortune to experience. We deserved so much more. When Brian O'Driscoll was concussed and needed to be replaced we had the option of putting Mike Phillips at 12 where he had played some time against the Golden Lions. That thought didn't cross our mind and moving Stephen Jones to 12 and bringing Ronan on probably didn't give us the physicality required. When I look back on it now, I think rather than kicking the ball out and it being a draw, Ronan was trying to do something special and unfortunately just got it wrong.

Yet those of us on the coaching panel knew something

else: that there was no room in international rugby, or anywhere else in sport at the top-level, for navel gazing. The Lions had now lost seven Tests back to back against the southern hemisphere elite. An eighth, to go with a second successive whitewash, did not bear thinking about, even though we had been ultra-competitive against the Boks for three halves of rugby out of four. To that end, we needed to flush the disappointment of Loftus Versfeld out of our collective system as quickly as possible and reload ahead of the series finale in Johannesburg. Yes, it was a 'dead rubber' game on paper but in our hearts, minds and souls, it was very much alive and full of meaning.

But how should we set about our preparations? A break from rugby at this point in the tour had been long in the planning, and we duly headed out of Pretoria for a two-day safari. A couple of hours up the road, some of the players made it clear that they had seen enough bloody big beasts for one weekend and would rather have some down-time at the hotel. Call it a Mutiny on the Buses. Soon enough, our convoy was parked on the side of the road while we sorted out who wanted to do what. Geech was spending a couple of days with his wife, so it was down to me to help manage the decision-making process. Along with the tour captain Paul O'Connell, Shaun Edwards, Paul Stridgeon (who had played his usual tireless and enthusiastic role as part of the fitness and conditioning team), virtually all of the Welsh players and most of those I'd coached at Wasps, I boarded the bus heading back to town. The rest disappeared into the wilds of the highveld. What they did with their cameras and binoculars, I have no idea. Us? We had a good drink in the hotel bar, sang an awful lot of songs awfully badly, and went to bed in dribs and drabs, dimly aware of the hangovers awaiting us. I can't claim it was the healthy option, but it did us the world of good. And it's a model we've stuck with on subsequent trips, with a 100 per cent success rate.

Changes had to be made for the Ellis Park match: our dressing room at Loftus had looked like a field station and it was obvious from very early in the week that several players would not recover in time. We ended up with a whole new threequarter line, with Shane Williams on one wing, Ugo Monye back on the other and a Tommy Bowe–Riki Flutey centre pairing; two fresh props in Andrew Sheridan and the returning Phil Vickery; and a pair of new flankers in Joe Worsley and Martyn Williams. The Boks also had a different look to them, but they felt they had a point to prove on behalf of Bakkies Botha, who had been banned for his demolition job on Adam Jones. When they took the field for their warm-up, they were wearing armbands with 'Justice 4' emblazoned on them. Bakkies' number? No 4.

To be frank, I was in no mood to see us pushed around by the South Africans. I felt we'd been a little too legitimate in the first two Tests, a little too compliant. It is of course important to have faith in referees and trust them to make the tough decisions, but if we're going to get real for a second, there are times in rugby when the toughness has to come from you. After Pretoria, the officials had expressed some concern about the 'amount of stuff that had been going on' and ventured to suggest that it might be nice to keep a lid on it in Johannesburg. My response was simple and straight-forward. As they'd been the ones letting all that 'stuff' go, they might look at themselves as well as the players. I certainly believed a firmer line should have been taken at Loftus Versfeld and I made the point with some force. I was equally forceful when I spoke to the team. I held up the Lions jersey. 'For most of you this is the last time you will ever wear this jersey. Losing this game isn't an option,' I said. 'The only way you earn respect from these ***** is to beat them. They won't respect you if you don't. Not a chance.' The players responded brilliantly, dominating the physical contest and running in three tries without reply for a 28–9 victory. It was a sweet moment, even if it could never have been completely satisfying.

Looking back on those weeks in South Africa, there is no doubting the lift it gave me as an international coach. I flew out as an outsider: before one of the games, Geech was kind enough to ask me if I'd conduct the jersey presentation ceremony. It was an offer I humbly declined, on the grounds that I was a newcomer to Lionhood and hadn't yet done enough to earn such an honour. When I returned, I felt I had a sound idea of what the Lions meant, why they mattered and how they should be handled. I also believed that we had gone some way towards restoring the Lions' lost identity on that trip. There was more to do and further to go, but the road ahead was clear.

8

THE HUMAN FACTOR

We are living through a new age of rugby. An age of statistical analysis, of research and development, of the appliance of science. There are ever-expanding legions of backroom staff whose job it is to compute, collate and calculate – to put every player under the microscope in an effort to identify not just his major strengths and weaknesses, but his tiniest frailties and foibles. In the world of the geek, everything is measurable. Soon enough, there will be a version of a GPS system that tells us what a player is thinking, as well as doing. George Orwell would have loved it. Or maybe not.

I would hardly be doing my job properly if I failed to keep abreast of technological advances and I have been fortunate to work closely with some outstanding people in the field, most notably Rhys Long, who played rugby for Bridgend and spent almost a decade crunching the numbers in the Wales set-up before joining the Football Association as their grandly titled 'head of performance analysis and insight'. Rhys did some brilliant work with us across multiple World Cup cycles, which was why I insisted on including him in my Lions party when we toured Australia in 2013.

All that being said, the sport still has a place – a central place – for instinct, for gut feeling, for the ability to reject orthodoxy and back a hunch. Contrary to modern thinking, rugby has a large number of unmeasurables. It is not track cycling or Formula One, where every pedal stroke and engine beat can be logged, pored over and assessed. It may be possible to gauge a player's aerobic capacity in ideal conditions, but it is very difficult to know how the fittest of individuals will perform once they have taken a smack on the nose at the first ruck. The human factor will always play a large part in our game, as the 2011 World Cup in New Zealand reminded me all too painfully. In one sense, our fate was defined by numbers: a centimetre or two here, a degree or two there. But in the end, it came down to the decisions of referees standing in the middle of a full stadium, not boffins sitting in a laboratory. And referees are human beings. Most of them, anyway.

Would we have won the Webb Ellis Cup had those decisions gone the other way? No. I wouldn't argue for a moment that we would have beaten the All Blacks in a final in Auckland, even though they struggled with the weight of expectation on the big night. But we would certainly have been on the field that evening but for Sam Warburton's dismissal in the early stages of our semi-final against France. I don't think any fair-minded rugby follower would disagree with me on this matter. We were a better side than the French and while they had developed a useful knack of extricating themselves from difficult situations during the tournament and possessed some very influential players in key positions, they would not have stopped us had we kept everyone on the pitch. But we didn't.

Sam was so important to us at that stage, both as a captain and an open-side flanker of the highest quality, that our chances of surviving his sending-off were virtually zero. (The fact that we gave ourselves chances to win even in the face of such a crushing setback says something about our courage and determination, but more than anything it re-inforces my point about the relative merits of the two sides.) Yet when I returned from the Lions tour in the summer of '09 and turned my thoughts to building for the World Cup two years distant, Sam was not in my thoughts as a leader. His rise to prominence was remarkably rapid.

We knew about him, of course. He had captained Wales through the age groups, had played in a couple of Junior World Cups and was a highly valued member of the Cardiff Blues academy. While I was away with the Lions in South Africa, he travelled to North America with the rump of the Wales squad for full international matches against Canada and the United States. He sat on the bench in Toronto, but wasn't used. A week later in Chicago, he won his first cap as a substitute for Ryan Jones and played his part in a 48–15 victory. He was just twenty. Come the autumn series at the Millennium Stadium, I started him against Samoa – not one of my happier days as Wales coach, although we just about scraped home by four points – and brought him on against the Wallabies in a game we lost pretty heavily. Sam still had plenty to learn, but his potential was plain to see. He was on his way.

As we had already lost to the All Blacks, albeit narrowly, that run of pre-Christmas matches was something of a disappointment. There were extenuating circumstances. Rest and recovery time is always at a premium following a Lions tour and a good number of our front-line players – Shane Williams, Jamie Roberts, Stephen Jones, Gethin Jenkins, Matthew Rees, Alun Wyn Jones, Martyn Williams – had already shouldered a heavy burden by the time the New Zealanders arrived in town. But I was absolutely committed to taking on the world's best teams whenever the opportunity arose. We could have chosen an easier road at times, playing weaker opposition and minimising our exposure to potential defeats. But to me, it was a question of pride. The most powerful southern hemisphere teams were beginning to field weakened sides on their European tours, blooding youngsters and experimenting with different combinations. My argument to the WRU hierarchy was that we should go full tilt at these people and let them know they would find themselves in a proper game every time they set foot in Cardiff. I certainly didn't want them thinking they could take us for granted.

In a way, our final autumn game against the Wallabies drew a line. The way I saw it, 2010 would have to be a year of transition: we were twenty months or so away from the

World Cup and there would be no better time to shake things up a little by making personnel changes. Our thirty-nine-man squad for the Six Nations featured a whole bunch of players in the single-figure cap category and some with no caps at all. Sam Warburton was among the fresher faces. So were a number of others who would go on to make a massive contribution to the Welsh game: Jonathan Davies and Dan Biggar, Ken Owens and Dan Lydiate.

I didn't expect a golden Six Nations and I didn't get one: we lost three of our first four games and ended up in the bottom half of the table. But by the end of the competition I'd at least given Sam his tournament debut against Italy, having run him off the bench against Scotland and Ireland. My first-choice back row featured Ryan Jones, still the captain, at No 8, with Martyn Williams and Andy Powell on the flanks. Remember Andy Powell? I do. How could I forget him?

He hit the headlines the day after our victory over the Scots, who were then being coached by Andy Robinson, the former England flanker and a member of the successful 1989 Lions party in Australia. If I'm honest, Scotland played us off the park that day. We were two tries down inside twenty minutes, nine points adrift at the interval and we would have been toast had they not completely butchered an overlap early in the second half. That error, along with a couple of yellow cards, gave us a way back into the contest, and after scores from Lee Byrne and Leigh Halfpenny, we pinched it at the death when Shane Williams – who else? – touched down at the posts in the final attack. Instead of losing by at least a dozen points, we won 31–24. There was a lot of relief in our camp that night. As it turned out, there was an element of mischief too.

At that point, we were employing a couple of security guards to look after the players on their after-dark ventures into Cardiff. This would always be followed by a management debrief on the Sunday morning. I'd heard my share of stories during these sessions and I recall one of the guards reporting back with the words: 'Oh my God. I've looked after plenty of people in my time. Footballers, musicians, movie stars. These guys are in a league of their own. There are women out there throwing themselves in their direction. No wonder they're so keen to get into town.' But on this occasion, after the Scotland game, all seemed quiet on the celebratory front. I met up with Alan Phillips over breakfast. 'Everything OK last night?' I asked. 'Yep, no issues.' I then drove home to my place in Cardiff Bay. England were playing Italy in Rome and I settled down to watch the match on television. It wasn't exactly a thriller. At the break, the score was 6–6 and I was only half paying attention when John Inverdale, who was hosting the BBC's coverage, mentioned something about Andy Powell being arrested for driving down the M4 . . . in a golf buggy. He said it in such a matter-of-fact way, I wondered if I had come in on the end of a joke. After another turgid spell of rugby from the restart, it occurred to me that I should check my phone, just in case. I'd left it in the car, so I went down to the garage and fetched it. The moment I switched it on, the truth dawned on me. Missed calls? There were fifty-seven of them.

It transpired that very late on the Saturday night – or, to be more accurate, shortly before dawn on the Sunday morning – Andy had felt in need of a smoke and left our Vale of Glamorgan base in search of a packet of cigarettes. He felt the most obvious source of tobacco products would be the service station situated one junction along the motorway, heading east towards the Severn Bridge. Intelligently, he decided that he'd had far too much to drink to even consider driving his car. Slightly less intelligently, he and a friend went for the golf buggy alternative, apparently on the basis that they couldn't be caught speeding. They were making their way along the hard shoulder, slower than tortoises, when some members of the South Wales constabulary caught up with them. As Andy was being driven to the station, slightly more quickly than he had been travelling in the buggy, the police van passed some of his teammates who were still out on the town! Really, you couldn't have made it up.

Looking back on it now, it is one of professional rugby's funnier stories. If I'm honest, it was pretty amusing at the time, and there was a part of me that wished he'd got away with it. But together with the WRU officials involved in the tidy-up, I felt there was no option but to ban Andy from the remainder of the tournament. If we'd shown even the slightest leniency, our critics would have mounted their high horses and spent the next few weeks talking about moral compasses, role models and road safety.

Unsurprisingly, the incident has gone a long way towards defining Andy's career, and as he's dined out on the story more than once, he's happy for the details to be trotted out every now and again. But there was more to Andy than a nocturnal adventure in the slowest vehicle known to transport. He was a lovable character and a good team man, popular with his colleagues. He was also a real powerhouse off the back of a scrum. When things were going well for him, as they were ahead of the Lions tour in '09, there were very good reasons to include him in any starting line-up. It is also true to say that while he struggled to settle anywhere for long at club level, apart from a five-year stint with Cardiff Blues, he had a good run with Wales. I picked him for the World Cup in 2011 and he was still involved when the Six Nations came around a few months later. That tells you something. He was never the most confident of players and often needed to be told how good he was, but when he had some self-belief on his side, he took an awful lot of stopping.

If Andy was a substantial specimen in back-row terms, George North was seriously big for a winger. The good news about George was that he was playing the house down for the Scarlets. The bad news? He was English-qualified. He'd been born in Norfolk and his father was a Yorkshireman, so even though he had been raised in Anglesey and was a fluent Welsh speaker, there was a danger that he'd play his international rugby in a white shirt. And there was no doubting his Test credentials. He was 6 ft 4 in, 17 st plus, formidably strong in contact, unusually fast and, it seemed to us, more or less fully formed. Extraordinary. As we set about piecing together our squad for the 2010 autumn series, we quickly reached the conclusion that we had to cap him as soon as possible. He may have been only eighteen, but who cared? The last thing I needed was this kid ripping up trees in Heineken Cup rugby, with Martin Johnson and the rest of the Twickenham hierarchy looking on admiringly and whispering sweet nothings in the ears of his parents. When we unleashed him against the Springboks, he scored a try after five minutes and another after fifty-six minutes. We lost the game by four points, largely due to the punishing goal-kicking of our old friend Morne Steyn, but we had found ourselves a player.

More than one player, as it happened, for Dan Lydiate was also emerging. Like George, he had been born in England but represented Wales in the lower age-group levels. Unlike George, he played for the Under-20s before he played for the grown-ups. He had suffered a very serious neck injury early in his career, and at that point, his rugby future had looked bleak. But Dan was made of strong stuff. He was also the epitome of a model professional, one of the new breed who took fitness and conditioning extremely seriously. Even though the amateur era was long over, some of the older players clung to the time-honoured ways. Not Dan. The way he trained and recovered and thought about the game was at the cutting edge. He was the future.

There was definitely an air of the changing of the guard about us as we moved into World Cup year. Our first match of 2011 was a Six Nations opener against England, just as it had been in 2008, my debut fixture as head coach. Only four players – James Hook, Shane Williams, Mike Phillips and Alun Wyn Jones – started both games and of those, Hook was in a different role. I don't have too many fond memories of that fixture. For one thing, we lost. For another, the whole event was dominated by the Dylan Hartley Affair. It stemmed from a Heineken Cup game between Northampton and Cardiff Blues a few weeks previously, after which one of my scrum-halves, Richie Rees, was suspended for allegedly gouging Hartley. Dylan told the disciplinary hearing that he had felt pain around his eye, but when I watched the tape of the incident, there was no reaction from him at all. As a front-row forward on the wrong end of such an assault, he would surely have called Richie a 'dirty bastard' and gone after him. Was this a conspiracy to get one of our blokes suspended before a big international? There was suspicious talk of it among our group, certainly. Richie picked up a twelve-week ban and I wasn't happy at all. In my dumbness, I had a real crack at Dylan at a press conference, flagging up his weakness as a line-out thrower under pressure and effectively questioning his manhood. He did have issues with his throwing, so that much was accurate, but the rest of it was miles over the top and indefensible. Needless to say, I had my pants pulled down in a humiliating fashion. Dylan threw exceptionally well against us, turning in a top performance all round and helping England win the game.

I spoke to Graham Rowntree after the game and he told

me I'd gone too far in criticising Hartley. It was a fair comment, so I approached Dylan and told him how well he'd played before acknowledging that I'd said too much. I'd got it completely wrong and I'd have been pathetically small-minded if I hadn't admitted it. Since then, we've had a good relationship, as New Zealand-bred hookers should. Dylan had learned his rugby at Rotorua Boys' High School, so contrary to my suggestion, he was no shrinking violet. He was tough. When you're given a rugby upbringing in Rotorua, you quickly learn how to look after yourself. There aren't many wimps in that neck of the woods. He dug deep against us in Cardiff that night and I respected him for it.

Another hooker, Matthew Rees, was our captain during the tournament, having taken over when Ryan Jones picked up an injury in 2010. I had no problem sticking with Matthew through the Six Nations, even when Ryan came back into the side. He was a quality player, a quality person and he did an excellent job with an evolving side. But Matthew suffered a neck problem that ruled him out of the 2011 World Cup and I saw an opportunity to try something fresh. A lot of people expected me to turn to Alun Wyn Jones, who was already a Test Lion and would be travelling to New Zealand as a fifty-cap lock. But there was something about Sam Warburton that set my mind racing. I knew some of the most influential players in the competition would be No 7s – Richie McCaw of New Zealand and David Pocock of Australia being the most obvious examples – and I felt Sam was cut from the same cloth. He was powerful, absolutely outstanding over the ball and would be spending his time at the centre of everything. He wasn't the finished article, as we say in the coaching trade, but he was a quick learner – Martyn Williams, his mentor at Cardiff Blues, had told me that – and there was good reason to believe he would grow with the team as the team grew with him. Yes, it was a risk. But I convinced myself it was a risk worth taking.

I remember my first conversation with Sam about the captaincy. His initial response was to turn it down. He felt he wasn't ready for it, that he was new on the scene and considered himself too quiet by nature. He was in need of some convincing, clearly, and it was down to me to sell him the role. It became something of a game between us – a cat-and-mouse situation. The breakthrough came when I showed him a video clip of us winning a turnover that he hadn't been directly involved in achieving. Even so, he was sufficiently pumped up to go around smacking everyone on the backside and geeing them up. 'It shows you that leadership isn't always about talking,' I told him. 'It's about actions and encouragement and setting an example through attitude and body language. It's about how hard you train. It's about the standards you set as an individual and your ability to carry people with you.' It did the trick. I think Sam agreed at least in part because of the transitional nature of the team. Had we been going to the World Cup crammed full of seventy-cap players with long-service medals pinned on their chests, he might have found it too much. But this was a less established playing group in which a majority saw their futures stretching out in front of them. Sam was of their generation and while it took him some time to understand the role fully, he always had the support of the group.

I can't pretend that we headed to New Zealand with a completely settled side, pieced together with tender loving care over a period of years. To a certain extent, we were making decisions on the hoof. Take Rhys Priestland, who to all intents and purposes had been the chief back-up to Stephen Jones down in Llanelli after making his way through the academy. We capped him off the bench during the Six Nations and he generally did what we asked of him, but it was not until the pre-World Cup training camp that he really set me thinking. Rhys worked his butt off as we prepared for the big tournament and while he didn't strike me as the complete package – he did not exactly exude confidence, being a diffident character, and he certainly wasn't the greatest goal-kicker I'd ever seen – there was an intelligence about his rugby, a subtlety and sophistication that was far from common. I remember saying to Rob Howley: 'You know, I think he may be our best No 10.' Rob looked at me sideways. He wasn't convinced. What I didn't know was whether he could produce the best of his game under the pressure of Test conditions. He gave me the answer to that conundrum in our first warm-up match, against England at Twickenham. Stephen was on the starting list, but he pulled up with a calf problem shortly before kick-off. Rhys took his place and performed exceptionally well. So there he was, suddenly: a nailed-on member of our World Cup party.

It wasn't only Rhys who worked hard that summer: our conditioning trip to Poland, based around the cryotherapy work carried out at the Olympic Sports Centre situated on the banks of the Pilica River not far from Lodz, was no one's idea of an all-inclusive five-star holiday. Sam called the cryotherapy chamber an 'evil sauna' and he had a point. And the chamber was in keeping with the centre itself. Someone once described it as a masterpiece of brutalist architecture. They had a point too. This was a university campus, not a hotel. There were two single beds in a shared room, a television with nothing to watch except Eurosport – most of the players had a PhD in Tour de France studies by the time they left – and the dining arrangements were strictly communal. There again, we weren't there to enjoy ourselves. We were there in search of results, and results were what we achieved.

Cryotherapy is not at the forefront of sports science in the way it once was – everything becomes old hat over time – and even back in 2011, the beneficial effects were familiar enough to those in the know. But the fact remains: the effect on the blood vessels of exposure to very low temperatures allows athletes to recover extremely rapidly from their previous training session. Which means they can train again in next to no time, instead of being as sore as hell, or just plain injured, and unable to set foot on a field for a week. They are able to operate at high intensity for longer, and spend far more time doing quality work. During our pre-World Cup camp, the players were undergoing two rounds of cryotherapy a day. It was tough, but they knew it was good for them. Even Gavin Henson dug deep, albeit under protest, and put himself through it. By the end of their stay, the players were supremely fit.

That became clear in our opening pool match against South Africa, the title holders, in Wellington. Even though the Boks were awash with experience – more than half of their starting line-up had been at the heart of their triumphant campaign four years previously – we had enough belief in our physical capabilities to keep the ball in hand and move them around the park. One of the newer South Africans was the flanker Heinrich Brussow, a nose-to-the-ground turnover specialist who was fully equipped to mess opponents around on the floor. But we neutralised him with our back-row balance: Dan Lydiate had become perhaps the game's leading specialist in the 'chop' tackle, while Sam was as good as anyone in the 'jackal' role. It worked time and time again. The moment Dan took someone out at the ankles, Sam was over the ball with an 'I'll be having that, thanks very much' glint in his eye. South Africa scored an early try through the powerful Frans Steyn, but we had the better of the first half in most respects and were pretty unlucky to go into the sheds 10–6 down. Especially as James Hook had a successful penalty disallowed by Wayne Barnes, the English referee, even though the television footage suggested the kick had sneaked inside the post. Neil Jenkins, down on the touchline, was going bananas and approached Wayne in the tunnel as he headed in for his interval drink. 'Why didn't you go upstairs to the TMO?' said Neil, close to spontaneous combustion. 'That kick definitely went over.' He had unexpected support from Frans Steyn, who was standing right next to the two of them during this rather one-sided exchange. 'Yeah,' he said with a smirk. 'I reckon it went over as well.'

In the end, we lost by a point. It was disappointing, of course, but only in terms of the scoreboard. The performance had been excellent in many areas and it gave us a springboard into the tournament. However, we knew we'd find ourselves diving into an empty pool if we failed to get it right in our second game, against Samoa in my home town of Hamilton. We received a wonderful reception in general and as a local boy made good, I could barely take a step outside the hotel without being showered with good wishes. I think the suited and booted committee men in New Zealand union circles were quite surprised by this, but a Mooloo Man has Waikato rugby in his blood and the rugby community will always show him some love.

This was no time to mess around in selection. The islanders were dangerous – they had a back division of rich talent, with players such as Kahn Fotuali'i, Seilala Mapusua, George Pisi and Sailosi Tagicakibau; they had a back-row of massive hitters, with Ofisa Treviranus and Maurie Fa'asavalu flanking the ultra-aggressive George Stowers at No 8 – and there was an obvious risk of damage, not least in terms of the body count. But in a four-match pool programme, we were already in must-win territory and had to field the same side. All of which left me feeling nervous, and with good reason.

The contest was highly physical (no surprise there) and come the interval we were points down, Anthony Perenise scoring a try in first-half overtime. In the dressing room, Sam took over in the most emotionally charged way. In doing so, he raised his level of authority as a captain by an astronomical degree. 'We are NOT going home,' he told the players. 'We haven't worked this hard and sacrificed this much to go home now.' He was right. Had we been beaten, we wouldn't have made the quarters. It was exactly what I wanted from my skipper, because only he could have made that speech. Why? Because he'd gone through the pain and sacrifice of the training camp in the same way as his teammates had gone through it. He could speak from the heart. As a coach, I couldn't have addressed the players in such a fashion – I would have been expected to pick up on something far more game-specific. With Sam, it was direct: a brilliant message, brilliantly delivered. We were better in the second half, denying the Samoans any further points and scraping home through a couple of penalties from Rhys Priestland and a Shane Williams try thirteen minutes from time. Shane was around 12 st 8 lb during that competition, but he could have taken the field at 22 st 8 lb – or even 122 st 8 lb – and still have been worth his weight in gold. He really was some winger.

Namibia, the eternal whipping boys, were next up. They had Jacques Burger on the open-side flank, and to be honest, he played us on his own. I had tremendous respect for Jacques: Test rugby is tough enough without taking the field knowing you're going to lose, yet he seemed to relish every unequal challenge he ever faced. If he'd found himself in a team with an even-money chance of winning some games, he'd have been an international legend with his off-the-scale work rate and a raw form of courage that to my mind bordered on insanity. Interestingly, I saw many of those qualities in Sam, who went toe to toe with him that day in New Plymouth. We scored a dozen tries, of which Sam contributed precisely none, but he thrived on the physical challenge of his individual battle with Burger. It was a vital part of his make-up, that overwhelming passion for the battle. Yet when it came to the parts of the game that demanded cool-headed restraint, he was doing that too. It may sound ironic, given what happened at the business end of the tournament, but I was already picking up good vibes from top referees who credited him with an excellent on-field manner. Sam had a polite and respectful approach to interaction that persuaded them to engage with him rather than dismiss him with a wave of the hand. It is impossible to over-emphasise the importance of this aspect of captaincy. Not every skipper is born with the ability to keep referees on-side. Alun Wyn Jones has become an outstanding captain for Wales in recent seasons, but he could be too confrontational in his early days and paid the price for it. We've seen something similar in England with Owen Farrell. Sam was a natural. When officials told me how much they enjoyed working with him on the field, it wasn't because they'd been presented with a façade. It was genuinely Sam's way to be quiet, reasonable and sparing with his requests for clarification. And while the referees were giving me all this positive feedback, they were also telling me how good a player he was. Right up there with McCaw and Pocock, they said. And they were in a good position to make that judgement, because they were closer than anyone to the action.

Our final group-stage game was against Fiji, who were having a disappointing time of it. This was probably our best performance yet, a 66–0 demolition job with George North on fire. Every time he laid hands on the ball, he was making thirty or forty metres. At one point we had feedback from the medics to say he'd hurt his ankle and was struggling a little. My message back? 'Tell him to stop making forty-metre breaks then!' That's player management at its best: get a message on to your main strike-runner, ordering him to stop being as good as he is! Happily, George was right for the quarter-final against Ireland, of all people, in Wellington, where the red shirts were horribly outnumbered by those of the green variety. Every Irish man and woman in the southern hemisphere must have been in town for the game – a four-to-one advantage, easily. What was more, Ireland were favourites to win. They'd topped their pool, having beaten the Wallabies in Auckland, and clearly fancied their chances. It put me on edge, and my mood was seriously fractious by kick-off because of an incident on the way to the ground.

Tony Bedford, our liaison officer, told us there would be a police escort from the team hotel to the stadium. When we boarded the coach, the escort was nowhere to be seen.

I wasn't too keen on hanging around before a knockout game of such magnitude so I asked the driver to get going. The trip was a short one and it wasn't as if I didn't know the way. Halfway through the journey, the police outriders showed up. It turned out they had been asked to escort both team buses, starting with Ireland's, and that there had been a delay because there had been so many Irish supporters in our opponents' hotel, the players had taken an age to find a way out of the lobby. When we arrived at the stadium, all hell broke loose. The police officer in charge of the security operation boarded our transport and hollered at Tony: 'LO off the bus NOW!' He couldn't have been more aggressive if he'd been Bakkies Botha. I was a little shell-shocked, as was Tony. Alan Phillips, our manager, was just plain angry. Before I knew it, Alan and the policeman were nose to nose and engaging in an almighty row, watched by a group of highly-strung players preparing for one of the biggest matches of their careers. An ideal situation? Not quite. It could have completely broken the mood we'd spent the last few days creating and it was only the professionalism of the players that prevented a meltdown in the dressing room. Before the game, I saw Neil Sorensen, a one-time Wellington scrum-half who was now in the middle of a long stint as the New Zealand Rugby Football Union's general manager. 'Neil, that was completely unacceptable,' I said. 'I know,' Neil replied, and to give him credit, he took that message back to the proper authorities. Afterwards, we received a formal apology from the police.

That apology wouldn't have counted for much had we been knocked out of the tournament, but our tactics were sound enough to see us into the last four. Primarily, we wanted to blunt the edge of Ronan O'Gara's outstanding kicking game, so we doubled up in the full-back department as a means of stopping the Munster No 10 from pinning us in the corners. Leigh Halfpenny was asked to cover one fifteen-metre area, with each wing on alert to hang deep and cover the other. Ronan was a little bemused by all this and must have kicked out on the full three or four times. I could sense his frustration from my seat in the coaches' box: try as he might, he just couldn't find the grass he was looking for because it wasn't available to him. Just to rub it in, our own kicking game was bang on the money, not least because Jonathan Davies gave us a valuable left-foot option. We also switched the wings knowing that they would have probably planned a kicking game on Shane Williams. Shane scored yet again, early rather than late this time, but I knew there would be moments in the game when they applied pressure. Which they did, for long periods of the second half. We held them up over the line three or four times. Dan Lydiate was outstanding, coming off his line and chopping people down with relish.

We also did well in distorting Ireland's defensive shape. In the build-up, we'd spent a lot of time studying Brian O'Driscoll's 'spot blitz' routine – his way of putting himself into the opposition passing lane and making a nuisance of himself. We decided that Rhys Priestland should play flat to the line at No 10, with our midfielders staying unusually deep. It worked a treat. By the time Jonathan Davies at outside centre received the ball, he had a lot of space on Brian, who couldn't get to him. Jonathan was really developing at that stage: he was very strong and far quicker than people imagined. In fact, he was more of everything than people thought, as O'Driscoll, magnificent though he was, would continue to discover over the coming years. Jonathan scored a second-half try, as did Mike Phillips, and we won 22–10.

Immediately after the final whistle, Roger Lewis was suddenly right in front of me. The CEO of the Welsh Rugby Union was so excited by what had just happened, he completely unnerved me. 'Roger, please don't kiss me,' I said. Luckily, he settled for a man hug. While he knew there was more work ahead of us, he was also aware that whatever happened from hereon in, this was our most successful World Cup campaign since the first, way back in 1987.

By this point in proceedings, it was patently obvious to everyone watching that we were as fit, if not fitter, than anyone, including the All Blacks. That gave me a sense of pride. It wasn't simply a matter of being running fit. We were contact fit too, and that had given us the edge over the Irish. Under the circumstances, there was no reason to fear the French, our semi-final opponents. Yes, they had some brilliant individuals, in the pack as well as the back division; yes, they had size and power and a formidable set-piece game, particularly at the scrum. But fitness was not considered to be their trump card, and as they had already been spanked by New Zealand and lost to Tonga in the pool stage, there were reasons to question their staying power. In addition, there were strong rumours that the relationship between Marc Lièvremont, their head coach, and the senior players had broken down irretrievably.

The French were already bedded down in Auckland, having beaten an even more fragile and undisciplined England side in their quarter-final at Eden Park. We were happy for them to stay where they were, at the big SkyCity Hotel smack in the middle of town, but the tournament organisers insisted they should move out to make way for us. It seemed pointless, especially as our opponents liked the hustle and bustle of their accommodation, with its bars and restaurants and casino. We had benefited from our quiet, out-of-the-way establishment in Wellington – exactly the kind of place the French would be checking into once we arrived! Why not leave them be and allow us to take over their booking? It seemed an easy, pain-free solution, but rules are rules.

Despite the noise and distraction, we trained well ahead of the semi-final, which was to be refereed by Alain Rolland of Ireland. Initially, it seemed that the South African official Craig Joubert would be in charge, but he'd run our match with Ireland and the organisers felt that if we made it through to the final and Craig was awarded that match, as seemed likely, we would somehow have an unfair advantage. I didn't quite understand the argument, but I thought little of it. We

I love my rugby, but family comes first: with Trudi on our wedding day (*above, left*); with Bryn after the Lions had played his NZ Provincial Barbarians side during the 2017 tour (*top, right*); and with Gabby at the Wales team's 2019 World Cup departure banquet in Cardiff (*above, right*).

Trudi's fiftieth birthday bash at Waihi Beach. My family should have told me that dressing up as Captain Hook was a bad idea . . .

Arriving at the highest point in Africa after the hardest walk of my life. Rob Howley joins me on the summit of Kilimanjaro.

Talking the forwards' language on the 2009 Lions tour of South Africa. *Above:* a one-on-one consultation with the Ireland prop John Hayes. *Below:* a mass meeting with Phil Vickery, Gethin Jenkins, Alun Wyn Jones and Donncha O'Callaghan, among others.

If rugby is a thinking man's game, it is also about heart and soul. *Above:* a tactical discussion with Graham Rowntree (*left*) and Ian McGeechan during the 2009 Lions tour of South Africa. *Below:* firing up the players ahead of the final Test in Johannesburg.

The Lions decider against the Wallabies in Sydney in 2013 was an emotional journey like no other. Alex Corbisiero set us on the right road with a first-minute try.

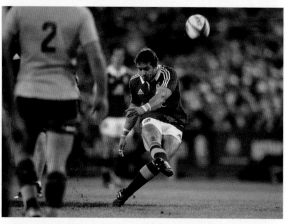

Leigh Halfpenny contributed 21 points with a brilliant kicking display.

George North was a stellar performer in the series with the Wallabies and his try in Sydney was a game-breaker.

After the final whistle, Alun Wyn Jones shared the trophy-kissing duties with our injured captain, Sam Warburton.

Tough week, triumphant weekend. Celebrating our series victory with Brian O'Driscoll.

A family reunion. It was wonderful to spend time with my dad Dave and sister Micharn during the tour.

Above: despite the mind games with Steve Hansen, the New Zealand coach, we found time for a civilised chat before the first All Blacks-Lions Test at Eden Park in 2017. *Below:* if that result went against us, Owen Farrell's kicking helped us square the series in Wellington a week later.

Above: the series decider in Auckland was an epic occasion, graced by Toby Faletau's wonderful try in the corner. *Below:* as the two captains, Kieran Read and Sam Warburton, were sharing the spoils, I reached the conclusion that a draw was the right result.

In Downing Street with Sam Warburton, holding the Tom Richards Trophy after the Lions' victory over Australia in 2013.

In Leeds a few months later, after winning the coaching award at the BBC Sports Personality of the Year ceremony.

At Buckingham Palace in 2014, after receiving the OBE.

studied Alain closely in the build-up: there were a few throw-away jokes about him being half-French and someone came up with a statistic about the All Blacks being the only side to beat France when he was the man with the whistle, but he was an experienced operator and I had no problem with his appointment. However, I did have some small concerns after Sam and I met him for the usual eve-of-Test chat – always an important part of the build-up because it gives you the chance to seek clarification on specific technical aspects of the game and offers a valuable insight into the general approach a referee is planning to take. We steered a diplomatic course in our dealings with Alain that evening: instead of pushing him hard on his intentions, we were very much in listening mode. But when we emerged from the meeting, Sam turned to me and said: 'I didn't get a good feeling from that conversation.' It was an interesting reaction, and a slightly worrying one. Sam was my captain and he didn't feel comfortable. Not great.

During the early stages of the game, any fears I had seemed misplaced. I remember sitting in the box as the first quarter unfolded and thinking: 'We'll win this, definitely. We'll be in the final.' Then, it happened. We knew the French had a habit of bringing Vincent Clerc, the dangerous wing from Toulouse, on a tight inside track off line-outs and we'd spent a good deal of time preparing our defensive response. Sam was the man charged with looking after this particular piece of business whenever it cropped up. Which it did, after seventeen minutes. Clerc took a short pass from Dimitri

Yachvili and Sam hit him with a tackle – solid, but nothing out of the ordinary. Down went Clerc. It was pretty clear that he hit the ground hard, and that his legs had flicked up beyond the horizontal. It was also clear that the French were keen to make something of it, with Lionel Nallet, their lock, first out of the blocks in showing his displeasure. But a red card? A sending off? At no point did that possibility cross my mind. I don't think anyone expected it. When Sam trudged towards the touchline, I assumed he was heading for the sin bin. When someone alongside me shouted 'Rolland's shown him red', I lost it. I stood up, kicked a table across the box and said: 'That's it. It's gone.' I couldn't believe the decision and unless I'm much mistaken, neither could the vast majority of those watching, either live in the stadium or on big screens and televisions around the world. Even the broadcasters were shocked. Look up the footage on YouTube. You'll see what I mean.

Sam was knocked sideways by Rolland's call, and in the emotional sense he fell far harder than his so-called 'victim' had done. The way he told it to me afterwards, Clerc had seen him lining up his tackle and almost jumped backwards. When contact was made, Sam said, there was nothing there – no forward momentum, no resistance, nothing. He felt he was tackling thin air. When I reflect on it now, I think Alain overreacted. He could have taken his time, chatted things through with his touch judges, considered the fact that this was a major sporting event with an audience of God knows how many – there were more people watching on a big screen in the Millennium Stadium in Cardiff than there were at Eden Park – and shown a card of a different colour. Instead, he went for the nuclear option. Have I ever gone through it with him? Asked him to explain his reasoning? No. To this day, we haven't discussed the matter. Why bother? It's gone. Over and done with.

If anything about that game still frustrates me, it is the fact that we lost 9–8. I may have given up on our chances in that eighteenth minute – if I'm being honest, I was sure we would lose by lots – but France really weren't much good and when Mike Phillips scored a lovely try down the left in the second half, the game was there for the taking despite our disadvantage. Stephen Jones rushed his conversion a little, but we were only a point down and on the front foot. At the death, we had an attacking line-out in drop-goal range. I thought to myself: 'Right, here we go. Off the top ball, Jamie Roberts up the middle, Stephen back in the pocket, kick to win it.' The first two parts of that equation went pretty much to plan, with Jamie carrying two defenders into the 22 along with the ball. But Stephen never attempted the drop goal. Instead, he ran up the short side after a number of phases and turned the ball over. I can't explain it. I don't suppose Stephen can either. The pressure of the moment does funny things to players, even the most experienced ones.

Despite that little mess-up, we still earned ourselves one last shot at a place in the final. Unfortunately, it was a long shot – a penalty from miles out. Leigh Halfpenny gave it everything he had, but the ball dropped a few inches short. I'm not saying we'd have beaten New Zealand in the final: after all, there were good reasons why they hadn't lost a Test at Eden Park since 1994 and some of those reasons – Richie McCaw, for instance – would be taking the field on a mission. But we wouldn't have looked out of place in that game, even without our captain. When the French took the field that night, I couldn't help thinking that it should have been us.

Not that there was too much time available for self-pity. There was a third-place game with the Wallabies ahead of us, not to mention Sam's disciplinary tribunal. The two of us with Alan Phillips and our lawyer walked to the hearing from our hotel, dressed in our best suits. As we turned into a side street full of restaurants and coffee shops, many of them with outside seating, we received a standing ovation. And the vast majority of people applauding us were not Welsh, but New Zealanders. Clearly, we'd earned some respect in the country through the way we'd conducted ourselves on and off the field. There had been a lot of behavioural issues around the England team and the locals had not been sorry to see the back of them. We'd been different. A lot of New Zealanders were hoping we'd make the final – they'd taken us under their wing. The prospect of a bronze medal play-off match may have been dispiriting, but at least we'd got something right.

Under the circumstances, our performance against Australia was more than satisfactory, even though we went down by three points. The Aussies always seem to turn up relaxed and play well in such circumstances. We, on the other hand, were still trying to find a way through some issues as a group after what had happened a few days earlier.

Before the tournament was over, I had to deal with one more unwanted distraction, this time of the journalistic variety – another skirmish in a long-running conflict. Sam's father had flown in for the semi-final and seen his son play next to no rugby, so I gave my final tickets to him and headed down to Waihi Beach in the Bay of Plenty, where we had bought a place next to Trudi's parents' house. Her uncle Kevin was fixing up a viewing area for friends and family at his place across the road – welcome respite from the extreme demands of the previous few weeks. Except that Trudi had just received a phone call from the *Herald on Sunday*, informing her of a story they were planning to run that weekend. According to them, I'd had a blazing row with a supporter in the SkyCity casino the night before the semi-final and been escorted from the premises. All very interesting. At least, it would have been had it been true.

I don't do slanging matches in public and I don't create scenes – anyone who knows me will confirm that much. I hadn't been in the casino anyway. In fact, I hadn't felt well that evening and after popping in to see the team doctor, I'd taken some headache pills and hit the sack early. Despite my straight denial of the story, the *Herald* insisted it would be published. So I threatened legal action, which did the trick. It wasn't my preferred course of action, but the paper left me with no choice. It gets under your skin, this kind of thing, and by that stage, I'd had enough of it. There were moments when the media circus got me down in Ireland and I'd also struggled with it in Wales. In some respects, it's been my biggest challenge. I've said some controversial things down the years, some of them calculated but most of them in the form of an honest answer to a question. I like to tell it the way I see it if I can, largely because I don't want to spend my life remembering what I said the last time I was interviewed. If I get it wrong, I'm happy to put my hand up. The Dylan Hartley Affair proved that much. What I don't see too often is the press putting its hand up. There are journalists who I like and respect, but there are also journalists I dislike. One or two, I despise. I've been on the rough end of some poor reporting, and with social media as it is, I now do as little as I can on the media front. A shame, but that's the way of it.

With the *Herald* business out of the way, I was able to enjoy the final down there at the water's edge. I had no doubt that the All Blacks would win, for the very good reason that they were the best team in the tournament. They were not, however, the best team in the final – and I say that as a native Kiwi. France dredged up a really resourceful, committed performance from somewhere that night and should have won. I know so many Kiwis will rubbish this, but that is my opinion. Anyhow that's sport, and while I feel New Zealand may have been lucky to win, they were the best team in the World Cup so probably deserved it. Bryn was watching alongside me and at half-time I said: 'Right, try to watch the next forty minutes from the French perspective.' Which he did. And all I heard from him during the second half was 'that should have been a penalty to France . . . and so should that . . . and so should that.' He was right. The French lost by a point in a low-scoring contest and had good reason to feel hard done by. Please believe me when I say that I knew how they felt.

9

RISE AND FALL

Rewind to the early autumn of 2010. Huw Evans, an excellent sports photographer and a popular figure around the Welsh rugby scene, has persuaded a bunch of former national captains to join him on a charity hike up Mount Kilimanjaro, the highest peak in Africa at almost 6,000 metres, in aid of cancer research in memory of his wife. He also invites me along for the ride – or rather, the vertical slog – and I am happy to accept. It is as tough a physical challenge as I've ever encountered and I know that the only way I'll make it to the top is to put myself in an All Black frame of mind. It is a matter of accepting the pain and the suffering in pursuit of your goal and slogging your way through it. Just like playing rugby under Grizz Wyllie. Not everyone reaches the summit but I manage to get there, and while I am exhausted by the time we complete our descent, I know I've achieved something and feel elated. I must be fit for my age.

Now, fast forward to Easter Monday 2012. The World Cup frustration is well and truly behind us and the whole of Wales is back on top of the mountain that matters most, having won another Six Nations Grand Slam. What is more, the British and Irish Lions have been in touch with an offer I really cannot refuse: the head coach's position for the tour of Australia in 2013. These really are golden days, I think to myself, as I spend some down-time with Trudi and the kids at our holiday home at Waihi Beach.

Then she asks me to clean the windows.

The house is about an hour and twenty minutes from Hamilton. Trudi's family had been going to the area for years and while I was coaching in Ireland, we had bought a site not far from their place and spent a good deal of time and money developing it. We had not long finished the project when Trudi phoned me out of the blue and told me she had swapped it for a property next door to her parents' house. It was a little, old, single-storey 'bach' (beach house), nothing like the home we'd just made for ourselves. But it was right on the beach and there was a big shared lawn where the whole family could get together and enjoy life. It was one of the best moves we ever made. Over time, we extended it, adding a storey and turning it into somewhere special for us, the kids and their friends to make memories.

'Warren, the windows are dirty with the salt from the sea and the photographer is coming today.' We are lying in bed and I'm in no hurry to move, but this is the third time Trudi has mentioned it and I'm beginning to realise I'm better off just getting up and getting on with it. She has given an interview to *Home and Garden* magazine and they are heading our way to do the photoshoot of the place. Eventually, I cave in. 'Would you like me to get up and clean the windows, Trudi?'

'That would be lovely.' I throw on some shorts and a T-shirt and walk outside in my bare feet. We have a long hose with a brush attachment and I set about my domestic chores, most of which can be conducted from ground level. Most, but not all. There are a couple of small windows at the rear of the upper deck that I can't quite reach, and as I've never been one to do half a job – I can be quite OCD in some respects – I climb up onto the deck railing to get at those annoyingly inaccessible panes of glass. At which point I lose my balance and fall three metres, landing on the concrete below. It happens in slow motion: I think about clinging to the rail, but know it won't hold my weight and fear that I'll smash my chin on it and lose all my teeth. When I land, it is at an angle of about twenty degrees. Everything goes through my heels and the pain is horrendous, way beyond anything I ever experienced on a rugby field. An elderly couple are walking past as I fall and come hurrying up.

'Are you all right?'

'No.'

'Shall we call an ambulance?'

'Yes.'

That is the conversation in its entirety, word for word. The woman goes to the front door, and not getting any answer wanders into the bathroom where she can hear a shower going. Gabby's poor boyfriend Zane gets a hell of a fright when he pulls back the shower curtain and this old lady says 'the man outside has broken his legs'. Trudi leaps into gear with blankets on me while we wait for the ambulance as she knows the shock will set in shortly. Half the neighbourhood gather and before I know it, I'm on my way to Waikato Hospital, a drive of about ninety minutes, accompanied by my wife and dosed up with a hefty supply of morphine.

The first doctor I see is German. 'I'm looking at your X-ray results and you've done a good job of this,' she says. 'In fact, you've munted it.' By 'munted', a time-honoured term among New Zealanders, she means 'wrecked'. By 'it', she means my right heel. My left heel is none too good either: it's well and truly fractured. But the right one is the real problem. The heel bone is the hardest in the body, yet I've managed to completely destroy it. After a few days flat on my back, with morphine pump attached, the surgeon arrives to run me through the options. 'We need to operate quite quickly, before the bones begin to reform,' he says. 'But there's so much swelling, I can't do it right now. You'll need plates, but there's a lack of good blood supply in this area of the foot and with the likelihood of infection, it's pretty risky.' He is pretty blunt . . . and then gets blunter. 'There's a good chance you could lose your leg if you get an infection,' he says and then pauses, so the information can sink in. 'So,' he continues eventually, 'we could attempt the operation, or you can take your chances without surgery. Up to you.' Trudi is really shocked and pretty tearful at this point, and I'm not feeling so brilliant myself. I look up at the surgeon and say: 'I think I'll take my chances. Forget the operation.'

There you have it: the full story of my fall, certain details of which were widely reported in every corner of the rugby landscape. I was in a wheelchair and off my feet for a good twelve weeks, with wires inserted into my heel to hold the bones together, and for some time afterwards I needed a mobility scooter to get around. The pain took a long while to ease, but that wasn't the half of it: the worst part of my recovery was the constant feeling of pins and needles in my foot. That was unbelievably uncomfortable and I really struggled to handle it. At one point, I told the Lions that I wasn't sure I would recover sufficiently to undertake the 2013 tour. They were incredibly understanding in putting things on hold until I was able to give them a clearer idea of my situation. More than anything, it was a wake-up call for me – a brutal lesson in how quickly your life can change.

There was a postscript, some months down the road. The force of the impact had left me with impact blood blisters on my heel and instep. Not just any old blood blisters, but bloody great big ones that caused me serious discomfort. Originally, I was advised that they would dry up naturally and could then be peeled off. That didn't quite happen. While the blister on my instep behaved itself, the one on my heel proved to be almost as stubborn as I am when it comes to rugby matters. When a nurse examined it, there was a tiny hole that hadn't healed. My specialist was worried about the potential for osteomyelitis – infection of the bone, in layman's language, and something to be avoided at all costs. It turned out that surgery would be required after all and the operation was carried out in Bristol. The doctor cut a big hole in my heel, cleaned the bone and took a graft from my instep. As a result, I have an indentation on my instep and a lump on my heel the size of half a squash ball. New shoes are a challenge. So too is a round of golf when I reach the back nine. I cannot walk for more than ninety minutes without considerable discomfort. There is still a numbness in the affected area and I have some movement problems with my toes. For years afterwards, I experienced the odd sensation of touching my heel and feeling it in my instep; something to do with the way the blood vessels had been reattached. When I look back, three thoughts occur to me. I'm thankful for my good fortune in getting through those long years as a rugby player without suffering a serious injury. I also know that whatever happens, I won't be climbing Kilimanjaro again. As for housework . . . well, that's a dangerous business. Avoid it if you can.

My contract with the WRU had been due to expire after the World Cup, but I agreed an extension just before the tournament. This was not a foregone conclusion. I was still of the view that stays of three or four years anywhere were long enough and besides, there was interest in my services from New Zealand. Ian Foster had ended his long coaching career with the Chiefs and joined the All Blacks, so there was a chance of running the show at Super Rugby level. I talked it through with the Chiefs, and there was a big part of me that fancied the job. The pull of home was strong, especially as the kids were at important stages of their lives. But the contract New Zealand rugby sent through would have left me on less money than I'd been earning in 2007, when I was in my joint Waikato–Chiefs role. I told Trudi that if they upped their offer by another five grand, I'd sign. But New Zealand Rugby wouldn't move. Not a cent. So I re-signed with Wales, who, besides giving me a platform at international level, had always been brilliant in allowing me plenty of opportunity to fly back to New Zealand to spend time with my family. When I thought about it, I was clearly in an enviable position. When I was at work in Wales, there were minimal distractions; when I was in Hamilton, the time I was spending with Trudi, Bryn and Gabby was quality time. When my friends asked me about the way I was living my life, I always used the same joke. 'It's not too bad: I get six honeymoons a year!' I believe it has strengthened my relationship with Trudi. As for the kids, family life in Hamilton was right for them. They were in the thick of their education and sport, the house was a magnet for their friends and Trudi was always there, fully involved in all their activities. Our food bill each week was huge, but I wouldn't have had it any other way.

The World Cup cycle being what it was, I felt it was reasonable to agree a four-year extension. I was working with quality players and coaches, we'd enjoyed some success together and I felt the Wales team was at the start of something rather than at the end. I was also confident in my relations with the movers and shakers on the union, especially with Roger Lewis, although there was the odd spat between us. One of them had occurred during the World Cup, just after I had put pen to paper on my new deal. Roger felt the coaching team had been in place for a long time and was in need of freshening up after the tournament, when all contracts would be up for renewal. It was a perfectly reasonable argument and completely within his remit as CEO, but I had plenty on my plate at that point and was more interested in getting him off my back than engaging seriously with the subject. 'We could let Shaun Edwards go,' I told him, just for something to say. After we beat Ireland in the quarter-final, with the help of a great defensive performance right out of the Shaun playbook, Roger attended a press conference and was asked about the coaching arrangements going forward. Given that Shaun was still a part-timer with us due to his Wasps commitments, his position was of particular interest. Roger announced that Shaun would be re-signing with Wales. Had he discussed this with me? No. I wasn't best pleased at him saying this in public without any kind of consultation and I told Roger so in pretty blunt terms, within earshot of various staff and players who happened to be hanging around at the time. 'Warren, let's go outside and talk about it,' Roger said. 'I don't want to talk about it,' I responded. Roger kept asking. I kept refusing. Eventually, I brought the discussion to a close by saying: 'Roger, just f*** off and leave me alone.' Which he did, presumably deciding that discretion was the better part of valour.

Even when things are going well, World Cups are a pressure cooker for the emotions.

There was precious little time for relaxation with another instalment of the Six Nations just around the corner – a competition with plenty riding on it. Our first game was against Ireland, of all people. In Dublin, of all places. It was a massive game for us. The Wellington quarter-final still rankled with the Irish and we knew they would be looking to take us apart as payback. It was also the case that there was an experience deficit in our squad. Only five players had won fifty caps or more. By contrast, there were thirteen in single figures. Some of the newcomers were high grade – Liam Williams and Rhys Webb were uncapped; Alex Cuthbert, Ken Owens and Justin Tipuric, all Lions of the future, had four caps between them. And then there was the wider issue of structure. We'd had our successes against the Irish because of intelligent game planning and the brilliance of one-off players like Shane Williams, but how long could we live with rivals who had everything securely in place behind the scenes? It was a big question then, and while we've made some progress in Wales, it still is.

In terms of international rugby, two countries in the world have a structure completely fit for purpose. New Zealand is one. The other is Ireland. It has been that way for years and everyone else is playing catch-up to some extent. I don't blame any of the money men who came into the game when it was opened up to professionalism and seized the day, either in Wales or in England. Indeed, the contribution of individual financiers in the late 1990s and 2000s was one of the major reasons why the sport has survived at a professional level in Wales. At the time, the union was in dire straits financially and in urgent need of support. Ireland was, and remains, in a different place. The people running the game there did not rush into professionalism because they didn't have to do so. The country already had an established provincial set-up, with history and tradition and a strong connection with the public. Just like New Zealand. That enabled them to create a pyramid structure with Test rugby at its apex, which put them ahead of the game. The other model – the club-driven 'football' model – took hold in England and France. But those were countries with big rugby economies; the biggest anywhere. Wales had neither the provinces nor the money.

What Wales did have was talent, despite its relatively small playing base, and an immense amount of local rivalry, bordering on tribalism, that stretched back a century or more. The rivalry underpinned the golden age of the 1960s and 70s: there was a hard edge to Welsh rugby then and it was reflected in results. But when the economics of the professional game began to bite, the politics kicked in as well. If you look at it now, are the regional teams in the right places? Does it really make sense to have two sides, Ospreys and Scarlets, separated by nine miles of motorway and fighting over the same supporter base and the same commercial opportunities? A single team in that area could develop into something very strong indeed. But if you try to make that happen, as the two regions did in early 2019, you find yourself walking across a minefield of rugby loyalty and heritage.

I think we've papered over a lot of cracks with our achievements at Test level, but there have been times when I've found myself in that minefield and had to tread extremely carefully. What would I do to strengthen the regional game in Wales? Being frank about it, I wouldn't start from here. But that's a joke, not an answer. It goes without saying that you'll always need a team in Cardiff. If it incorporated the disenfranchised rugby community of Bridgend, that might be a step forward. There's an argument for a team based in Newport taking in not only the whole of Gwent, but also some of the forgotten valleys teams, most notably Pontypridd. With a single team in the west, that opens up possibilities for something in the north of the country too. This is contro-versial stuff, but professional rugby naturally gravitates towards population. It happened in Scotland and it's happening in France. The Welsh regions need average crowds of between 12,000 and 15,000 to make a proper go of it financially, and they're a long way off that at the moment. Somewhere along the line, the emotion will have to be removed from the decision-making. That means hanging tough when it comes to tinkering with identity and tradition, as the Ospreys did when they forged the bond between the old Neath and Swansea clubs and dropped the 'N' word and the 'S' word from their name. That was enlightened thinking. Welsh rugby will need more of it over the coming years.

But back to Ireland in Dublin. I felt good about having them first up, even though we were playing them over there. Down the years, Ireland have had a good deal out of the Six Nations draw: if you look at the records, they've opened up against Italy twice as often as us, while we've played England on the first weekend three times more often than them. As the Six Nations is all about momentum generated from the outset, that's a big advantage. Yes, we were in high risk territory in 2012. There again, so were they. It was a fair fight and I've always been able to live with that.

It was a proper contest at the Aviva Stadium and this time we came out on the right side of it. Just. Not only did we need a late try from George North to give us a shot at victory – George's finish as three tacklers converged was nothing short of outstanding – but we also required a leg up, so to speak, from Stephen Ferris, the tough Ulsterman on the Irish flank. Ferris tipped up our lock Ian Evans in the tackle and was shown a yellow card. Yellow, mind you, not red. That gave Leigh Halfpenny the chance to decide it with a penalty with around a dozen seconds left on the clock. A routine shot on the face of it, but there is nothing routine about any kind of kick when the shape of your season rests on it.

After that, the remainder of the tournament fell into place. We were poor at times: it took us too long to get away from Scotland in round two; we needed a slightly unorthodox try from our substitute centre Scott Williams five minutes from time to see off Stuart Lancaster's new-look

England side at Twickenham (he ripped the ball from the arms of the substantially larger Courtney Lawes, kicked ahead and was quick enough to beat the covering Chris Ashton); we were only six points ahead of the Italians in Cardiff until Jamie Roberts broke the game open from distance midway through the third quarter. Yet once again, we were demonstrating a mastery of the mental side of the game. Strong leadership, cool-headedness in important positions, an instinctive feel for the dynamics of rugby and an eye for the main chance – these were the things that pushed us towards a Grand Slam meeting with France on home soil. Not forgetting our reliability in defence. We'd conceded only three tries in those first four games and we didn't crack once in the finale. Alex Cuthbert, a real find for us, scored the only five-pointer of the match after twenty minutes and Leigh Halfpenny did the rest from the kicking tee. That 16–9 victory, coming off the back of our World Cup run, meant a hell of a lot to all of us.

It meant something to the British and Irish Lions too. My name was being linked with the head coaching job on the 2013 tour of Australia with ever greater frequency, but the Lions hierarchy decided to wait until after the Six Nations to make a final call. Declan Kidney of Ireland was under consideration, and it may have been that, had Scotland performed strongly, Andy Robinson would have been given the nod. I certainly picked up that vibe before the start of the competition. But as it turned out, the Scots drew a blank by losing all five of their games and finishing bottom of the pile. The Lions' offer was not long in coming my way. There again, neither was my calamitous window-cleaning mishap. That fall could easily have cost me the trip and had it done so, my career might have taken a different turn.

Happily, I was able to start putting weight on my left foot in time to cast an eye over Wales on their summer tour of Australia. If I'd already been in Australia, I would happily have hopped to each of the three Test venues. Unfortunately, I was still in New Zealand and couldn't make the opening game in Brisbane. Wales, with Rob Howley in charge, lost 27–19, but they'd been only a point adrift after an hour and had given a good account of themselves. I flew over the 'Ditch', as we call the Tasman Sea, for the matches in Melbourne and Sydney and while I had no direct involvement – I had a seat in the coaches' box but there was no chance of me negotiating the stairs in time to offer any suggestions to the players at half-time – I was completely caught up in the emotion of it all. We should have won both games. As it turned out, we lost by two points, then by one. In Melbourne, we won the try-count by the odd score in three but were beaten at the death when Mike Harris, who had just appeared on the field at No 10 as a substitute for Berrick Barnes, kicked a wide-angled penalty with the clock in the red. It was a similar story in Sydney, with Barnes snatching victory off the tee on this occasion. What was it with us and the bloody Wallabies?! Time and again, we were putting ourselves in a position to beat them. Time and again, we were letting it slip, often through technical indiscipline at close quarters. It was too frustrating for words.

That being said, Rob relished the opportunity to run things his way and the Wallaby series was a priceless experience for him. Many people have him down as a reserved character and it's true that he doesn't give much away to outsiders, but in the Wales set-up he makes his views known. And those views command respect. The rugby intelligence that put him in the front rank of international scrum-halves has lost none of its sharpness and his contribution to Wales during my time has been very significant indeed.

As I would be taking a break from Wales duty at the start of 2013 to concentrate on Lions affairs, I was more than happy to give Rob further time in the hot seat during the autumn internationals. We agreed to split the four-match programme between us, with Rob taking charge of the opening games with Argentina and Samoa and me returning for the headline fixtures: New Zealand and, you guessed it, Australia. It was some way short of a triumph for either of us. All four games were lost, and not in good ways. We went into our meeting with the Pumas without some important players, including Jonathan Davies, Adam Jones and Dan Lydiate, but that didn't explain the lethargy and lack of conviction we showed in front of our own supporters. Maybe it was a case of World Cup–Grand Slam–Wallaby tour fatigue catching up with us. The Samoa defeat was worse, prompting 'Wales in crisis' talk in the papers. I took no notice of the 'crisis' argument, but I couldn't mount much of a meaningful defence against the criticism. When I returned to the group, we promptly lost 33–10 to the All Blacks, who scored twenty-three of their points without reply in the first half. The fact that the result came as no surprise to the pundits made it even more painful than it should have been.

That left the game against Australia as our one shot at salvation. We'd come home from tour knowing that we'd messed up, but it wasn't as if the Wallabies had played us off the park. The defeats had been down to game management and there is only so much of that stuff a coach can teach. You can go through every scenario under the sun on the training field, but decision-making at the back end of a tight contest . . . that's a different thing entirely. So we talked about it a good deal in the build-up in an effort to maximise the players' understanding of what to do, and what not to do, in the event of it going down to the wire once again – especially as our opponents had the ability to attack from deep.

In common with recent meetings, there was precious little between the sides. Leigh Halfpenny kicked penalties for us; Kurtley Beale kicked penalties for them. It was desperately tight and very low scoring, to the extent that Leigh's fourth penalty after an hour gave us a 12–9 lead which we held all the way into the last couple of minutes. At which point we were so deep in their half, they would have to run scrum ball from behind their own sticks if they wanted to turn things around. That much was obvious to me in the stand and should have been equally plain to the players down on the field. Yet we lined up at the scrum as we would have done for an exit kick at any time in the game. 'What are we doing?' I yelled to anyone and everyone within earshot. 'Get up in the front line, make your tackles and don't let them out of their 22.' We should have had one player in the back field as sweeper and everyone else flat. Instead, both Alex Cuthbert and Liam Williams were with Leigh in the deep. The Wallabies made too much ground off the scrum because of the width and space we'd handed them and when they broke open near halfway, Liam was still too deep and Beale cut a top-class line to score the winning try.

How did I react? Not in the way of old. On arriving in Wales in 2007, I was told that when they last lost a game to the Springboks in Cardiff, the players had been seen high-fiving and congratulating each other on how well they'd performed. When my Welsh side first lost against the South Africans, there was no high-fiving. Instead, they had to listen to me going berserk in the changing rooms. 'Don't any of you make the mistake of thinking that was good enough,' I said. 'We're at home. We should expect to win.' Having established that particular ground rule, I had no need to repeat myself. This latest painful defeat at the hands of the Wallabies hurt them, and it still eats away at me. But we reviewed it quietly, dispassionately and without argument. We had grown up a good deal as a side in the space of five years and now was the time for everyone to treat each other like adults.

10

A DIFFERENT SHADE OF RED – PART TWO

There are times in sport when you perform and deliver beyond your wildest dreams – when things go better for you and your team than you could possibly have imagined. Did I confidently anticipate landing a Six Nations Grand Slam within weeks of taking over in Wales in 2008? Hardly. After our opening half against England at Twickenham in my debut as head coach, the only thing I had a right to expect from my new rugby public was a free ticket back to New Zealand.

Then there are the occasions when you achieve your heart's desire, only to find that achievement tarnished by forces beyond your control. That's what happened to me in Australia in 2013. A series victory with the British and Irish Lions? As head coach? What's not to like? It should have been the most satisfying moment of my career. Instead, I ended the trip in a dark mood. When I look back on those events now, I am able to put them in their proper perspective and take pleasure in the results we put together and the style of rugby we played. But it's been quite a long process. When you find yourself sitting in the coaches' box with ten or twelve minutes to go in the third and deciding Test against a team as good as the Wallabies, and you're winning 41–16, and you see yourself on the big screen behind the posts, and your first thought is to raise both arms and aim two massive V-signs into the night sky . . . well, I think that tells a story.

It had been a demanding job for all sorts of reasons. There were difficult decisions to be made before departure, there were complications early in the schedule and there was the bitter disappointment of losing the second Test in Melbourne by a point – a defeat that persuaded most pundits that our goose was well and truly cooked. But all that was as nothing when set against the outpouring of vitriol that followed my decision to drop Brian O'Driscoll, the great Irish centre, from the winner-take-all finale in Sydney. I had never experienced anything remotely like it and have no wish to do so a second time. No one actually died as a result of that team selection, but there were plenty of people in the parallel universe of social media who would have been happy to see me on Death Row. All this anger and bile over a game of rugby? I can't pretend that I didn't find it disturbing.

Of course, I saw none of this coming when, after getting the Kurtley Beale sucker-punch try out of my system and enjoying Christmas with the family, I turned my thoughts full-time towards the upcoming Lions tour. Rob Howley, who would take the Wales team through the Six Nations while I cast my eye over the entire field of runners and riders for the tour, was always going to be on my coaching roster for the Australia Lions tour. I also felt Graham Rowntree was a natural fit. Graham had spent a good deal of time as a scrum specialist, but he now had a wider-ranging forwards role with England and had forged a good reputation as a technician, as well as being a positive character with a gift for camaraderie. Neil Jenkins on the kicking front? That was a no-brainer. Rhys Long on the analysis? Ditto.

If there was a coaching conundrum to be solved, it was on the defensive side of things. On the face of it, Shaun Edwards was the obvious choice. After winning big trophies with Wasps and taking Wales to two Grand Slams and a World Cup semi-final, we clearly worked well together. In addition, we'd picked up valuable Lions experience under Ian McGeechan in South Africa in 2009. So who did I pick? Andy Farrell of England. Why? There was nothing dark or Machiavellian about the decision. From my own point of view, I wanted to upskill myself. The quickest way to do that was to open myself up to new ideas from someone who had made a name for himself in a rival set-up. From the Lions' side of things, diversity is important. With Rob, Neil, Rhys and one or two other members of the Wales backroom team on board, there had to be some balance. Shaun was seriously disappointed when I gave him the news: he was as completely gutted as I'd ever seen him. He's an emotionally charged bloke at the best of times, and this was a bad moment for him. The fact that he and Andy were like two peas from the same pod – both of them born-and-bred northerners from Wigan; both of them rugby league legends who had broken into professional sport in their mid-teens and played many an epic match together for club and country; both of them ploughing a similar furrow in rugby union – may well have made it harder for him. Did he see it as a betrayal? Probably. If he did, I can't blame him for it. All I can say is that I made the call for what I believed were the right reasons.

Once the front-line coaching team was settled we met every three or four weeks, selecting a squad on each occasion based on the most recent evidence. Meanwhile, I tried to win some battles with the Lions hierarchy on the outstanding personnel issues. Everything had to be run past the top brass. Andy Irvine, one of the great names of Scottish rugby and a member of the unbeaten Lions party in South Africa in 1974, had been named as tour manager. Gerald Davies, one of the most revered wings in rugby history and a major contributor to the Lions' victory over the All Blacks in 1971, had headed up the 2009 tour and was still a major force on the board. So too were Tom Grace of Ireland and John Spencer of England, along with the CEO, John Feehan. Whatever it was I wanted, I would have to clear it with them.

I had three requests. Paddy O'Reilly, known throughout northern hemisphere rugby as 'Rala', was my first choice as baggage man. It may seem odd to outsiders that I should place such emphasis on this role, but unless the nuts and bolts are right, a Lions tour can go off the rails in no time. Rala was the most dedicated, thorough, completely reliable of organisers. For a game kicking off at 6 pm, he would be at the ground eight hours earlier, making sure our equipment was in full working order and the changing room was set up correctly. He was also an energiser, a paragon of positivity, and the players loved him. If they wanted a cup of tea or coffee, a spare pair of socks, or some fresh underwear, they would go straight to him. If they were feeling down and needed words of reassurance, he offered that service too.

Talking of energisers, Paul Stridgeon was also on my list. Nicknamed 'Bobby' after the Adam Sandler character in the sports comedy movie *The Waterboy* (those who have seen the film will understand), it is possible to feel close to exhaustion after a brief conversation with him, let alone a night out, but more often than not you emerge refreshed, such is his enthusiasm for life. An international wrestler back in the day, he has long been a top-class fitness coach with an impressive CV. But he is more than that. Far more. In every environment we've shared, he has lifted the collective spirit of the group. That's a rare gift, and an important one.

My third go-to man was Richard Smith QC, a successful barrister specialising in sports law as well as criminal law. A good rugby player in his time, Richard had been drafted into the England set-up as a travelling advocate by Clive Woodward and quickly demonstrated his expertise across the full range of disciplinary and regulatory issues that have a habit of cropping up during high-profile tours and competitions. He was an obvious choice as far as I was concerned, especially as he had always been willing to throw himself into tasks outside his professional remit. Both Andy and Graham had spent a lot of time in his company and trusted him completely.

When I ran the names past the board, there was some resistance to each of them. That's what board members do: they don't like to think of themselves as mere rubber-stampers. Rala was thought to be too old and there was a view that Bobby was prone to over-exuberance – that there was too much of the 'one of the lads' spirit about him. As for Richard, concern was expressed over his handling of the many and varied controversies that had so badly undermined some of England's recent trips to the southern hemisphere. In the end, I won the arguments over Rala and Bobby, but had to admit defeat when the board went for Max Duthie, who had played professional rugby in both England and France, ahead of Richard as legal officer. It could have been worse, so I cut my losses. As the old Meat Loaf song reminded me: 'Two out of three ain't bad.'

This was a crucial tour for the Lions. I was clear about that, as were the grandees on the board. After the miseries of the 2005 hammering in New Zealand, things had changed for the better in South Africa in '09. There had been a restoration of traditional values – a single cohesive coaching unit, a move back to shared rooms for the players as part of a renewed emphasis on togetherness, a fuller engagement with the wider rugby community in the host nation. We all felt we had put some pride back into the jersey, which was the minimum requirement on that trip. But when all was said and done, we had flown home defeated. Yes, the Lions had ended a seven-match losing streak with that well-earned victory in Johannesburg. But they had not won a series since

1997. This time, we had to win. That was the bottom line. Why? Because a fourth successive failure was unthinkable, especially with the All Blacks next up in 2017. This was a pressure situation, for sure.

It was a slightly odd few weeks for me, watching Wales play their Six Nations games while keeping an equally close eye on every fixture involving the other three home countries. But there were classic moments. As I was watching the France–Wales match on television, I thought I recognised the bloke who ran onto the pitch in Paris to celebrate George North's brilliant match-winning finish in the left corner and was promptly marched back off again by a blue-jacketed security man. I was right. It was George's dad, Dave, his hat pulled down over his ears but unmistakeable all the same. There was something else I recognised when Wales hosted the Grand Slam-chasing English in Cardiff on the final weekend. It was the raw passion of a Welsh crowd with the scent of white-shirted prey in their nostrils. The Millennium Stadium roof was shut for the game and the noise level was off the scale. Even though I was sitting in the stand, away from Rob and Shaun and the others at the heart of the action, I will never forget the buzz I felt as a result of that immense performance – one of the best for many years. The impact of the events of that night in mid-March were still being felt Down Under in early July. They certainly had an effect on Lions selection.

I can confirm that some Welsh players – Alex Cuthbert on the wing and Justin Tipuric on the flank being prime examples – were picked directly as a consequence of their displays against England. The way the match unfolded also confirmed my view that Chris Robshaw, the England captain, should not be chosen. This had nothing to do with Robshaw's efforts in Cardiff: he had been one of his side's better performers and without his tremendous energy and resilience, their 30–3 defeat might have been even worse. But Rob Howley played both Tipuric and Sam Warburton, two genuine open-side flankers, in that game and they made Robshaw look like a No 6 in a No 7 role. A six-and-a-half, at best. As the Wallabies would be running genuine break-away forwards as good as Michael Hooper, George Smith and Liam Gill against us, we couldn't afford to be found wanting on the floor.

It was tough on Chris, the latest in a long line of England captains who could not quite crack it with the Lions. (Will Carling had been dropped from the Test team in 1993, although he played like a hero in defeat against me and the rest of the Waikato boys, earning our respect in the process. As for Phil de Glanville and Steve Borthwick, they missed out on selection in 1997 and 2009 respectively.) It was also hot news. The England captaincy is one of the biggest jobs in world rugby, and the press being what it is, any whiff of rejection makes headlines for weeks. But I was absolutely sure I'd made the right call. Because of the way the game was being refereed in the English Premiership, with the breakdown decisions generally favouring the side in possession, club coaches were picking big back-rowers at the expense of smaller, more mobile turnover specialists. Goodbye, Neil Back; hello, James Haskell. It has never been my place to tell England who they should be picking, but for much of my time in Europe, they were behind the curve when it came to No 7s.

Which takes me back to Sam Warburton and his potential as tour captain. Sam had suffered some injury hassle since the World Cup and while he had started the Six Nations as skipper, he broke down again after the first match and saw the leadership duties pass first to Ryan Jones and then, for the mighty match against England in the final round, Gethin Jenkins. The fact that Sam was happy to play that game from the ranks said much about his humility, but there were those outside the group who took it as proof that whatever gifts he had brought to the Wales captaincy had diminished and that the Lions job should go to someone else. Brian O'Driscoll's name was widely mentioned, inevitably. So too was that of Paul O'Connell. Both men had performed the role on previous tours, but what did that matter? Hadn't Martin Johnson led the Lions in 1997 and again in 2001? And besides, the two Irishmen were stone-cold Test certainties, weren't they?

I saw it differently, not least because Sam was not alone in spending as much time in the treatment room as he was on the field. Brian had missed Ireland's international programme before Christmas through injury, while Paul's fitness issues kept him out of the Six Nations. Indeed, there were serious concerns that he would not make the Lions trip at all. It was not until he turned in some vintage performances for Munster around the time of the formal squad announcement that he booked his seat on the plane. I knew the captain should be able to justify his place in the Test team. There had been more than one instance of the Lions naming the wrong skipper and paying a heavy price, and I didn't want to select a modern-day equivalent of Ciaran Fitzgerald, the Irish hooker who was so badly miscast on the tour of New Zealand in 1983. Brian? Paul? Yes, they would be strong candidates for the Test elite. But to my mind, Sam was equally dominant in his position, if not more so. He was nowhere near as experienced as the two Irishmen, a thirty-capper rather than a 120-capper like O'Driscoll, but he had proved himself able to lead older, long-serving players into the heat of battle and to command their respect. He was also on a roll after the recent Welsh successes in the Six Nations. That swung it for me.

Sam was being asked about the captaincy at every press conference, but he couldn't give the game away because he didn't have a clue what was happening. I left it to the very last minute, then rang him on the Sunday before the announcement and asked him if he'd consider taking on the role. A couple of years previously, when offered the Wales job, he had hesitated. This time, he jumped at it. There was no pregnant pause on the end of the line, no request for thinking time. I knew then that I'd made the right choice. It showed he had grown as a man as well as a player – that he was a mature human being, confident in his own ability.

Needless to say, there was a good deal of media talk about one other big name: Jonny Wilkinson. The papers were always writing pages of stuff about the England No 10, even when he wasn't playing for England; or for anybody, come to that. He was in a different category to most rugby players in the sense that 'out of sight' did not necessarily mean 'out of mind'. Quite the opposite. The less the English press saw of him, the more they seemed to bang on about him. And with the Lions trip fast approaching, he was the talk of the town once again. Not least because he had signalled a desire to go on tour, even though he had called time on his England career after that car-crash of a World Cup campaign a couple of years previously.

Jonny was a magnificent player, no question. It is a little-known fact that during my time at Wasps, I tried very hard indeed to bring him to the club from Newcastle. We had lost a Premiership game against them – or rather, against him – at Kingston Park, even though the Falcons never managed to set foot in our 22. While we played all the rugby, and I mean all of it, Jonny simply banged over penalty after penalty from miles out. 'He's the man for me,' I thought and contacted his agent. Not for the first time during my stay in London, I had to point out that we couldn't afford to pay top dollar. 'It's not about the money,' his agent told me. 'He's earning plenty off the field. It's just that he's committed to Newcastle.' And there he stayed, probably for too long. It was not until 2009 that he packed his bags and moved across the English Channel to Toulon, who were busily spending a fortune building a side strong enough to win multiple European championships.

In different circumstances, a fit and firing Wilkinson would have been well worthy of consideration. But I didn't see him as a 'must have' player – Jonathan Sexton had been a key figure in a strong Ireland side for some time while Owen Farrell was fast turning himself into a true Test-class No 10 with England. The plain fact of the matter was that Jonny's first loyalty was to Toulon, and that meant he would almost certainly be tied up in play-off rugby when we were already in Australia. I had to go through the motions of calling him to check his availability, of course: if I hadn't, I'd have been back behind bars on the front pages of the newspapers, facing a charge of 'crimes against rugby'. But I knew the answer before I asked the question. Jonny signalled his interest in touring, but he also confirmed his unavailability while Toulon were still in the hunt for the French domestic title. So that was that.

Had we been going to New Zealand, where there is no let-up in intensity and no respite even for the midweek side, I might have thought about taking a third No 10. Jonny could have done a job for us, as could someone like Danny Cipriani – a game-breaker with a different skill set to his rival international playmakers. We did talk about Danny, briefly. He had just returned to England after a spell with the Melbourne Rebels, so he was familiar with the Wallaby rugby zeitgeist – not to mention the best nightclubs in town. But Australia wasn't New Zealand. There were one or two soft spots in the programme, games where an occasional No 10 like Stuart Hogg of Scotland could fill in. That created some space elsewhere in the party.

Once the thirty-seven-man squad was finalised, there were clear indications of where we thought the strengths of the respective nations lay. Of the ten English players, six were tight forwards. All but one of the back-rowers were from Ireland and Wales. There was a fairly even split across the scrum-halves and No 10s, but there was only one English threequarter in Manu Tuilagi. By contrast, the entire Wales combination from Nos 11 to 15 were on the plane. There were the usual rumblings about coaching bias, but did anyone really imagine that Leigh Halfpenny, George North, Jonathan Davies or Jamie Roberts would miss out? As for Alex Cuthbert, his Six Nations form more than compensated for his relative lack of exposure at Test level.

The first game was not played in Australia at all. Hong Kong was the location – an obvious tilt of the cap to our major sponsors, HSBC, whatever the Lions hierarchy may have claimed when the itinerary was announced. I wasn't at all keen on playing in the heat of the Far East at first, and it soon became clear that certain players, most notably the scrummaging specimens, would suffer the torments of hell during our stay. Adam Jones, a tight-head prop of the substantial variety, sounded off in the press about the misery of training in such unforgiving temperatures, while Richard Hibbard, his fellow front-rower, found life even more difficult. The heat really got to Richard: during one training run, his eyes glazed over and he looked on the point of collapse. But in retrospect, it wasn't a bad way to prepare for the rigours ahead. A little discomfort ahead of business can be beneficial, as our Polish cryotherapy trip had proved before the World Cup.

Our opponents in Hong Kong were a Barbarians team who, on the face of it, were plenty strong enough to give us a meaningful game. They had some big names: Joe Rokocoko of New Zealand on the wing; another New Zealand international in Nick Evans at outside-half; the crafty French playmaker Dimitri Yachvili at No 9; and a useful pack of forwards drawn from all parts, including the Italian folk heroes Martin Castrogiovanni and Sergio Parisse. Counter-intuitively, it was said that the Baa-Baas had imposed a drinking ban on themselves. I didn't believe it myself, but the fact that such a rumour was running showed how seriously they were taking the fixture.

To make matters more complicated still, I stuffed up royally on the evening of the match. Some of the backroom staff had been to the stadium early in the morning and informed me it was a twenty-minute trip by bus. I allowed an hour, just to be on the safe side, which enabled me to call a team meeting a little later than usual. When we finally left the hotel, we found ourselves smack in the middle of rush hour, Asia-style. The traffic was horrendous – a problem not lost on Andy Irvine, who descended into a blind panic that was somewhat at odds with his usual relaxed managerial style. 'How the hell are you staying so calm?' he barked at me as the bus moved forward another inch and the clock ticked down another five minutes. 'Andy, there's nothing you can do about a traffic jam,' I replied. 'We'll get there eventually.' Which we did, after a ninety-minute crawl through the worst congestion in the whole of the continent. The kick-off was delayed and as a consequence, our preparations were truncated. The players could have reacted negatively and started the game badly. In the event, they were completely professional and delivered an excellent performance, winning 59–8 and scoring eight tries to the Baa-Baas' one. I learned something important that day, namely that this group did not need to be wet-nursed or spoon-fed. They could look disruption in the face and still put on a show. It was a reassuring thought.

There would be one more transport issue before we reached Australia and this time, there was no escaping the consequences. There were not enough business class seats for the entire party on the flight from Hong Kong to Perth, so a decision had to be made: either we split the party in two and travelled on separate planes, or we kept everyone together, which would mean some people turning right rather than left at the top of the steps – never a popular walk for those familiar with the splendours of life towards the front of an aircraft. I decided that the players should travel business with the staff in economy. Which almost worked. Unfortunately, one player would have to join the dispossessed in the back. Who should it be? Being an ex-hooker, I chose poor old Richard Hibbard. I can't say he was overjoyed at being forced into this sacrifice and I saw his point. He was the biggest of the hookers in a party that included a small scrum-half in Ben Youngs and a slightly-built full-back in Stuart Hogg. I don't think I was picking on him in any way: I must have done it for comic effect. Whatever, he had his revenge. Richard was a member of the tour fines committee and he hammered me hard in the pocket for the rest of the trip.

The first game of the tour proper, against Western Force, was not as demanding as it could or should have been, thanks to the decision of their coach Michael Foley – yes, another member of the international hooking fraternity – to field a weakened side ahead of a Super Rugby game he considered, for his own reasons, to be far more important. We scored even more points and even more tries in a 69–17 win, but lost Cian Healy, the Irish loose-head prop, to mangled ankle ligaments in the process. We immediately called up Alex Corbisiero of England, an unusually talented front-rower who would go on to make a big impact, particularly in the final Test. There was a second significant development over the course of a disappointingly low-key game on the banks of the Swan River, and it surrounded Leigh Halfpenny and his goal-kicking. Leigh couldn't miss from the tee, nailing all eleven of his shots at goal, and that pushed him to the front of the queue for the No 15 shirt against the Wallabies. Rob Kearney of Ireland, a big player in South Africa four years previously, was the other prime candidate for the role, but he hadn't been fit for the Hong Kong game and was still struggling. After Leigh's performance, Rob's chances of making up the lost ground were very slim indeed. In effect, his ambitions for the tour were dead and buried before he had set foot on the field.

The rugby quickly grew more meaningful the moment we set foot in Queensland, traditional union territory and home of the Reds. They had Quade Cooper, a real bag of tricks, at No 10 and were obviously planning to run us off our feet. Fortunately, we had our Hong Kong fitness in the tank and we were able to match them around the field while outmuscling them at close quarters. It was a far tighter game and we lost the try-count, but Owen Farrell's kicking, every bit as faultless as Leigh's had been in Perth, saw us home 22–12. Then it was into New South Wales: a 'soft' game against a Country XV in Newcastle, followed by a seriously hard outing in Sydney against the Waratahs, who had every intention of making things lively as a means of softening us up ahead of the first Test. It didn't quite work out the way their coach, Michael Cheika, planned. We were exceptional, none more so than Jamie Roberts and Jonathan Davies in midfield. Indeed, Brian O'Driscoll made a point of saying to me afterwards that the centre unit had been brilliant. 'How well is Foxy playing?' he said, referring to Jonathan. He had a point. Just how strong a point, he had yet to discover.

Leaving that aside, there was a more pressing midfield problem to be solved. Jamie Roberts hadn't lasted the game in Sydney, his outstanding performance ending prematurely when his hamstring went in the final quarter and he limped from the field in considerable discomfort. With the first meeting with the Wallabies a week away, we were left with one of the most experienced outside centres in the world in Brian, a relatively young outside centre playing out of his skin in Jonathan and a third specialist No 13 in Manu Tuilagi, who had started only one match and had fitness issues of his own. There were one or two other makeshift options available to us, but the No 12 position is of the utmost importance in the modern game and life without Jamie was going to be a challenge.

When it came to our last midweek fixture before the Test series, a real bump-in-the-road match against a Brumbies side coached by a World Cup-winning South African in Jake White, who loved nothing better than to lure opponents up dark alleys with his clever strategies, I decided we had no option but to summon reinforcements from far and wide. When we took the field, we had a non-touring back line featuring Brad Barritt and Billy Twelvetrees in the centre, and Christian Wade and Shane Williams – yes, the real Shane Williams – on the wings. Shane had retired from international rugby in 2011 in a blaze of glory, putting a try past the Wallabies with his last touch in his last Test, and was now bumping up his pension pot in Japan. While he always planned to be in Australia for the big matches, he had been signed up as a broadcaster rather than a player. Still, needs must. He did us a great service by turning out against the Brumbies that night. It was hard on all the incoming personnel, who had minimal preparation and may well have been suffering from the effects of the air travel. It was even harder on them when we went down narrowly in filthy conditions, largely because we lost around sixty per cent of our own line-outs. I suppose we could have won had I taken bigger risks off the bench, but was it really worth exposing potential Test contenders to an entire half of rugby none of them needed? It wasn't my most enjoyable night as a coach: Lions defeats hurt. But I felt I made the right calls.

Happily, I felt a whole lot better a few days later, enjoying a few glasses of red wine after victory over the Wallabies at the Suncorp Stadium. It was a top game all round – tough, tense, a real grind of a contest, interspersed with moments of attacking genius. You often get that from the Wallabies: think of Mark Ella and Michael Lynagh and Stephen Larkham, of Tim Horan and David Campese and Joe Roff. This time, they unleashed an attacking sensation by the name of Israel Folau on the wing, and he scored a try with his second touch in international union after a break from the scrum-half Will Genia and then doubled his tally with a jaw-dropping finish from distance before half-time. Yet we had a jaw-dropper of our own in George North, and his score, running back a defensive kick and leaving the fragmented Wallaby defence for dead with an in-out run to the left corner, was probably the try of the night. George remains a quality player to this day, but he was at his best between 2011 and 2014 – big, physical, fast, fearless . . . as good as anyone in the world. Opponents could take the field knowing everything there was to know about him and still have no answers to the problems he posed. That's the mark of a great rugby player and at that point in his career, before the injury problems kicked in, George was touching greatness. His fellow wing Alex Cuthbert also crossed the Wallaby line and with Leigh Halfpenny landing five from six off the tee – by contrast, the Aussie kickers managed only four from nine – we found our way home 23–21. It was a feather in our cap, especially as we had been forced into an O'Driscoll–Davies centre partnership that was not ideal in terms of their positional preferences.

As every Lions coach knows, a first-up win in a three-Test series is crucial. It keeps the tour alive until the last weekend, come what may, and piles the pressure on the hosts ahead of the second match. It might therefore be assumed that game eight of a ten-match programme – the midweek fixture before the second Test – is of minimal importance, but any such assumption would be wrong. In fact, our Tuesday night meeting with the Rebels at AAMI Park in Melbourne was as significant as any game outside of the Wallaby contests. There were lots of people with plenty to prove after the Brumbies setback and as this would be the last action for a good number of those involved, the incentive was there to turn on a show. It was important for me too: a big performance would help hold the squad together for the remainder of the tour, always a challenge when a party is split between those with something to live for on the trip and those whose day is done. Dan Lydiate was my captain that night and he really took me aback with his emotional address before kick-off. The dressing-room atmosphere was electric and we won 35–0, with Dan just one of those forcing his way into Test contention with the quality of his performance.

The second Test, in the same city, was every bit as fiercely fought as the one in Brisbane, but with Sam Warburton performing at the very peak of his powers, I felt we were in a good place to wrap things up there and then. Sadly, Sam suffered an injury early in the final quarter, when we were leading 15–9, and with the Wallabies cranking up the intensity in a desperate search for a match-winning, series-saving breakthrough, we finally cracked a few minutes from time. Adam Ashley-Cooper's try down the short side and Christian Leali'ifano's conversion left us a point down, and even though Leigh Halfpenny had a shot to pinch it at the death, it was well over fifty metres out, to the left of the posts, and the ball dropped short. The feeling of disappointment ran deep, but something struck me in the minutes after the game. I walked past James Horwill, a big bruiser of a lock who had just skippered the Wallabies to victory. He was crying with relief. Real tears. My mind flashed back almost a decade to that Wasps–Leicester rivalry at the top end of the Premiership, when the same thought occurred. 'We may have lost this one, but they've given everything to win. How much do they have left? Not physically – we're all tired – but emotionally. I don't think it's possible for them to go that deep again in the space of seven days.'

Following the non-safari tactic from 2009, we headed for

Noosa Heads on the Queensland coast for three days of rest, recuperation and refreshment – a good deal of which involved alcohol. There was a time when this kind of relaxed approach to final Test preparation would have been universally frowned upon. Even now, I don't suppose it would attract majority support. But unless you're on the inside track with the Lions, it's impossible to understand exactly how much the players and staff put into a tour, or quite how much they need a release of the pressure valve after almost seven weeks of relentless commitment. The fact of the matter is that in the last week, there is almost nothing left to do except patch up the walking wounded, stage a couple of run-throughs and, when the time is right, start concentrating on the last eighty-minute effort. As there is always a danger of playing the game too early in the mind, I don't see much point in forcing detail down the players' throats on a Monday or Tuesday.

One mistake we made was putting up Brian O'Driscoll for a press conference on our arrival in Noosa, less than twenty-four hours after the Melbourne Test. We were operating a rota system for media work, but I should have thought more carefully about the implications: not because the coaches were still undecided whether to drop Brian for the last Test, but because the media knew that Sam Warburton was out of contention and were keen to install Brian as favourite to take on the captaincy. They would therefore be certain to ask him lots of questions he had no way of answering. Also, he was bitterly disappointed at losing to the Wallabies and had taken the defeat to heart. He knew that this was the last of his four Lions tours and his final shot at a series victory. Looking back, he could have done without the added burden of interrogation by press.

We didn't finalise selection until the Tuesday night, by which time we had done two things: established that Jamie Roberts would be ready to play after recovering from his hamstring problem, and reviewed the footage from the loss in Melbourne. That review revealed just how hard the Wallabies had gone at Brian, who to a certain extent had been nursed through the tour because of his fragile fitness. He had completed a massive number of tackles in the second Test and been characteristically brave in throwing his body into the fray, but when Ashley-Cooper scored that crucial try in the last six minutes, Brian had been slow to get back after making a hit on halfway. To be fair to him, he was honest about it. 'My legs had gone,' he said when Rob Howley showed him the clip.

With the speculation over selection gathering pace, I called the coaches in for the big discussion. We decided that changes should be made to the front row and that in Sam's absence, Sean O'Brien of Ireland should wear the No 7 shirt, with Dan Lydiate on the blind-side flank and Taulupe Faletau at No 8. When it came to the midfield pairing, the conversation was brief . . . and unanimous. Jamie should come in at 12, with Jonathan Davies at 13. And as I felt that Brian was a starting midfielder or nothing, I went for Manu Tuilagi as a more potent last-quarter option off the bench.

There were no arguments from any of my coaching colleagues. Brian was out, not just of the starting 15, but of the 23.

The one area where unanimity broke down was over the captaincy. No Sam, no Brian . . . what now? I asked each man in the meeting to write down the initials of the name of his preferred leader on the back of his hand. Rob Howley opted for Sean O'Brien while Graham Rowntree went for Geoff Parling, the England lock who had performed really well for us as our go-to man at the line-out. Andy Farrell, Neil Jenkins and yours truly formed a meeting of minds, all three of us agreeing that the other lock, Alun Wyn Jones, was the correct choice. He had been in South Africa in 2009 and had been a first-choice forward here. Decision made.

The task now was to tell Brian, which I did in company with Rob Howley. I wasn't relishing the task. Leaving any player out of a match of such magnitude is awkward, and I was very aware that the phrase 'any player' was not relevant in Brian's case. He was in Jonny Wilkinson territory in terms of his stature on the international stage. In Ireland, he was a genuine legend. And contrary to popular opinion, especially as expressed in the Emerald Isle, I cared. I was the coach who had first capped him, we went back a very long way and I had the greatest respect for him. Now, I was the first coach to drop him. Any idea that I didn't understand the significance of the decision was nonsensical. As it turned out, our conversation was pretty short. He was profoundly disappointed, of course, but his reaction was everything I hoped it would be. Brian O'Driscoll was always a class act and when Rhys Long, our analyst, told me of that comment in the lift – 'I've talked the talk, now I have to walk the walk' – my level of respect, already stratospheric, rose another notch.

Before the team was announced and the frenzy kicked off, I had one other interesting chat, with the England hooker Tom Youngs. He had been brilliant for us all tour, emptying the tank in the first two Tests and leading the way with his heart-and-soul performances. On this occasion, we felt Richard Hibbard would offer that little bit more and promoted him to the starting line-up. When I told Tom, he breathed deeply, looked me in the eye and said: 'That's the right decision, Warren. My body is absolutely f***ed.'

'Thank you,' I replied. 'But what about sitting on the bench? Can you do that for us?'

'Yes,' he said. 'I'll give you everything I have for as long as you need it.'

It was a quality reaction from a quality bloke. When I informed Richard, he went quiet.

'This is a big game, isn't it?' he said eventually.

'Yep, it's a big game.'

'OK.'

What did that mean? Had I made the right move? Richard had been perfectly comfortable in the substitute role, but now I was asking a whole lot more of him. As it turned out, he played outstandingly well.

Once the team was in the public domain, there was some

initial surprise at the midfield combination. This was only to be expected. What I didn't know was that the immediate reaction in Australia was just the beginning. When the news reached the United Kingdom and Ireland, I found myself in a different place entirely. There was an extraordinary level of hostility to the decision, way beyond anything I'd ever encountered. It was wild, vicious and, in my view at least, miles over the top. Criticism is one thing. This was something above and beyond, something else entirely. Social media meant nothing to me then – it doesn't mean a great deal now, if I'm honest – but however much of a technophobe I might have been, there was no escaping the anger, the insults, the torrent of accusations about being anti-Irish – that this was a naked act of revenge aimed at those who had sacked me in Dublin all those years ago. I couldn't believe what I was reading and hearing. Genuinely, it came as a huge shock to me. The night before the announcement, Andy Irvine had said: 'We're backing you 100 per cent, Warren, but I'll give you this: you've got some balls.' Maybe that should have prepared me for the outrage ahead. But it didn't. Within a few hours, my head was spinning from the abuse.

It was still spinning on match day, by which time the media had gorged themselves to the point of bursting. Most pundits had the Wallabies down as favourites and I knew that if we lost, I'd be on a hiding to nothing. The record books tell us that we didn't lose. We won 41–16 – a record-busting effort. We outscored the Wallabies by four tries to one, Leigh Halfpenny kicked eight from nine, we scrummaged our opponents into the New South Wales dirt and we ran them ragged. It was a wonderful performance, from the moment Alex Corbisiero capitalised on Will Genia's fumble from the kick-off to the coup de grâce from Jamie Roberts on sixty-seven minutes. But I was not as overjoyed as I should have been, hence the temptation to throw those V-signs towards the screen.

At the final whistle, I made my way down to the field to congratulate the players and be a part of the moment. All I could see as I emerged from the tunnel was a mass of camera lenses. I must have walked twenty metres, this way and that, but there was no way past. 'Come on, boys, give me a chance here,' I said to the cameramen. No movement. 'Ah, f*** you,' I snapped and turned around. I went to the changing rooms, sat down alone, cracked open a can of beer and reflected, with a tear in my eye, on the events of the week. When I arrived at the press conference, the first question was predictable. 'Warren, do you feel vindicated over your decision to drop Brian O'Driscoll?' My heart sank. What was I supposed to say? Yes? I could see the headlines from where I was sitting. 'Gatland: I told you I was right.' No, thanks. There was no way I was going to play that game, so I refused to engage with the subject.

The good news was that Trudi and Gabby were both in the stadium. As far as they were concerned, all the heat and unpleasantness of the week was so much water off a duck's back. 'They can say what they like,' Trudi told me. 'You won.' Bryn was also in town, belatedly. He had been playing an important game back in New Zealand, but Michael Holland, a good friend from my days at Wasps, organised a helicopter to get him from Tauranga to Auckland Airport in time for a flight to Sydney. The helicopter worked, but the flight was delayed. As a result, Bryn missed the game. What he didn't miss was the celebrations afterwards. I think he enjoyed it. In fact, I know he did.

Did the journalists who had been so critical of me enjoy it too? I'm not sure I care, frankly. Some of them were big enough to admit they'd got it wrong, but others didn't. For all I know, those people were devastated by our success. I thought back to a conversation I'd had with the Welsh broadcaster Phil Steele, who told me about covering a World Cup game in 2007. Wales were playing Canada and were losing at the interval. 'I was chatting to someone in the studio and told him how terrible it would be if Wales lost,' he recalled. 'The reply? "Yes, but it would be a great story for us."' Which tells you something, I think.

As for the Irish rugby community, have they ever put it behind them? A long time after the tour, I was invited there as a guest on *The Late Late Show* with Ryan Tubridy, one of the longest-running talk shows of its kind in the world. It seemed like they wanted me to get on my hands and knees and beg forgiveness. I'll always be grateful for the time I spent coaching in Ireland. Without the opportunities I was given there, I wouldn't be where I am today. I just hope that most reasonable followers of the game in Dublin, Limerick, Galway, Belfast and all points in between will accept that I made a tough call for the right reasons. Roger Lewis subsequently told me that when he met Sir Alex Ferguson, one of the greatest of all football managers, at a race meeting, Alex said: 'That O'Driscoll thing. Your coach made the right decision.' What I took him to mean was that coaches are there to make the hard judgements and stand by them. Anyone can make the easy ones.

11

ALL ROADS LEAD TO TWICKENHAM

By the standards of modern travel, the distance from Australia to New Zealand is nothing more than a hop – even if you go via Fiji, the perfect place for a spell of rest and reflection at the end of a hard road. Yet when I made that trip in 2013, it was like landing on a different planet. Never in my rugby life had I been more in need of a break from the game. The O'Driscoll affair was still blazing away uncontrollably when I left Sydney with Trudi and the kids, so I was grateful for the outbreak of sanity when I returned to Hamilton after our island break. The local rugby folk told me I should stop worrying about it: I was a professional coach, I'd picked a side to win a match as per my job description, the task had been successfully completed, end of story. 'This is how it should be,' I thought, praying that the craziness had been left behind. But it wasn't like that at all. On the other side of the world, there was no let-up. The English papers, such an influential collective voice in the sport, were still full of the controversy. As for the sporting people of Ireland . . . the word 'apoplectic' barely scratched the surface of their mood.

On top of that there was another World Cup on the horizon – a World Cup that was certain to be more highly charged than any I had previously experienced. Thanks to our poor autumn series in 2012, which culminated in that Kurtley Beale try at the back end of the Australia game, we had slipped below Samoa and Argentina in the rankings and ended up being drawn with England, the tournament hosts, and our old friends the Wallabies in a particularly gruesome 'pool of death'. Which meant more pressure, more scrutiny, another few thousand circuits of the goldfish bowl in full public view. Most of it I could handle comfortably: after all, this was my chosen career. Right from the start, I had wanted to challenge myself, to pit my wits against the best in the business, and I accepted the exposure that came with it. But with social media's takeover of the known universe gathering pace, the nature of that exposure had changed. It wasn't just me who struggled with the sheer volume and intensity of the criticism online. It also had an effect on some of the Wales players, to the extent that Rhys Priestland and Alex Cuthbert, important contributors at key moments in recent times, sought escape routes. Rhys, in particular, took it to heart. He was in danger of falling out of love with rugby and moved from Llanelli to Bath in search of a reconnection. Happily, he found it. But for a while, there was a danger he would be lost to the game.

When you've been through the kind of upheaval I experienced with the Lions in Australia, close family means everything. Trudi, Gabby and Bryn were fantastically supportive, and by the end of my break, I felt better about things. In fact, I felt absolutely on top of the world when, a couple of months or so after the final Lions Test, I returned to Sydney to watch Bryn play for New Zealand Schools against the Wallaby age-groupers. In a different life, I would have been on the touchline or in the stand for all of Bryn's games, like any proud sporting father. He spent three years in the Hamilton Boys' High School first XV, so there would have been plenty for me to watch. As it was, I'd spent count-less hours on the phone at the dead of night in Wales, speaking to Trudi in New Zealand and receiving running updates on his matches. In 2013, his last year at school, he dropped a goal in the last minute against St Kentigern's College from Auckland to win the national title. To see him wearing the black shirt of New Zealand later that same season gave me the warmest feeling imaginable, especially as he was on the field at the death and helped secure a single-point win for his team.

Like the livewire All Black Damian McKenzie, the other No 10 in that talented schools squad, Bryn subsequently made it into the professional ranks and is now forging a career for himself in Super Rugby. That's no mean feat: New Zealanders do not throw around full-time contracts like confetti. I'm often asked how a hooker like me produced a fly-half like him. My stock answer? 'He has his mother's build . . . and my skills!' Talking seriously, he's a good pro, dedi-cated to his work, and he has a very good rugby brain. He understands the game – its dynamics, its intricacies, the shape of it. He'll be an excellent coach one day if he wants it, although having seen what I've been through, I'm not sure he'll ever sign up as a head coach. He has a level head on him and is already using his earnings to secure a future for himself. He's not one for flash cars or spending 20,000 bucks on a watch. He's a saver.

Talking of which, he turned out to be something of a lifesaver as far as I was concerned. Why? Because by making his way into that NZ Schools squad, he spared my liver a terrible battering. The aforementioned Michael Holland, my close friend from Wasps days, owns a lovely property in southern France, down near Perpignan, and he made it available to me and a group of old schoolmates for a post-Lions reunion and a celebration of our fiftieth birthdays. I enjoy a drink as much as the next man, but the alarm bells started ringing when the blokes back home thought it would be a good idea to break the trip to France by stopping off at the Munich beer festival. I needed an escape route and Bryn provided me with one, bless him. When we eventually gathered at Michael's place, it was blindingly obvious that my friends' attempts to pace themselves in southern Germany had not been entirely successful.

Back in Wales, I set about building towards the World Cup. The situation in 2013 was very different to the one in which I had found myself at the same point in the previous cycle. In 2009, the national side had been in a state of flux: within two years, we would travel to the global competition with a reshaped threequarter line and a new back row. This time, no major surgery was required. Our biggest names – George North and Jamie Roberts, Gethin Jenkins and Alun Wyn Jones, Dan Lydiate and Sam Warburton and Taulupe Faletau – were hardened international performers and would be even more firmly established by the time the World Cup came round. We would have been more settled still had Leigh Halfpenny and Rhys Webb stayed healthy, but when they broke down just before the tournament, we at least had good alternatives to hand. The years either side of 2011 had been crucial in the team-building sense and we were now in a position to reap the reward. Ten Welsh players in the starting line-up for a Lions series decider? That told a tale.

I had no intention of changing my coaching style, either, despite the upheaval in Sydney. I felt I'd been true to myself and my rugby values during the Lions tour and saw no reason to tinker around. When I thought about the O'Driscoll business – and yes, I was still thinking about it in my quiet moments – I kept reminding myself that the choices made for the Sydney Test had been collective in nature, completely in keeping with my approach to selection. I understand the responsibilities of the role of head coach and I have never shied away from them. I also consider selection to be one of my strengths and would always be prepared to make my own call if necessary. But as a general rule, I like to seek consensus. I choose my coaching teams with great care, on the basis of trust and respect as well as ability, and therefore see no point in shutting down discussion or pulling rank when it comes to the difficult decisions. Would I have dropped Brian from the Test side had I been in a minority of one at the selection meeting – had Rob Howley and Andy Farrell insisted that with Sam out injured, Brian was the only possible captain and that they'd seen enough from him in the Melbourne Test to believe he had enough in the tank to go up a level in the decider? Would I have dug my heels in had they said: 'We see where you're coming from, Gats, but Brian's the man for this game.'? No. Almost certainly, I would have changed tack and gone with them. If people are really passionate in their opinion and back it up with a strong argument, proper account must be taken.

That is not a sign of weakness. Top coaches are like top professionals in any walk of life: they want to have a voice, to be given a hearing. I know there are plenty of successful head coaches out there who argue that only one man can pick a team – that in sport, committees never achieve anything. I'm not that kind of autocrat. Or any kind of autocrat, come to that. I'm genuinely interested in what my colleagues think. If I wasn't, I wouldn't have invited them onto the panel in the first place. With Wales, some selection meetings lasted five minutes flat. But there were many occasions when Rob pushed someone forward from an attacking point of view, while Shaun Edwards pulled back from a defensive perspective. Then, it took a lot longer. We might have sat there and thrashed it out for hour after hour, or agreed to sleep on it and then reconvened over breakfast to chew the fat some more. I was completely comfortable with that. It was the glue that held us together as a coaching team.

We spent more than a decade with the Wales team and achieved a good deal. None of that was down to one man alone.

I always tried to show the same openness and under-standing when it came to the players, especially when they were being tempted away from Wales by wealthy clubs in England and even richer ones in France. When I named my first Six Nations squad in 2008, only two players were playing their rugby outside of the country: the two Gareths, Cooper and Delve. Both of them were at Gloucester, so they weren't exactly a thousand miles away. We held that number fairly steady right the way through to the 2011 World Cup. Then, the line on the graph started heading more sharply in a northerly direction. By the 2015 Six Nations we had nine so-called exiles. Leigh Halfpenny, Jonathan Davies, Jamie Roberts, Mike Phillips and Luke Charteris were at Clermont Auvergne, Racing Metro or Toulon; George North, Paul James, Richard Hibbard and Bradley Davies were playing Premiership rugby with Northampton, Bath, Gloucester and Wasps respectively. Was that too many? Was it good for the game in Wales? A hell of a lot of influential figures took the view that it was very bad news indeed and made a lot of noise about it. Me? I had a more nuanced attitude.

You can mount your high horse on the subject as often as you like, but it's very difficult to stand in the way of market forces. And market forces were at the heart of it. Before 2011, we'd had limited success at a global level, and as a result, there wasn't too much in the way of international demand for Welsh players. Post 2011, the Norths and Warburtons and their high-profile countrymen had made a significant dent on the wider consciousness. They were big names, capable of attracting equally big contracts, and there was a part of me that felt they should be able to cash in on their success. They'd worked hard enough for it, so who was I to undermine their earning power? Almost to a man, those who were considering moves out of Wales made a point of talking it through with me. Almost always, I would give them the same response: 'You're in this game for a relatively short time and you don't know what's going to happen with injuries. You have to make the best decision for you and your family. Now, you might not hear me saying this out loud. In public, I have no choice but to say how disappointed we are to be losing you. But the reality of it is that I'll support you in the decision you reach.'

For all that, it is a complicated and highly political business and has been one of the principal issues at the heart of the Welsh game across the last two World Cup cycles. When players leave, there is undeniably a downside. Especially when they go to France. With the possible exception of Leigh Halfpenny, who signed for Toulon in 2014, no one has travelled back across the English Channel a better player. For Leigh, there was the benefit of joining a very high-powered squad of players brought together from all corners of the rugby landscape with the specific aim of landing major trophies. With Leigh being a kind of Jonny Wilkinson 2.0 in terms of dedication and the will to improve, he revelled in the seriousness of the Toulon approach and the ruthlessness of their ambition, which in many respects was completely un-French. For the other Wales players who crossed the water, I saw no such benefits. Their experience of life may have been broadened and enriched by the time they returned, but there was no improvement in their skill levels or their physical conditioning. Quite the opposite, in some cases. For those relocating to the far side of the Severn Bridge, it was a different story. As long as they had a full release clause in their contracts with English clubs, as George North did at Northampton, there was no great problem from my point of view. Such clauses were not always easily negotiated, however, and as a result, there was more than one outbreak of hostilities between the various interested parties.

Generally speaking, I was relaxed about it. The people who were not relaxed were those running the four regional sides. The union, and by extension me, came under huge pressure to restrict international selection to those players contracted to one of the home teams. I was dead against that idea for a number of reasons. As I took the view that the players were not commodities, I didn't want to see them being taken advantage of by their employers, who could easily low-ball them on the salary front if their Test ambitions depended on them staying in Wales. Also, I didn't think it was fair on the likes of Charteris, Faletau and Lydiate to hold them under lock and key in Newport when the Dragons were under-performing so badly on the field and faring even worse as a business. Like every other player, they had their ambitions. How could I look them in the eye and tell them to stay put when everyone in rugby knew that their chances of winning something meaningful at Rodney Parade were more remote than the planet Saturn?

It's the easiest thing in the world to call for a 'home players only' policy, but it's extremely difficult to implement. Even the All Blacks have moved a little towards accepting the reality of a market-driven professional sport. They still pick from inside New Zealand and I don't see that changing any time soon, but they embraced the idea of sabbaticals for the top players more than a decade ago – the great fly-half Dan Carter made his temporary move to Perpignan as long ago as 2008 – and they were happy to draft the flanker Jerome Kaino into their 2015 World Cup squad despite the fact that he had spent a good deal of his recent time playing club rugby in Japan. As for the Wallabies, they modified their selection criteria before the last World Cup in order to arm themselves with such France-based internationals as Matt Giteau and Drew Mitchell. England are still digging in their heels in this area, but they have more top-end players available to them than virtually any other nation. For a country like Wales, with only four professional teams and a small pool of talent, a balanced approach has always been essential.

That balance has not been easy to find. I was heavily involved in the discussions around the introduction of National Dual Contracts, the first of which was offered to, and signed by, Sam Warburton in 2014. Under its terms, sixty per cent of Sam's salary was paid by the union, with his regional side, Cardiff Blues, picking up the remainder. As the system was rolled out to more of the best players in the country, we found we were able to compete with the moneybags clubs in England and France – to make a strong case to our most sought-after Test performers that by staying in Wales, they could have most of what they felt they needed. There was still a trade-off to be made in terms of hard cash, but under the new policy, we could bring our own points of difference to the table. I was able to say to a player with a written offer from London or Paris or Toulouse burning a hole in his pocket: 'Look, if the extra £100,000 a year, maybe even £200,000 a year, is what matters most to you, we can't begin to match it. But if you stay here, you're guaranteed the right amount of rest, the best medical care and the finest facilities, together with an excellent financial deal. Also, your Six Nations and World Cup and Lions chances will be strengthened rather than compromised. As well as asking yourself what you'll earn by heading out of Wales, you should also ask yourself what you'll be giving up.'

I'm happy to say that we came out on the right side of quite a few of these conversations. Why? Because we had some important facts on our side, and those facts will continue to count for something. For instance, it is completely true to say that today's Wales squad bears more resemblance to a club set-up than it does to an exclusive Test concern, with the Wales-based players within a forty-five-minute drive of the Vale of Glamorgan, which in turn means minimal disruption to their home and family circumstances. They also like the taste and smell of success, which, to say the very least, is not always there for them at regional level. When they arrive in camp, they're often switching from a team that doesn't believe to a team that expects to win. That's a big thing.

Not that there isn't room for improvement. I still feel desperately sorry that Rhys Webb, every inch a scrum-half of international calibre, has fallen victim to our 'sixty-cap rule', which states that for people playing their rugby outside of Wales, only those with that number of Test appearances or more can be picked for their country. I believed from the start that it was too high a figure and I've continued to back a cut to thirty caps. Rhys had already agreed to join Toulon when the rule was introduced in 2017. At the time, he had thirty-one caps to his name. He could have pulled out of the deal and remained available for Wales, but to his credit he felt he had made a commitment to the French club and should honour it. I can't pretend I agree with the situation and I've made my feelings known, but as some influential figures in Welsh rugby originally wanted a seventy-five-cap cut-off, it was never going to be an easy argument to win.

As far as the regions are concerned, the policy on over-seas imports remains flawed. When I first arrived in the country from Waikato, I was alarmed by the fact that in some positions, most notably the back row, two-thirds of the starting players on any given weekend were not qualified to represent Wales. Simon Easterby, an Irish international, was usually to be found in the Scarlets pack; Marty Holah and Filo Tiatia, both from New Zealand, and Hale T-Pole, who played World Cup rugby for Tonga, were among the first names on the team sheet at Ospreys; Xavier Rush, another New Zealander, and Maama Molitika, another Tongan, were important figures at Cardiff Blues; the Dragons had Nic Fitisemanu, a Kiwi of Samoan descent, on their books. Before long, the celebrated hit-'em-hard All Black flanker Jerry Collins and the Wallaby No 8 David Lyons turned up in Wales too. This concentration of imported talent in one positional area was hardly designed to make my life easier. There has been a similar problem in France, with all those Fijian wings and Georgian props plying their trade far from home, but at least there are fourteen top-flight clubs over there.

The situation in Wales has stabilised in recent years, but they're still spending some £5 million a year on around thirty overseas players across the four regions. I have no problem with hiring foreign talent in principle – indeed, I believe players like Xavier Rush were brilliant for the game in Wales and more than justified their salaries – but if that kind of money is going to be splashed out, I would prefer it to be on a smaller group of extremely high-calibre performers. Maybe ten or twelve players who drive up professional stand-ards, bring on the youngsters, put plenty of bums on seats and win some games. Unfortunately, too many of the imports during my time in Wales were middle of the road, pretty average performers charged with filling a hole in the side for short-term gain. I don't place all the blame on the regional coaches: their jobs depend on results, and if it comes down to a choice between signing a quick-fix option from abroad or placing trust in a kid from the academy, most of them will see it as no choice at all. But the fact remains: while there have been some striking successes, the general approach to overseas signings has not played any significant role in pushing Welsh rugby a step further up the hill.

When it comes to hills, the ones you face as a coach immediately after a Lions tour often seem steeper than usual. Your best players are pretty tired physically and often wiped out emotionally – the after-shocks of an all-out effort that tend to be reflected in performance levels and results. This is not exclusively a Welsh problem. You can see the same syndrome at work in England. There was a reason why France had a long run of Six Nations success following Lions series, winning the title in 1998, 2002, 2006 and 2010. In my view, they would have taken a lot of beating in both 2014 and 2018 as well had their confidence levels been higher.

We had a difficult autumn series straight off the back of the Lions' triumph in Australia, with the Springboks and the Wallabies book-ending meetings with Argentina and Tonga. Sure enough, we started poorly against the South Africans, conceding early tries to Jean de Villiers and Bismarck du Plessis, and also suffered four injuries in the opening half. Under the circumstances, we showed a good deal of resilience in making a proper fight of it for the rest of the contest, largely through Leigh Halfpenny's brilliant marksmanship from the tee. It was at times like this when I fully appreciated the contribution of Neil Jenkins as kicking coach. Like Dave Alred, the Englishman who had such notable success with Jonny Wilkinson and a handful of others, Neil was clearly on top of things in the technical department and understood the mechanics of kicking as well as anyone in the business. But unlike Dave, he had been an international goal-kicker himself – indeed, his accuracy had been the centrepiece of the Lions' series victory in South Africa in 1997 – and had an instinctive appreciation of the psychological side of the job. During my time with Wales, he has always been down there on the touchline, in close proximity to the action. There were a number of aspects to his on-field role, but the most important of them was to offer immediate feedback and, if necessary, reassurance to our kickers. Having a good communicator like Neil on the spot and able to tweak things in real time was a massive advantage.

The other autumn games were up and down. We put four tries past the Pumas in a record 40–6 victory, struggled past the Tongans by ten points with what amounted to a shadow side and then lost by four to the Australians – yet another nearly moment, a game in which what might have been and should have been failed to happen. George North, absolutely at the peak of his powers and playing some stunning rugby, scored two tries, the first of them a blinder from long range in the opening minute, but the Wallabies had Quade Cooper at No 10 and he had one of his golden days. Just our luck. It was a compelling match and we had all the momentum in the closing stages, but as so often against these opponents, almost was not quite enough.

It was beginning to hurt quite badly, coming up marginally short time after time against the southern superpowers, but I felt we were closing in on the Wallabies and the Boks and as the clock ticked over into 2014, I knew there would be further opportunities to catch up with one or both of them ahead of the following year's World Cup. After an in-and-out Six Nations – we played really poorly in Dublin and lost heavily as a result, but produced something like the best of ourselves with big home wins over France and Scotland – we travelled to South Africa for a two-Test series. There was a lot of negativity about our prospects, not least from inside the international coaching set: Gary Gold, who had been part of the Springbok panel when the Lions toured there in 2009 and at the World Cup two years later, went public with his theory that we simply didn't believe we could win against any of the SANZAR countries and were therefore destined to lose to them. It was not an opinion I shared. In fact, I felt we could go toe to toe with the Boks on this occasion. But for an excruciatingly painful turnaround at the back end of the second Test in Nelspruit, I would have been proved right.

We went virtually fully loaded into the opening match in Durban – although Leigh Halfpenny and Sam Warburton were missing from the line-up, all the other big guns were in place – but when it comes to heavy artillery, the Boks are tough to match. They fielded a massive pack, with the du

Plessis brothers in the front row, Bakkies Botha and Victor Matfield in the engine room and Willem Alberts and Duane Vermuelen together in the back row. That's a lot of poundage. Not for the first time after a break of a few weeks, we were slow off the mark. As a result, the Boks went along at a point a minute for the first quarter, aided by the early sin-binning of Jamie Roberts for a mid-air challenge on Willie le Roux, and were 28–9 up at the break. That turned into 38–9 soon enough, and while we picked up the pace in the last quarter and scored a try of our own through Alex Cuthbert, whose solo effort from his own 22 was quite something, we finished a distant second.

We needed a positive response in Nelspruit, where the Boks had played only one previous Test and were almost as unfamiliar with the surroundings as we were. We picked Samson Lee, just twenty-one, ahead of Adam Jones at tight-head prop and drafted Josh Turnbull into the back row alongside Dan Lydiate and Taulupe Faletau. Otherwise, we stuck to our guns in selection: I knew we would be better for another week together and sure enough, the improvement was there for all to see. Towards the end of the first quarter, Cuthbert performed another minor miracle to create a try for Roberts, and then scored one himself three minutes later. We were all over the Boks, who didn't like the pace we were putting on the game and had no answer to Cuthbert's physicality. Their response was to rein things in by going to their set-piece game, and this gave Steve Walsh, the referee, all the opportunity he needed to get stuck into us. Luke Charteris and Dan Biggar saw yellow within moments of each other, and the inevitable followed: a penalty try for the home side, followed by a score from the wing Cornal Hendricks. From 17–0 up, we were back at 17–14. It didn't seem right, given the quality of our rugby, but having pretty much won the game once, we would now have to win it again.

Which we almost did. Ken Owens made it over the line for a fingertip try and with Dan Biggar back on the field after his enforced absence, the conversion was nailed. So too were a couple of penalties. Suddenly, we were 30–17 up with a quarter of an hour left. A first-ever Welsh victory in South Africa seemed not only possible, but probable. And then it slipped away. On seventy-one minutes, Willie le Roux dummied his way over our line after a long spell of Springbok pressure, and they were back to within a score. That score duly came in the most heartbreaking of circumstances, Liam Williams conceding a penalty try after barging Hendricks into touch at the corner flag with the clock on seventy-seven minutes. Almost four decades had passed since Liam's namesake and predecessor as Wales full-back, the celebrated JPR, famously secured a Grand Slam with a shoulder barge on the French wing Jean-François Gourdon. But rugby was different then. Thirty-eight years on, we had no choice but to suck up Walsh's decision and curse our cruel misfortune. I felt sorry for Liam, who had always been prone to the odd rash decision but was fast turning into a player of serious quality, with a deeply competitive spirit and a thrilling sense of adventure. At the same time, I was disappointed at our management of the closing seconds, during which we showed a lack of patience in opting for a couple of long drop-goal attempts, both of which proved too much for Dan Biggar. If we were going to be the best we could be at the forthcoming World Cup, this was something we would have to address.

We didn't address it quite quickly enough to end our run of defeats against the Wallabies, who sneaked past us yet again in the opening autumn Test with a couple of late kicks from Bernard Foley, their latest first choice at No 10. We outscored them by four tries to three, we were leading deep in the final quarter . . . but once again, we failed to close it out. Yet I saw enough to believe it could be different when we faced them in the World Cup pool stage. What we needed, pretty much at any price, was a victory over one of the big three from the southern hemisphere, and both New Zealand and South Africa were on the immediate horizon. And it was there, against the best of the best, that things began to move in our direction. The All Blacks came to Cardiff close to full strength, and that meant we were playing opponents in a different league to everyone else. For more than an hour, we matched them everywhere. For more than an hour, it really seemed as though we might win. Jamie Roberts and Rhys Webb delivered big, big performances, and with thirteen minutes left we were up by a point at 16–15. But teams as good as the All Blacks can do a lot of damage in thirteen minutes and once Beauden Barrett, that high-voltage livewire of a running fly-half, took advantage of a fortunate bounce to turn the tables, the scoreboard started to leave us behind, two more tries at the death giving it a lopsided look that did us no credit whatsoever. Steve Hansen, the All Blacks coach and a predecessor of mine in the Wales job, gave it the usual dead bat treatment, stating afterwards that rugby matches lasted for eighty minutes and that points scored at the back end of a contest counted for just as much as those scored at any other time. Me? I cast my mind back to my days in the Waikato front row – days when we could not beat our great rivals from Auckland for love nor money. 'The first one is the toughest,' I said. 'Once you've done that, the rest gets easier.'

Joyously, we made our breakthrough seven days later against the Boks, winning 12–6 in a tryless encounter that was just about the polar opposite of our meeting with the All Blacks. Did I care about the nature of the victory? Did I hell. We had lost sixteen games on the bounce to the South Africans, and when you looked at our statistics against the southern superpowers as a whole since the end of 2007, it was an ugly sight: twenty-seven matches, one victory. The pundits had been going further than Gary Gold in questioning our mental aptitude for the big occasion. They were calling us chokers. If we were going to head into the World Cup 'pool of death' year feeling as good about ourselves as we would need to feel, we had to change that perception. Not for the first time, Sam Warburton found the right words in the build-up. 'It's not a matter of *if* we beat one of these sides, but *when*,' he said. Dead right. And in beating the Boks with four penalties from the boot of the ever-reliable Leigh Halfpenny, we took a mighty step forward. I couldn't bear to watch the last couple of minutes, but the players filled their shirts with pride and made it through to the final whistle. None more so than Dan Biggar, who played magnificently. The security of his tactical kicking, the courage of his defensive work and the athleticism of his aerial game established him as our number one 10. At the World Cup, he would more than justify that status.

The 2015 Six Nations was a funny old tournament. Once again, there was a performance gap between the last game of one series and the opening game of the next: we lost to England on opening night, at home. Not by much, but defeat by England leaves the whole of Wales hurting whatever the margin. Jérôme Garcès, the French referee, had a reputation as a good officiator of the scrum, but some of his calls against us that night left me confused. Apart from that, however, I had few complaints: England played pretty well in the second half and managed the big moments better than we did. If there was a bright side, I knew we would be spending a lot of time together over the coming months and that our form and fitness would improve.

That improvement kicked in immediately. We saw off Scotland at Murrayfield – Alun Wyn Jones was nearing the peak of his powers and turned in a superb display against the Gray brothers in the opposition second row – and produced a superior scrummaging display to beat the French in Paris. I had no reason to think we wouldn't win on the road again in round five: Italy in Rome held no fears for us. So if we were to put ourselves in with a shout of the title, we had to beat Ireland at the Millennium Stadium. It was a big game for Paul O'Connell, their magnificent captain: he was making his 100th appearance in the green shirt. Likewise, it was a landmark occasion for our own Sam Warburton. This was his thirty-fourth game as Wales skipper, a record. At the end, Sam was the man with the smile on his face. A try from Scott Williams on the hour, a drop goal from Dan Biggar and a flurry of Leigh Halfpenny penalties, four of them in the opening few minutes, saw us home 23–16.

So to Rome, on the weirdest of days. The Azzurri had a few of their old warhorses left in the team, from Martin Castrogiovanni at prop and Mauro Bergamasco on the flank to Andrea Masi in midfield, but they were not the strongest Italian side of all time, and after a tight first half, they couldn't handle our tempo as the game went deeper. We played some sensational rugby to run in seven tries after the break – George North grabbed himself a hat-trick in the space of ten minutes – and there was an eighth on a plate when Gareth Davies zipped off into the distance. Unfortunately, he spilled the ball on his way under the sticks. That cost us seven points. Another seven went against us when, in the final minute, the Italian wing Leonardo Sarto broke free and claimed a try, converted by Luciano Orquera.

This fourteen-point turnaround didn't seem to matter much, but when the calculators came out later on Super Saturday, after the Scotland–Ireland and England–France games, it suddenly mattered a lot. Had our match finished 68–13, as it should have done, we would have won the title on points difference. Instead, the Irish sneaked it by winning 40–10 in Edinburgh, just edging out England, who came out 55–35 victors in a twelve-try contest at Twickenham. Twelve tries? In an elite Test? Please. I'm too much of an old All Black to trust games where there are more tries than tackles. Still, it was an interesting experience.

My gut feeling about the World Cup ahead of our warm-up games – two against Ireland, home and away, and a send-off match with Italy in Cardiff – was positive. There was no doubting that the group stage would be massively challenging, but I felt our chances of surviving it were lifted by the shape of the fixture list. I hadn't realised at the time that the host nation, England in this case, had a say in the order of matches and in my opinion, they made a massive mistake in allowing us a soft opening against Uruguay instead of pairing us with the Wallabies. If we'd lost to Australia in round one, we would have been playing catch-up far earlier than we would have liked and been under intense pressure. By choosing to play us before we'd faced the Aussies and leaving their own match with Uruguay until last, presumably because they felt the pool might come down to points difference, they undermined their own campaign. When I arrived in Tokyo for the 2019 World Cup draw, the Japan coach Jamie Joseph, a fellow Kiwi, took me to one side and said: 'If you were with Japan as World Cup hosts, who would you play first: Ireland, or Scotland?'

'Neither,' I said. 'Make them play each other first and give yourselves a fixture you know you can win.'

It seems he took my advice.

I played hard ball in selection for the first warm-up against the Irish, putting a handful of players in a 'succeed or fail' scenario. A couple of them, James Hook and Richard Hibbard, were big names: they had played a lot of international rugby and had been on Lions tours, so leaving them out would leave me open to some flak from the media. In the event, we played very poorly in the opening half and lost 35–21. Together with the likes of Tyler Morgan, Nicky Smith and Dan Baker, neither James nor Richard did enough to make me revise my thinking and would not make the final cut. A week later in Dublin, it was a different story. I named a much stronger side, gave the players four days off to replicate World Cup conditions – we didn't train until the Thursday morning – and was rewarded with a top performance. It gave us a big spike in confidence, winning 16–10 over there against the Sextons, the Murrays, the O'Connells and the Heaslips. This was more like it. We were on a roll. All we needed now was a smooth run-through against the Italians. Which didn't happen. We were outscored two tries to one in a sub-standard contest and although we clung on to win by four points, we were laid low by the sight of Leigh Halfpenny and Rhys Webb being stretchered off the field and out of the World Cup. Two of our form players, gone. It was not the most enjoyable day I'd ever spent in Cardiff, by a very long way.

Very few people believed we could beat England at Twickenham in the pivotal game of the pool stage, but there were reasons why I felt we could fly in the face of public opinion. For one thing, the hosts had not been especially impressive in beating Fiji on opening night, even though they secured a try-scoring bonus point in the final seconds. For another, I knew they were under immense pressure. On the eve of the game, the Vunipola brothers, Mako and Billy, turned up at our hotel in Weybridge for a chat with Taulupe Faletau. The three of them were close friends: their families were distantly related, and as Tongans growing up in Wales in the 1990s, they spent a lot of time together with and without a rugby ball. I had no problem with them shooting the breeze over a coffee, despite the proximity of the game, and at one point during their discussion, I butted in to tell Taulupe that he'd have been free to pop over to the England base in nearby Bagshot had he wanted to do so. At which point, Mako piped up. 'Do you think he'd have been allowed in, the way things are with us right now?' he asked. 'There's no fun or smiling over there.' Then, when we were travelling to Twickenham, something passed us in a white blur. It was the England team bus. By all accounts, it was the most important thing in the world for them to get in front of us. I don't quite understand the point they were trying to make, but it said something about their mood of desperation.

Then there was their decision to pick Brad Barritt and Sam Burgess in a new midfield partnership. They had never started a Test together before that night, and while they both had their qualities in terms of ball-carrying potency and physicality, they didn't bring much in the way of mystery to the table. I can't say I was unhappy about the selection, because it gave me a massive clue as to how England intended to play the game. Forewarned is forearmed.

In the event, we won the game on our backsides in the face of considerable adversity. It was our fitness that allowed us to hang in there, even when injuries threatened to completely destabilise us and left us fighting for our World Cup lives with a No 10 at No 15, a wing at centre and a scrum-half on the wing. If anyone still wonders why I place so much emphasis on conditioning and preparation ahead of a major tournament, the explanation can be found in this game. I had no doubts that the Wales players would last at least as well as England and probably better. More importantly, the players themselves had no doubts. Why? Because they had trained at altitude in Switzerland, then in forty degrees of Arabian Gulf heat in Doha and been through all kinds of pain together. They could look into each other's eyes and know there was a special bond between them. That bond was what allowed them to man the barricades and defend for their lives, even though so many of them were performing unfamiliar roles – and, what was more, to show the patience and precision to strike when the match-winning opportunity presented itself. England helped us by making some poor choices at the end of the game, and the fact that they didn't think clearly underlines my point. When we broke out for the crucial try, Dan Biggar, Jamie Roberts, Lloyd

Williams and Gareth Davies made all the right choices at all the right split-second moments. That was the difference.

Our three-point win, 28–25, meant so much to me. Look at the tape: if you've ever seen me as animated as I was at the final whistle that night, you know more about my life than I do. It called for a proper celebration and we enjoyed it to the full, knowing that we had given ourselves every chance of making the knockout stage. Not that I escaped entirely trouble-free. On the way out of Twickenham, I ran into Kenny Logan, the former Scotland wing with whom I'd worked closely during my days at Wasps. He persuaded me to do an online interview. When it went out on Instagram, what was the most prominent object in the background? The England team bus, that white blur from earlier. I was accused of staging things so I could inflict maximum agony on our hosts. It wasn't true, but when did that stop those determined to dish out criticism?

The job was not yet done, of course. Our next game, midweek, was against Fiji. Not just any old Fiji, either. They had given England some trouble and pushed the Wallabies hard. They had the best scrummaging props in the tournament in Campese Ma'afu and Manasa Saulo, they had some fantastically explosive open-field runners – Leone Nakarawa, the lock, was off-the-scale dangerous with ball in hand – and they knew what it was like to bomb Wales out of a World Cup, having done precisely that in 2007, just before my arrival. Sure enough, they sucked us into a South Seas-style game during the second half and made things a little delicate for

Right: my first game as coach of Wales was against England at Twickenham, where we were rank outsiders. Shaun Edwards looks equally anxious.

Below: a Grand Slam is no mean achievement. Ryan Jones, our captain, was the first to make the most of it.

Trudi joined me for the celebrations. I tried my best, but she looked better than me on the red carpet . . .

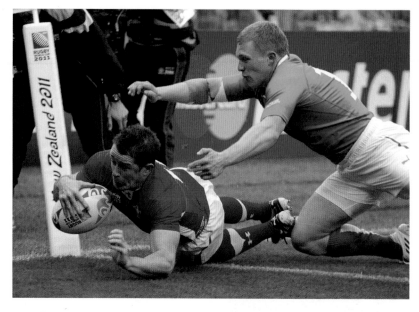

Shane Williams, doing what he did best. The opening try in our 2011 World Cup quarter-final with Ireland.

Mike Phillips also knew his way to the corner. Our second try in a great performance.

Mike Phillips puts us within touching distance of the final with an individual score against France.

Left: Sam Warburton tackles Vincent Clerc – the decisive moment of the game.

Below: if the semi-final in Auckland was a sell-out, even more people – 60,000 of them – watched live on the big screen at the Millennium Stadium in Cardiff.

Three folk-hero forwards – Gethin Jenkins, Ryan Jones and Adam Jones – celebrate our Six Nations Grand Slam in 2012.

From the Millennium Stadium to the Welsh Assembly. Sam Warburton holds the trophy aloft in front of the politicians.

Shaun Edwards (*left*) and Rob Howley were at the heart of the Wales project. We went through a lot together.

Laughing with Eddie Jones before the 2019 Six Nations game with England in Cardiff. Only one of us was laughing afterwards.

The third and final Slam. Alun Wyn Jones had become a world-class leader on the field.

GRAND SLAM
CHAMPIONS 2019

The roof is open and the rain falls in torrents. Do the players look as if they care?

Thoroughly bedraggled and very emotional, I reflect on my final Six Nations outing with Wales.

Hitting the ground running at the 2019 World Cup: Hadleigh Parkes (*above, left*) celebrates his early try in the epic pool game with Australia; Gareth Davies sets sail for the line (*top, right*) to put us 23–8 ahead.

Fighting for our lives: Aaron Wainwright feels the force of Sebastien Vahaamahina's elbow (*centre, right*) – a violent act that helped turn the quarter-final in our favour; Ross Moriarty (*right*) wins it with a late plunge for the line.

The ecstasy: Josh Adams nails a brilliant semi-final try under pressure to draw us level with the Springboks.

The agony: for all their heroics, the Wales players know it's over. Alun Wyn Jones in the middle with, clockwise from top right, Hadleigh Parkes, Justin Tipuric, Rhys Carre, Adam Beard and Rhys Patchell.

The respect: a grateful team of Welshmen thank the wonderful Yokohama crowd in traditional Japanese style.

those of us watching from the coaching box before we made it home 23–13. It was not a vintage performance in anyone's book, but I have no doubt that the Fijians of 2015 were the best side ever to finish fourth in a World Cup pool. By far. With a little more preparation time and some better resources, they would have undoubtedly caused more damage.

There was a nine-day gap to our final pool game with Australia, so it was with some relief that I clocked off for a spell of quiet reflection. Forty-eight hours after Fiji, I found myself sitting at home watching the England–Australia game on television. Out came the red wine. Why not? I felt I deserved a glass or two of something decent. The Wallabies were warm favourites to win the game and knock the hosts out of their own competition and with Bernard Foley scoring tries and kicking goals in the first half, there was no reason to think it would be anything other than a straightforward Aussie victory. But England inched their way back into range with a try from the Bath wing Anthony Watson and that left me feeling a little nervous.

'It's almost as if I'm sitting in the coaches' box, I'm that edgy,' I said to Trudi.

'Yeah,' she replied. 'But if you were in the coaches' box, you wouldn't have had a dozen glasses of red, would you?'

At the final whistle, I stormed off to bed in a mood. Blame it on the tension.

With the Wallabies winning 33–13 against England, it meant that victory over the Aussies in our final pool game would earn us a quarter-final against the Scots. Defeat would pitch us in with the Springboks. I felt we could win either way, but topping the pool would put us in the softer half of the draw. We drafted in some reinforcements for training purposes, which caused a row. The Rugby World Cup media department announced that there was an investigation in progress, which was not terribly helpful, not least because we had informed the appropriate people in advance and acted entirely within the rules. Angry, I demanded an apology. There was none. I was not best pleased with the tournament hierarchy anyway, World Rugby chief executive Brett Gosper having made a comment bemoaning the prospect of the host nation failing to make the knockouts. What kind of message did that send out? I felt it was completely unacceptable and said so. One way or another, things were getting fraught.

We could have beaten the Wallabies that day. We should have beaten them. Down by six points, we were playing against thirteen men for a period either side of the hour mark and well placed to capitalise, especially as the players in the sin bin were not any old absentees. They were Will Genia and Dean Mumm, two of the clearer thinkers in the Aussie line-up, and as a result, the massively influential David Pocock found himself being substituted. Talk about an open goal. Unfortunately, we stuffed it up. There's no other phrase for it. We had them under all sorts of pressure and while I take my hat off to the Wallaby scramble defence, which was out of this world at times, we had every opportunity to put them to the sword. In the end, they found a way out of their own red zone, advanced up the field and coaxed a penalty decision out of Craig Joubert, the South African referee. The goal was kicked by Bernard Foley and that was that. It was a crushing disappointment.

I was not at all convinced about that penalty decision – an offside call based on minimal evidence. And that's putting it kindly. Therein lies a story. We always did a lot of analysis on match officials and during our research on Craig, we formed the view that he had never overseen a genuine shock result. When he was awarded the Australia–Scotland quarter-final and the Scots looked well set to turn the form-book on its head by winning, a few of us commented on this unusual situation. 'Jeez, this is Craig's first upset,' said one of my coaching team as we watched the drama unfold. What did we know? The game was finally decided by a deeply controversial penalty resulting from a Joubert error. Craig sprinted off the field in the end, which was not a good look. Clearly, the pressure was getting to everyone.

We were not in the best of physical shape ahead of our quarter-final with South Africa: Dan Lydiate took the field with a metal plate in his eye socket and there were all sorts of other fitness issues. But by that stage in the competition, everyone was suffering to some degree. With the autumn victory behind us, we dominated the Boks in the first half, to the extent that they looked more than a little bewildered. I remember walking down the Twickenham steps at half-time and passing Lood de Jager, their lock. 'He looks shell-shocked,' I thought to myself. 'He doesn't know what's hit him.' Yet we were only a point up at 13–12. Even though our most deeply competitive spirits, the likes of Sam Warburton and Dan Biggar and Alun Wyn Jones, were throwing everything at the game, we never quite found a way of breaking free. The South Africans did not do anything particularly dynamic in that second half, but they dredged up a hell of a lot of fight and slowly turned the territorial battle in their favour. Then, five minutes from time, Duane Vermeulen broke off the back of a scrum and flicked a behind-the-back pass to Fourie du Preez. The scrum-half breezed over and that was the game, 23–19. If I'm being critical, the try should have been stopped. Lloyd Williams, on at half-back for our own try-scorer Gareth Davies, tried to take the mighty Vermeulen low rather than high – to bring him to ground rather than prevent the pass. Alex Cuthbert, faced with a split-second decision on the wing, came in when he should have stayed out. But look, I couldn't have asked for a whole lot more from anyone in a red shirt that day. What was more, the number of walking wounded had risen sharply once again. I wasn't sure we would have been in a position to field a side against the All Blacks in the semi-final, let alone beat them.

12

A DIFFERENT SHADE OF RED – PART THREE

Now I've had time to think about it, I believe the photograph will come to be seen as one of the great images in the history of rugby union. As iconic in its way as the one that captures South African captain François Pienaar receiving the World Cup from his president, Nelson Mandela, in Johannesburg in 1995, or the Fran Cotton 'swamp monster' snap taken in the midst of a Wellington mudfall in 1977. I am talking about the gathering of the Lions and the All Blacks in Auckland at the end of the drawn 2017 series – two teams entwined in mutual admiration following a momentous Test series neither side was prepared to lose.

When the French referee Romain Poite blew his whistle to bring proceedings to a close, I'm not sure any of those directly involved in events knew how to react to the indecisiveness of the outcome. Steve Hansen, the New Zealand head coach and my opposite number, walked towards me across the Eden Park field and asked me how I felt. 'It's a bit like kissing your sister, isn't it?' I replied, falling back on the stock standard response to a drawn contest. I wasn't the only one struggling to gather my thoughts. Some people felt there should have been extra time or some kind of shootout. The American solution, in other words. Draws don't happen in American sport, which probably explains why cricket will never take root there. A five-day Test with no winner? They would rather see a communist in the White House.

But when I look at that photograph now, I feel nothing but pride and positivity. If it is true that some of the players mingling together beneath the floodlights seem less than ecstatic at having to share the spoils – the All Black flanker Sam Cane appears to be a little down in the mouth, while the ultra-competitive Lions fly-half Johnny Sexton looks shell-shocked rather than merely bemused – there are warmer, happier details elsewhere. The flashing smiles of Owen Farrell and Jack Nowell, Charlie Faumuina and Ardie Savea; Jerome Kaino's gentle placing of hands on the shoulders of Taulupe Faletau after eighty minutes of thunderous physicality in which they had been anything but gentle with each other; the comradely way in which Rhys Webb drapes his arm around Israel Dagg while Codie Taylor, the New Zealand hooker, does the same to both Rhys and Jamie George; the spontaneous clap of the hands by Jonathan Davies, our player of the series. Knowing 'Foxy' as I do, he was applauding everyone.

Only once before in almost 130 years of Lions touring had there been a tied series: in 1955, when the team led by the Ulster and Ireland lock Robin Thompson fought the Springboks to a standstill in a classic four-Test match-up in

South Africa. Nothing like this had happened under the three-Test format or in the professional era. But then, this had been an unusual trip all round. We flew in the face of received wisdom by bouncing back from a heavy defeat in the opening Test; we survived and thrived despite a fixture list that might have been designed to make our lives impossible. Graham Henry, who coached the Lions against the Wallabies in 2001 before running the All Blacks against the Lions four years later, had publicly used the word 'suicidal' in connection with the itinerary, and no one gave us a prayer of emerging in one piece from a ten-game schedule that featured meetings with all five Super Rugby franchises and a 'fourth Test' with the New Zealand Maori as well as those three run-ins with the All Blacks themselves, two of them in Auckland, where they had not lost a single match against anyone for almost a quarter of a century. Funnily enough, even I said it was 'crazy'. That was before I accepted the role of head coach, of course, but I must have meant it at the time!

On top of all that, there was the personal challenge of leading the Lions in New Zealand – of heading up an assault on my own homeland, of attempting to inflict some serious damage on the very teams, Waikato and the All Blacks, I had been so passionate about representing during my playing days. Sending out sides against the All Blacks was not new to me: I had done it once with Ireland and plenty of times with Wales. But the Lions? That was different. They were the last of the old-style touring sides, drawing support from all four home nations rather than one. Even the Scots, so often infuriated by the lack of representation in Lions parties, would be fully and unquestioningly behind us – and believe me, there are plenty of people of Scottish ancestry in New Zealand, particularly in the South Island.

As it turned out, the rugby side of the trip was almost everything I wanted it to be – not just in terms of our competitiveness in the Test series, but also in terms of the support I received from the overwhelming majority of the New Zealand sporting public. My problem, not for the first time, was with the media, some of whom went out of their way to criticise and undermine me, to kick me around, to generally get on my nerves and under my skin. It was disappointing, to say the least. Accuse me of naïvety if you must, but before we set off on tour I had this romantic dream about rugby revelling in its internationalism, about an ex-All Black returning to his own shores to coach against the All Blacks being embraced as home-bred success. It didn't quite turn out that way because it wasn't portrayed that way in the press. Particularly in the *New Zealand Herald*, the biggest paper in the country. They gave me a really hard time and if it hadn't been for my family, first and foremost, and for the hundreds upon hundreds of locals who took the trouble to send texts and emails supporting me in the face of so much hostile 'journalism', I'm not sure what state I would have been in by the end of the tour.

What was it all about, this media aggression? I've spoken to people who felt it was part of a planned strategy to unsettle me. If so, it failed. With the players in their own bubble and largely unaware of the stick being dished out, I made a point of not mentioning it to them, of never appearing to be affected by it in the team room. But even though I knew that what was being reported had little in common with what was actually happening, there were times when I found it tough to take. Only Trudi, Bryn, Gabby and one or two very close friends realised just how tough.

The nonsense started early, long before we boarded the plane at Heathrow. As part of my preparations for the tour, I had travelled to Auckland the previous October for the Bledisloe Cup game between the All Blacks and the Wallabies. On the morning of the match, the *Herald* went to town on Michael Cheika, the Australia coach. Under the headline 'Send In The Clowns', they ran a cartoon in which he was dressed up in a frilly circus outfit and a bright red nose. New Zealand galloped away with the game, winning 37–10 and scoring six tries to one. Michael was pretty angry about his treatment and when I was questioned about the incident, I expressed the view that the paper had gone over the top. I also mentioned the booing of Quade Cooper, the New Zealand-born Wallaby playmaker, when he came off the bench late in the match. Cooper came from Tokoroa, little more than an hour's drive from my home town of Hamilton, and to my way of thinking the spectators who went after him that night should have remembered that. 'Come on, guys,' I remember saying to myself as the barracking began. 'We're New Zealanders here. We're better than this.' It was disrespectful, I was embarrassed . . . and I said so. The following day, the *Herald* ran a picture of me. Guess what? They had me dressed as a clown. So began the phoney war.

This was no time to think about the New Zealand newspaper industry, however. Among the many more important items on my agenda was the pulling together of a coaching and backroom team, a decision on the tour captaincy and the careful selection of a playing squad capable, emotionally and psychologically as much as physically, of taking on such a savagely hard fixture list. Some of these things, like the captaincy, would be more straightforward than others. While I saw no reason not to ask Sam Warburton to double down on his 2013 efforts and remain in the post – he had missed some rugby through injury, but I knew his skill-set would suit the environment and he had grown as a leader in the intervening years – the rest of the jigsaw required a good deal of thought.

The Lions hierarchy had not made an early call on the head coach position: I was interviewed on the same day in early July 2016 as my countryman Vern Cotter, a highly effective operator who had been doing good work with Scotland since moving to Murrayfield two years previously. (A third New Zealander coaching in the Six Nations, Joe Schmidt of Ireland, had decided against throwing his hat in the ring.) It was not until the end of the month that I was offered the position, so time was of the essence. The following weeks were something of a whirlwind, beginning with a reconnaissance trip to New Zealand in the company of Ger

Carmody, our director of operations – a key figure in the set-up and a thorough, resourceful, hugely loyal individual for whom I developed a great regard. There was also a good deal of rugby to watch, a large number of personnel decisions to be thrashed out and more commercial commitments than I could even begin to count.

There was neither the time nor the space to reinvent the wheel: a sense of continuity and a collective familiarity with the pressures of a Lions tour would be vital. I insisted that Paul Stridgeon should be on board once again – a priceless figure in every respect – and argued successfully that we should stick with the lion's share (no pun intended) of the medical, sports science and analysis teams who had dove-tailed so successfully in 2013, in so far as they were available. On the coaching front, Andy Farrell was always my prime candidate as defence specialist, as was Neil Jenkins on the kicking side of things and Graham Rowntree with the scrum-maging, and I was always going to take Rob Howley on attack. It struck me that as we were going to play a lot of ball-in-hand rugby, a second voice in that department might be useful. In the end, it didn't happen. Joe Schmidt stuck to his guns, deciding that he really did want to concentrate on building up Ireland's strength in depth ahead of the 2019 World Cup. Another pair of Kiwis with Super Rugby experience, Kieran Keane and Jason O'Halloran, also declined.

Most publicly, so too did Gregor Townsend, the first-choice No 10 when the Lions had won in South Africa in 1997 and one of the great names in Scottish rugby. Gregor sounded keen initially, but then said he needed to focus on Scotland, where he was succeeding Vern. I respected his decision, but I couldn't help wondering whether he had come under some pressure from his national union. If that was the case, there was the obvious counter-argument that a couple of months with the Lions would have sent his learning curve rocketing upwards. I don't know if I'd have been able to complete twelve years in Wales without the Lions to refresh and reinvigorate me, to give me a change of pace and perspective. Yes, Gregor was at the start of his career as a Test head coach, rather than in the middle of it. There again, there is no hothouse like the Lions hothouse, irrespective of the stage you have reached in your working life. Steve Borthwick of England certainly took that view. When I asked him to bring his line-out expertise to the mix, he grabbed the opportunity.

Even though Wales suffered a rough Six Nations in the run-up to the tour, finishing fifth on the back of three defeats, I wasn't unduly concerned by the form of the players. The year before, we had been pretty competitive in two of the three Tests we played against the All Blacks in New Zealand and there was also a convincing win over the Springboks in the home autumn series. Against the toughest opponents, we had turned a corner. England? They had been playing strongly enough under Eddie Jones, who had replaced Stuart Lancaster after the World Cup implosion. Ireland? They had been a little inconsistent, but their spikes in performance had brought them big results against all three southern hemisphere superpowers – most memorably in Chicago, of all places, when they had put five tries past New Zealand in a 40–29 victory. The interesting nation, if I can put it that way, was Scotland, who, during the professional era, had faced an increasingly uphill battle for representation in Lions squads. There were various reasons: often, their results did nothing to push the claims of potential contenders; sometimes, it seemed that the Scottish players were far stronger collectively than they were individually, which was not ideal in a Lions context, when the selectors are breaking down players piece by piece, aspect by aspect, in an effort to work out if they have what it takes to make a significant contribution on and off the field.

Stuart Hogg, the dynamic Scottish full-back, was one of the earliest names on the squad list for the 2017 tour. There was no questioning his capacity to make an impact. The other leading Scots – the likes of Finn Russell at fly-half and Jonny Gray at lock – were definitely up for discussion, but we wanted to take their measure under pressure and placed a lot of emphasis on the Calcutta Cup match at Twickenham in the fourth round of Six Nations matches. I didn't travel to London expecting Scotland to win the game, but I did want to see their big players make a scrap of it. What happened? They conceded sixty-one points, some of the top names disappeared from view and as a result, only Tommy Seymour, the Glasgow wing, joined Hogg on the roster. (Greig Laidlaw would also make it at scrum-half, but only after Ben Youngs of England pulled out of the trip before departure so he could spend time with his brother Tom, whose wife was fighting cancer.)

I can honestly say that I didn't want it to be that way. Part of the magic of the Lions is the coming together of four rugby nations, four grand traditions, four distinct cultures. If one quarter of the Lions community is allowed to flirt with irrelevance, what does it say for the basic concept? We had a discussion in selection on this very subject and kicked around a few ideas about representation. Should there be a minimum number of players from each country? If so, how many? If it's a forty-man squad, is five the number? There was no consensus. We simply had to pick the best men for the job, and Hogg and Seymour were the ones who met the criteria. Even then, there was a long and hotly contested debate about the wing positions. I didn't want us to go down to a single Scot, so I argued hard for Tommy and eventually got my way. He didn't make the Test side, but he left a mark with three tries on tour.

It did not require the mind of a rugby genius to work out that this tour posed unprecedented demands: one glance at the fixture list made the reality of the situation abundantly clear. But once we were up and running, the scale of the challenge registered with everyone. We did not assemble as a full group until our farewell dinner bash at the Roundhouse in London the day before the long-haul flight south. This was less than ideal for obvious reasons but a number of players – Conor Murray, Peter O'Mahony and C J Stander of Munster; Liam Williams and Jonathan Davies of Scarlets;

Elliot Daly and James Haskell of Wasps; and Jack Nowell of Exeter – had been involved in club finals that weekend and had therefore been off-limits to us. A shining example of joined-up thinking by the people in charge of rugby in Britain and Ireland? Not quite. Our prep time had been mind-blowingly inadequate, and things would have been even worse had Leinster and Saracens not lost their respective semi-finals. Had they made it through, almost a dozen players would have been taken out of Lions circulation until the very last minute, including such key figures as Johnny Sexton, Tadgh Furlong, Owen Farrell, Mako Vunipola, Jamie George and Maro Itoje. To add to our problems, we would not arrive in New Zealand until the Wednesday, barely seventy-two hours before our opening game against the Provincial Barbarians in Whangarei. I couldn't help wondering how things had come to this: I wouldn't have countenanced it as head coach of Wales and I couldn't imagine any other Test coach feeling differently. And we were supposed to be the best of the best! I remember saying to John Feehan, the Lions CEO: 'I'm concerned about the timings here. Some of the players will still be jet-lagged on match day, we're staying in ten different hotels in the first fortnight of the tour, there are no days off that don't double as a travel day . . . I'm worried that if someone picks up an injury early, they will have a legal case against us for inadequate preparation.' I wasn't joking. I was deadly serious.

Trudi was at the airport in Auckland when we landed: I hadn't set eyes on her since March and couldn't have been happier to see her again. I knew that on this tour of all tours, she would play an incredibly important role as a supportive figure, an organiser, an energiser, maybe as a shoulder to cry on. She is absolutely a people person, the most positive of spirits, and has always been brilliant in making everyone around us feel good about themselves. There were times on this trip when we were taking thirty or forty friends and family members to Lions matches – my ticket bill at the end was north of NZD$40,000! She then collected the money and distributed tickets to everyone. That in itself takes some arranging, but Trudi was so completely in control of the logistics, there was never a moment when things looked like veering off-track.

Only once was her loyalty tested, and that was on opening night – the match against the Provincial Baa-Baas. To my delight, our opponents had selected Bryn to start at No 10. It's a proud thing for any father to see his sports-mad son achieve such recognition on the big stage and I told him so when I heard the news. I was still telling him on match night. A few minutes before kick-off, as he was completing his warm-up routine on the field in front of a noisy crowd, I gave him a big hug and said: 'Mate, I hope you play well this evening.' Which he did. Bryn was vocal and authoritative, he kicked well, he took the ball to the line and he left the pitch satisfied that he had played his part in a strong team per-formance. Few expected a scratch side like his to finish within a score of the Lions, but they did. It was a dream evening for the Gatland family. Not even the *NZ Herald* could ruin it.

Which is not to say they didn't try. Their headline a couple of days before the match? 'Gatland finds Baa-Baas' weakness – his son.'

Jeez. What can you do? The premise of the piece was that I had instructed Ben Te'o, the England centre who would be starting his first Lions match, to target Bryn and expose him defensively – a claim based on a comment I had made during a press conference. My actual words had been as follows: 'I spoke to Bryn last night and he seems to be enjoying the week. He probably expects to make a few tackles on the weekend, but we haven't spoken too much about the game.' What fly-half doesn't make tackles in the modern game? Barry John and Phil Bennett may have had some help in this department back in the day, but rugby doesn't work that way any more. It was a crass piece of journalism, a cheap-shot article written for a reason, and it was far too close to home for me to let it go. The Lions press officers, Dave Barton and Luke Broadley, set about getting it changed and they succeeded to a degree, but the main thrust of it remained in print. I wasn't happy at all.

We were not exactly overjoyed at the nature of our 13–7 victory, either, but at least we were underway. Bryn told me that the wet conditions had played in the Baa-Baas' favour: on a dry field, our pace would have counted for more. He also said that when we ran into Super Rugby opposition who liked to play at a high tempo, we would have a better idea of where we stood. I knew this was true and understood the importance of the next couple of games, against the Blues in big-city Auckland and the Crusaders in poor earthquake-ravaged Christchurch. These teams would ask questions of the philosophy underpinning our whole approach to the Test series, which was constructed around the idea of playing a lot of rugby against the All Blacks rather than attempting to eke out victories on the basis of forward dominance and a siege-gun kicking game. My take on it was that a narrow approach would be fatal: their set-piece was too good to hope that we could edge a series through our scrum, maul and line-out. If we were serious about winning, we would have to threaten them with ball in hand – to get behind them, not play ten-man rugby in front of them.

As it was so early in the tour, the Blues were in a position to name a very strong side and did so: they picked Rieko Ioane and Sonny Bill Williams behind the scrum and Charlie Faumuina in the front row, all of whom were certain to feature in the Tests. As for us, I had gone on record as promising every player a start in one of the first three games and planned to stick to that pledge, fitness willing. But rumbling away beneath the 'surface' issues of training and selection and match planning, there was the problem of dealing with the media. One or two papers, in England as well as in New Zealand, picked up on my muttered comment to Ken Owens after the Monday press conference. 'F*** it,' I had said to him. 'I don't know why I have to keep f***ing defending myself.' It wasn't particularly poetic, I admit, but I was pretty hacked off with some of the questioning. It was also deliberate. My words may have seemed like 'noises off', but I was aware the microphones were still running and that offered me a different way of making my point.

At the conference I had been asked about 'Warrenball'. Yes, that old chestnut. Some of the media commentators had it in their minds that when I coached a team, 'Warrenball' would inevitably be the strategy. Most of them didn't have the faintest idea what 'Warrenball' was meant to be: when I pushed them on it, which I was doing with increasing frequency, they tended to mention Jamie Roberts crash-balling his way over the gainline at inside centre for Wales. As far as I understood it, the word was coined by Brian Smith, the Australian who was a senior member of England's coaching panel at the 2011 World Cup. If Brian was talking specifically about Jamie's ability to put a team on the front foot through his strength on the carry, fair enough: Jamie had been exceptional at it for years. Why wouldn't you use a weapon like that if you had it in your armoury? But Jamie wasn't with us in 2017, and anyway, I felt the 'Warrenball' thing was being used against me – that it suggested I was a one-dimensional coach with no Plan B. Even my opposite number here, Steve Hansen, had been digging away at me. Before the tour, he was quoted as saying: 'Unless Gatland has an epiphany, we pretty much know what to expect.' To which I felt like saying: 'Just a minute. I won big trophies with Wasps when we had a back line of Rob Howley, Alex King, Stuart Abbott, Fraser Waters, Tom Voyce, Josh Lewsey and Mark van Gisbergen. They weren't the biggest players, or the most powerful.

Where's the "Warrenball" there?' I felt it was becoming derogatory and disrespectful, and it annoyed me.

That night, we lost 22–16 to the Blues, which was a body blow. Out of contention in the Super Rugby competition, this was the Aucklanders' chance of taking something from the season and they went after it with a passion. Rieko Ioane scored an early try and Sonny Bill Williams scored a freakish one while I was in the changing room preparing for the half-time talk. I knew the Blues had been awarded a shot at goal and assumed they would nail it, but the ball hit a post and Sonny Bill claimed the touchdown in the frenzy that followed. Having got ourselves back in front during the second half, we were very disappointed when Ihaia West latched onto a trademark Sonny Bill offload at pace and wrapped up victory late in the game. I wasn't the best of company when I caught up with the family late that night, but Bryn gave me a reason to feel better about life. 'The Blues want me in their full squad next year,' he said. Ironic, eh? But brilliant, too.

The Crusaders match, an important game from the moment the fixture list was finalised, was now massive for us. We had to win. There would be only one more Saturday game before the opening Test and another defeat would open up a wound in our collective mindset. I knew that. I also knew that the Crusaders, always sharp on the tactical front, would react to what we had done in the opening matches and come up with a Lions-specific plan. Which they did. According to Bryn Hall, who played at half-back for them, they took the field believing that if they made 200 passes in the game, they would definitely win. It was a tough encounter: why would it have been anything else against a side boasting current All Blacks as good as Israel Dagg, Sam Whitelock and a top-line front row of Joe Moody, Codie Taylor and Owen Franks? But our set-piece work was terrific, especially in terms of Peter O'Mahony's raids on the Crusaders' line-out. We also managed the game intelligently and our defence was spot on. There were no tries, but Owen Farrell's kicking gave us the 12–3 victory we needed so badly.

And the best news? Johnny Sexton was back at the races. I'd been a little worried about him. By his own very high standards, he hadn't played well in Whangarei. Here, he came off the bench when Jonathan Davies picked up an injury just shy of the half-hour mark, teamed up with Owen in a 10–12 link and rediscovered some of the confidence that makes him tick. This was such a bonus. Johnny was a key figure for us: a big voice, a forceful personality, a driver of standards. When he's on a rough run, however, the sense of frustration wells up in him and he's not quite the same player. After Whangarei, I found myself wondering if he'd resigned himself to playing second fiddle to Owen, to being on the down slope. By making a significant contribution when it was really needed in Christchurch, he reclaimed the best of himself. As I said to the media after the game, he had his mojo back.

I should mention here that there was a third contender for the No 10 shirt in the hugely competitive form of Dan

Biggar, who had performed so magnificently for Wales at the 2015 World Cup. This tour was a serious challenge for him. He knew, as well as anyone, that Sexton was a proven winner in the uniquely pressurised Lions environment, and that Farrell was a growing force in the world game with his iron temperament and his overt physicality. Not for a moment did Dan settle for third best, and while the cards didn't fall his way in selection, my respect for him grew over the course of the trip. He took his disappointments on the chin, went straight back to work and redoubled his efforts. If he wasn't going to win himself a Test place, he was buggered if he was going to give the blokes ahead of him a free ride.

People often ask me whether I ever found it difficult, going back to Wales to work with people who had not achieved what they wanted in a Lions shirt and may have felt a sense of betrayal. The answer has always been 'no'. I think honesty is the key here. The one thing I never do is tell a player that he's the best in the world. I might say he's high quality, but I always add that there is room for improvement. The moment you start telling someone he's better than he is and then you don't pick him for a Lions Test, you're in a heap of trouble of your own making. Players know that with me, the best team will be picked in an objective, emotion-free manner. It's always been that way. If you're honest, if there's no favouritism or double-standards, there can be no come-back. They may not like my decisions at times, but I like to think they respect the reasoning behind them.

We were running fast towards the first Test now. Down

in Dunedin against the Highlanders, we managed to lose from a winning position. I felt we were on the rough end of some big refereeing calls, but there was also a good deal of self-inflicted damage, some of it caused by players experienced enough to have known better. Four days later, we were back in the North Island for the so-called 'Fourth Test' against the New Zealand Maori, in Rotorua, of all places – real Maori heartland, as the poor England tourists found out on their notoriously grisly 'tour of hell' in 1998, when they went down 62–14 and suffered the ignominy of being laughed at by the crowd. The Maori had a proud tradition of causing problems for the Lions, having beaten them in 2005 and pushed them really hard in virtually every other meeting since World War II. Weirdly, this turned out to be our easiest game. The Maori were in the same boat as us: a team drawn from far and wide, not terribly familiar with each other and struggling with limited preparation. They had some terrific players – Nehe Milner-Skudder on the wing, Damian McKenzie at 10, Liam Messam in the back row – but they were not as cohesive as the Super Rugby sides. With Leigh Halfpenny kicking goals for the fun of it, we won 32–10.

The following day was Father's Day – not an occasion I had celebrated often, generally being away with Wales while the kids were in New Zealand. This time, there was every reason to make something of it: I was back home in Hamilton for the forthcoming game against the Chiefs and with the First Test only six days distant, this would be the last opportunity to even pretend to relax. Trudi contacted most of the staff and players' wives and they all sent video messages with a montage of clips of kids wishing their dads a happy Father's Day from the other side of the world. It was an emotional moment. There were tears in the eyes of some tough men. Maro Itoje, young and unmarried, turned to me and said: 'Looking at this, I'm going to have to get myself a baby.' Trudi was in her element during those few days at home. The Chiefs game was always going to be a big Gatland family occasion – it's amazing how many long-lost relatives you rediscover when there are tickets to be had – so there was plenty to be done on the organisational front. We also hosted the Lions management and backroom workforce at our house for a couple of hours. Attendance wasn't compulsory, but just about everyone turned up for a bite to eat and a few drinks. The calm before the storm? It felt like that as our guests chatted away over their barbecued food or strolled, beer and wine in hand, to the bottom of the garden, where the Waikato River ran. It was a great night and a relaxed reward for the hard work everyone was putting into this tour.

It was around this time that the 'Geography Six' contro-versy unfolded. There was plenty of comment in the media about us bringing in a handful of reinforcements (true enough), presenting it as a sign of Lions panic after the defeats in Auckland and Dunedin (which wasn't true at all). I had always planned to summon extra players to help out in training and perform some bench duty when necessary as a means of taking the load off the Test squad and reducing the chances of them being asked to double-up on their match appearances. The full-time Lions were aware of the plan because I'd mentioned it right at the start. The men I called in were Finn Russell and Allan Dell of Scotland, plus four Wales players in Gareth Davies, Kristian Dacey, Tomas Francis and Cory Hill. That sparked a row. There were reports of rumblings of discontent from the English contingent, who felt that senior internationals like Dylan Hartley and Joe Launchbury had more of a call on a Lions shirt. But Dylan and Joe were on tour in Argentina, and I knew from my 2013 experience that people flying in from far-flung locations were not in the best place to acclimatise quickly and give of their best at short notice. I understood the criticism to some extent and I might do things differently now, but my decisions were based on logistics as much as anything else: the six call-ups were already on tour in our general time zone and were immediately available.

Our match-up with the Chiefs gave me most of what I wanted. This was a relief. I had admitted to Trudi on the day of the game that things were getting to me. 'How are you enjoying the tour?' she asked over a bite of lunch. 'I'm hating it,' I replied. Her face betrayed her shock at the extent of my stress levels.

'I love being involved with the team, but it's the external stuff . . . The last few weeks have been tough.'

'I had no idea,' she said. 'Don't let it get you down.'

The discussion cheered me up, and our performance made me happier still. The midweek game before a Test is always a tough one for those involved, because most know they won't be playing in the Big One a few days hence. Rory Best, the Ireland hooker, led the side well after speaking powerfully in the dressing room before kick-off. I was delighted for him. It was payback for the problems that beset him when he skippered the Lions against the Brumbies in Canberra at the same stage of the 2013 tour. The only slight downside to our four-try, 34–6 victory was an outbreak of hassle during the warm-up. Stu Williams, the manager of the Chiefs, approached me and said: 'What the hell are you doing?'

'Sorry?'

'You're videoing our warm-up.'

'I don't know what you're talking about. Leave it with me,' I said.

I knew Stu well enough to know that he wasn't trying to pull a fast one: we'd worked together during my coaching spell with Waikato and always got along and we will be working together again when I take up the Chiefs job at the end of 2019. It quickly transpired that Mike Hughes, one of our analysts, had indeed been recording the Chiefs' pre-match preparations. It wasn't a massive deal: whatever it was they were doing, they were doing it on the field before an audience of thousands. Still, it was unusual and just a little awkward, this being my home club.

'What's happening?' I asked Mike.

'Steve Borthwick told me to do it.'

This was news to me. 'Look, if you're going to record them, don't do it down on the field,' I said. 'Do it from the coaches' box.'

'I've been doing it for every game,' came the reply.

I had no idea. Honestly. To this day, I don't know what Steve was trying to get out of it. I apologised to Stu and then, the next day, had my moment of fun with Mike. 'The Chiefs have put in a formal complaint and the New Zealand union want you sent home,' I told him, with as straight a face as I could manage. Quite quickly, he realised I was kidding. But I knew he'd report back to Steve. How he reacted, heaven only knows. But I found out subsequently that England had been doing it for some time.

Now came the really difficult bit: selection for the first confrontation with the All Blacks. Right the way through, I'd insisted to the players that even if they found themselves playing in the midweek side ahead of the First Test, there was still an opening for them. If you put out messages like that, you have to live up to them. I think I did. Both Liam Williams and Elliot Daly started against the Chiefs. Both of them did enough to convince me that they should make a quick turnaround and start again against New Zealand. With Anthony Watson of England completing the back three, there would be no place for George North. That was a headline grabber. Nothing for George? From superstar on the last Lions tour to also-ran here? It was a tough message for me to convey. I took him to one side after announcing the side to the squad and told him that there would be another opportunity ahead and that he should make the most of it. I'd known him a long time and was aware he would take it hard. I'm happy to say that there have been no issues between us as a result of the decision. That's the mark of the man.

There was no room for Sam Warburton either. He hadn't played a great deal of rugby and was a little off his level, so we went with Peter O'Mahony as captain. There were long discussions about the midfield and the second row too. I'm not sure how long it took to pick the All Blacks side: more than half the line-up had started the World Cup final less than two years previously while others, like Israel Dagg and Sonny Bill Williams, had lifted the trophy back in 2011. They had masses of experience and the recent additions – Rieko Ioane, Beauden Barrett, Sam Cane – were serious propositions in anyone's language. Throw in the Eden Park factor and we were facing a proper challenge. That much was obvious.

They went after us in the areas they thought we thought we were strong, if that makes sense. They wanted to mess with our minds, undermine whatever assumptions we had about the way the series would play out. They were extremely physical and direct, running everything off Aaron Smith at scrum-half and attacking close to the tackle areas rather than out wide. We had the odd moment, including a try from Sean O'Brien that was almost certainly the try of the tour, if not the year: a courageous and adventurous 22 break-out from Liam Williams, maximised through magnificent length-of-the-field support work. But we finished a poor second at 30–15. We didn't match them in contact, we weren't nearly fast enough in getting off the floor and back into the game – the All Blacks were up on their feet one and a half seconds quicker than us on average, a huge differential – and we were far too quiet in the vocal sense. We didn't impose ourselves in any respect and that was bitterly disappointing.

One further thing alarmed me. I felt the All Blacks were just a touch over-physical when it came to putting the heat on Conor Murray close to the breakdowns. At one point, Jerome Kaino dived on our scrum-half just after he had put boot to ball and landed hard on his leg. It was dangerous, and I said so. The next thing I knew, Steve Hansen had contacted a radio station and rejected any suggestion that his players had acted in a questionable fashion. Why did Steve do it? Was he feeling the pressure too? It was an odd reaction. If he'd wanted to take it up with me, he had my phone number.

The final midweek game, against the Hurricanes in Wellington, was a whole mix of things: abrasive, free-scoring, strangely error-prone from our point of view. We were up 31–7 at one point, but we failed to think our way through the remaining minutes and ended up drawing 31-all. It was a flat way for those players to sign off, but they showed enough spirit at the back end of the game to shut out a twenty-one-phase attack before turning over the ball. That was brave. A whole lot braver, I felt, than the *NZ Herald*, which had trotted out the clown cartoon again on the morning of the match. It was getting personal. It was also out of step with the public take on the tour. In the real world, away from the parallel universe of the media, I was receiving heart-warming support from large numbers of New Zealand rugby followers who found a way to contact me by phone and online. If I was a clown, I was a popular one.

One down in the series with two to play, the next selection had to be right. No ifs or buts. We decided Maro Itoje had to play in the Wellington Test: we needed that extraordinary engine of his at the heart of the forward operation. But who to let go? In the end, we chose to play Alun Wyn Jones over George Kruis, preferring his international experience to the younger man's cutting-edge skills at the line-out. It was a close-run thing and Alun Wyn knew it. 'Thanks for sticking with me,' he said after the announcement. 'I won't let you down.' We also turned to Sam Warburton, who replaced Peter O'Mahony. This was difficult for Peter. Captain one week, nowhere the next. It wasn't that he hadn't done a good job for us at Eden Park, but given the nature of our defeat, it seemed to me that Sam offered the precise qualities we had been missing. The other change was in the midfield, where Johnny Sexton came in at 10 and Owen Farrell moved to inside centre in place of Ben Te'o. We needed to play some rugby and Ben wasn't really a passing centre. The Sexton–Farrell axis stood more chance of wrong-footing and stretching the All Blacks. They had more rugby in them in the footballing sense.

Interestingly enough, the flavour of the build-up changed abruptly two days before the game when Steve Hansen took a public swipe at the *NZ Herald* for their ground-breaking contribution to rugby journalism. He gave them both barrels. So too did my old colleague and rival in the hooking department, the great All Black captain Sean Fitzpatrick. Following a press conference, I saw Sean and Josh Kronfeld, another silver-ferned legend, at the back of the room. Sean had written a piece condemning the *Herald* for its coverage and I thanked him. It seemed I had some pretty big names on my side.

Despite the pressure, I felt good about the Test. I was aware that down the decades, Wellington had been the least forbidding of the great New Zealand rugby fortresses. In addition, the weather had turned sour: lots of wind, plenty of rain. That might slow the All Blacks' momentum. Most importantly of all, our opponents had been forced into back-line changes because of injuries to Ben Smith and Ryan Crotty. These factors wouldn't give us victory on a plate, of course: there had been plenty of great All Black performances in Wellington to set against the duds, and as we were the ones looking to play with width and tempo, the weather wasn't an unmitigated blessing. As for the new faces in the New Zealand side, neither Anton Lienert-Brown nor Waisake Naholo could be considered a weak link. But there was a shift in balance, all the same. I could sense it.

There were some thunderous hits early on – I remember Alun Wyn making good on his pre-match promise by smashing seven bells out of Owen Franks – and our carrying was far stronger than it had been at Eden Park. And then it happened. Sonny Bill Williams clattered Anthony Watson with a leading shoulder to the head, the Lions players reacted immediately, the French referee Jérôme Garcès asked for a closer look on the big screen and suddenly, the All Blacks were down to fourteen men. Red card for Sonny Bill, off you go. For good. To make matters better for us, they decided to remove the formidable Jerome Kaino from the back row and send on Ngani Laumape to shore up the midfield. That call surprised me at the time and still surprises me now. I would have kept a full pack on the field and made do and mended with clever positioning in the backs. From thereon in, we slowly chiselled out an advantage and made it pay in the last quarter. Taulupe Faletau scored a really good try down the left, running through and over Israel Dagg, and there was a big moment from Conor Murray deep in the game, dummying his way to the line after a strong drive from Jamie George. A nerveless Farrell penalty wrapped it up, 24–21. We were still alive. And as life is worth celebrating, I set about doing so. A magnum of champagne in the family room with Trudi, Gabby, Bryn and other members of the Gatland clan; a quick change of clothes and a 300-yard walk to an Irish bar called D4; a 3 am stroll back to the hotel; more wine in the team room with Graham Rowntree and Rob Howley; lights out at 4 am. 'Today makes up for all the disappointments of 2005,' said John Feehan at one point during the high jinks, referring to the 'blackwash' of Clive Woodward's party. I knew nothing about that. I was simply living in, and loving, the moment.

After the 'Mutiny on the Buses' episode in 2009 and the Noosa adventure in 2013, I felt we had a model worth standing by: some quality rest and relaxation away from the public frenzy between Test Two and Test Three, supplemented by liquid refreshment for those who wanted it. So it was that the entire party headed to Queenstown in the South Island. Or rather, almost the entire party. As Sean O'Brien had been cited for a 'swinging arm' on Naholo in Wellington, I was one of a small group of management who stayed in town for the disciplinary hearing at the head offices of the New Zealand RFU. It was a long hearing, but after a nervous wait the case was dismissed. Sean was not best pleased at missing out on the fun in Queenstown – I think it's fair to say that he has nothing against a social event – and I could have done without the hassle. Trudi and Gabby had headed down there on the Sunday. Me? I missed all the fun. Such is life.

At that late stage of an exhausting tour, there was not much to be done apart from naming an unchanged side and building up gently towards the decider. I knew the All Blacks would come back at us hard, but I also believed the force was with us and that we could be the first visiting side to win at Eden Park since the French in 1994. I felt we had them worried a little, that we were the ones going into the game with confidence. I even said to Gabby the night before the match: 'If it goes our way tomorrow, you can go shopping and buy whatever you like.' Her eyes lit up. Why do I do it to myself?

There was not much point in banging on to the players about the scale and importance of the match. That would have been stating the blindingly obvious. I simply stressed to them that they should under no circumstances allow such an occasion to pass them by. Sam, meanwhile, announced plans to stare down the haka – not to the extent that Ryan Jones and the Wales team had done on that famous day in Cardiff, but just for a few seconds to send out a message. 'I'll count to five and walk away then,' he said. The All Blacks broke up first. Excellent.

This was the biggest game outside of a World Cup final. Because of the twelve-year Lions cycle, many of the All Blacks may have considered it the biggest game full stop. It was certainly tense – you could see that by the number of mistakes from both sides – and it became incredibly attritional. The All Blacks scored an opening try after a long run from Laumape following Beauden Barrett's interception of an Owen Farrell pass, our concession of a line-out in the scramble defence and a cross-kick to the right corner, from which Laumape touched down. Afterwards, Jonathan Davies apologised to me. 'I should have stopped him on that cross-kick,' he said, 'but my legs had gone. I had nothing there.' When I looked at the tape, it was Jonathan who had chased back after a fourteen-phase Lions attack lasting the best part of four minutes to make a hell of a tackle on Laumape. No wonder he was knackered. That one conversation gives you an insight into what makes 'Foxy' a world-class centre.

Laumape was instrumental again when Jordie Barrett scored a second try before the break, the All Blacks sucking in our midfield and doing us for width. But Owen, not in the greatest form of his life in some respects, was in brilliant shape with the boot and his four penalties, together with a howitzer from Elliot Daly, meant we were all square at 15–15 in the final minutes. It was a zero-sum game now: every tiny mistake was a massive advantage to the opposition. And I have to admit that for a moment, I feared we had made the mistake that would really matter. The restart from Owen's last penalty a little over two minutes from time went high on Liam Williams, who spilled the ball in aerial contact into Kieran Read, the New Zealand captain. The ricochet fell to Ken Owens, on the field as substitute hooker, and at first glance it looked as though Ken had held the ball for a split-second before dropping it. The Kiwis, players and crowd together, appealed for offside and Romain Poite duly awarded them the shot at goal they craved.

I was in quite a state up there in the coaches' box. 'Please God, don't let us lose it like this,' I said, to everyone in general and no one in particular. At this point, Sam Warburton played a blinder, asking ever-so-politely if it might be worth checking upstairs as to the exact chain of events. There was plenty to check, in fairness: for example, it is clear now that Read was offside from the kick-off, and not so clear that he was ever in a position to catch the ball despite his head start. It is equally clear that Ken Owens thought on his feet by unplaying the ball immediately he had played it. The upshot was that Poite changed his mind on advice from his colleagues and awarded the All Blacks a scrum for an 'accidental offside'. This was his 'deal', as he interestingly put it. The All Blacks were flabbergasted – I don't think I've ever seen Kieran Read, a gentleman of the game, so unhappy at a decision – but for us, it was a result. They're still talking about it in New Zealand now and I can see their point: we were lucky to survive intact. There again, Aaron Paterson, a Kiwi friend of mine who does a lot of Television Match Official work, felt the ball had gone lateral off Liam Williams, not forwards. That was his take. I'm in no hurry to argue with him.

All that was left was to thank the players for efforts that had bordered on the superhuman – for the occasion, I donned my favourite tour burgundy smoking jacket – and get on with the enjoyable task of catching up with family and friends. Oh yes, I almost forgot. There was the press conference. After the last clown cartoon in the *Herald*, I'd asked Luke Broadley to source a red nose and a bow-tie straight out of the Big Top. 'You're not going to do this, are you?' people asked as I made my way to the briefing room. 'Yes, I am,' I replied. On went the nose – I didn't bother with the rest of it – and in I went. It generated plenty of laughs.

There was a post-trip hangover of the unfortunate variety when Sean O'Brien, who had performed outstandingly well, made some critical comments on an Irish radio station about the management of the tour. He was particularly hard on Rob Howley, claiming that Johnny Sexton and Owen Farrell had been the ones driving things forward. I took it personally and contacted him. 'What I can't understand, Sean, is your claim that we should have won the series 3–0,' I told him. 'That's pretty disrespectful. The ABs aren't a bad side, after all. You've also said that you were in the best shape of your life, so people must have been doing something right somewhere. What's the issue?' He said he felt we had taken too much time off in the week of the Third Test. I reminded him that we had done the same in 2013. 'Did we?' 'Yes, Sean, we did.' I could have done without it: as usual, public criticism of the coaching staff from a high-profile player meant 'open slather' (free rein) for the press. But leaving that aside, I took, and continue to take, great satisfaction from our achievement.

No one had given us a chance of avoiding defeat in the series. Not with that 'crazy' schedule, that 'suicidal' itinerary. Yet avoid it we did. We might even have won it. And if an outsider looks at the Test statistics without knowing which team is in which column, he or she would see that when it came to front-rowers carrying and passing the ball – indeed, when it came to passes and offloads overall – the figures favour the Lions, not the New Zealanders. We showed a lot of skill and attacking intent on the toughest tour of them all, as well as an ocean's worth of heart and character. If you can't draw satisfaction from that . . .

Incidentally, as no one, least of all myself, had considered a draw in that final Test match, my daughter reminded me of the 'shopping' promise if we won. Didn't it still count with a draw? Maybe I owe her.

13

TALES OF SADNESS AND JOY

Fifteen months or so after the emotional highs and lows of that Lions series in my home country, during which the love and support of my family had played such a fundamental role, my dad passed away. He was seventy-seven years old. Sadly, he had not been well enough to attend any of the 2017 tour games and had even stopped strolling down to the local working men's club for a few beers, a flutter on the horses and a chat with his mates. He was admitted to Waikato Hospital in Hamilton for checks on his blood circulation, then fell as he was leaving and suffered a broken pelvis. Doctors quickly discovered a whole lot of other issues going on. 'He really isn't a well person,' one of them told Trudi, who, along with other family members, was visiting him most days.

The decline was swift. I believe that once it became clear to Dad that he wouldn't be going home – that he would instead need round-the-clock care in a nursing establishment – he made his peace with the inevitable. He had always been an independent spirit, very much his own man, and the thought of being completely reliant on others must have horrified him. Meanwhile, I was on the other side of the world, wondering what to do. The answer came suddenly when, as I was talking to Trudi on the phone, my sister Kim contacted her to say he had died. That same afternoon, I was on a flight to New Zealand.

We decided to hold the funeral within a day or so of my arrival and then spend the weekend reminiscing and celebrating his life with those who knew and loved him. Dad's grandchildren, including Bryn, carried the coffin and we performed a haka as he left the club – a ceremonial, deeply personal way of bidding him farewell on his journey to a better place. He may have been an undemonstrative man, as I found out during my childhood, but he had always followed my fortunes closely and, in his own way, felt a sense of pride. I'm sure of that, just as I'm sure that he was proud of Bryn and Gabby. For the burial, we dressed him in a Wales polo shirt. He would have loved that.

All this happened in late October 2018, just about at the mid-point of my two-year cycle leading Wales into the World Cup in Japan. For more than twelve months, I had been concentrating on developing strength in depth within the squad as a means of maximising our chances of success at the global tournament, and while the initial results were mixed in terms of the numbers on the scoreboard, I was clear in my own mind that we were heading in the right direction. In the 2017 autumn internationals, there was another forward shift against the Springboks – a 24–22 victory built around a fast start and another flawless goal-kicking performance from Leigh Halfpenny. We scored three tries in the first half, two of them from Hadleigh Parkes on his debut in midfield, and that was enough to see us home. Hadleigh was born and raised in Hunterville, no more than 150 miles from Hamilton, and had played Super Rugby in both New Zealand and South Africa before moving to Llanelli and committing himself to the Scarlets. He qualified for Wales through residency and I saw him as a potential answer to the problem created by the slowly diminishing powers of Jamie Roberts as a Test centre. Subsequent events would bear me out.

Now that our record against the big southern hemisphere trio was looking a little more respectable – Wales had won three of their last four contests with the South Africans, having beaten them only once in twenty-nine previous attempts stretching back to 1906 – I was confident of generating further momentum through 2018 and hitting the World Cup at full gallop. I was even more convinced of something else, namely that the clock was ticking down on my long tour of duty in Cardiff. In recent times, I've lost count of the number of people professing their astonishment at my decision to leave Wales and head for home after the competition in Japan, but I'd made up my mind long before I made my intentions public. Why cut the cord at this point in my career? For one thing, the Welsh Rugby Union never asked me to stay on. At no point did they approach me with the offer of a further contract extension or even open discussions along the lines of 'could we tempt you . . . ?' or 'would you consider . . . ?' Hand on heart, I'd have turned down the opportunity even if it had been offered. By the end of the 2018 Six Nations, I knew I'd be on my way. The Wales experience had been fantastic for me and I'd fallen completely in love with the tension of the big occasion and the crackling electricity of sending out a team in front of full-house crowds at the best rugby stadium of them all, but I hadn't been involved in day-to-day coaching since 2007 and was missing it more and more with each passing season. I also felt I needed a break from the prioritising and compromising and corner-cutting that is part and parcel of the international scene. And yes, there was the lure of home to consider. While Gabby and her now fiancé Sam were staying with me during my last year in Cardiff, and working for law firms, my wife was living in New Zealand for most of the year and Bryn was playing his rugby there, going from strength to strength with the Blues and, latterly, in Dunedin with the Highlanders. The end of this latest World Cup cycle would be the perfect point to reintroduce myself to the normal rhythms of family life.

There was, however, still plenty of work to be done and it began with the 2018 Six Nations. Until the last minute of the opening game, against Scotland in Cardiff, we were 34–0 up. That's what you call a decent start. The Scots scored a late converted try, but we'd laid down our marker for the tournament and felt we had a more than reasonable chance of establishing ourselves as title favourites by winning at Twickenham the following week. We might have done it but for a bizarre call from Glenn Newman, the television match official, who denied Gareth Anscombe a perfectly good try on the grounds that there hadn't been clear downward pressure on the ball as it crossed the goal-line. As the incident was replayed on the big screen, Owen Farrell, the England centre and one of the big voices in their team, started to walk towards his own posts to await the conversion. He knew it was a try, as did I. Unfortunately, the one person who didn't know it was Glenn. And he was a New Zealander, too! He'd been flown all the way across the world to make the big calls, only to get the biggest one wrong. I called it out for what it was – a stone cold mistake – immediately after the game, and in the days following, World Rugby did the same. A fat lot of good it did us. Bang went the game. Bang went our best shot at the championship.

In the event, we finished second. There you have the margins in international rugby, in all their microscopic glory. Had Gareth been awarded the try he deserved and had we managed to complete a comeback after a really disappointing spell either side of half-time against Ireland in Dublin instead of having a crucial last-minute pass intercepted by the dangerous Ulster wing Jacob Stockdale, we would have been Grand Slammers once again. But that's sport. The Irish, fair play to them, rode their luck in that second half against us and then played some convincing rugby against Scotland and England to complete a clean sweep of their own. I was more frustrated with our misfortune than disappointed with our performance. The key outcome from my perspective was that we'd blooded a couple of new players, Josh Adams on the wing and James Davies at open-side flanker, and given more high-pressure experience to the likes of Hadleigh Parkes outside the scrum and Cory Hill and Josh Navidi in the pack. Our selection options were improving all the time.

The process took another upturn during the summer, when we played the Springboks in Washington DC – another of rugby union's attempts to secure a foothold in the vast American sports market – and then travelled to Argentina for a two-Test series with matches in San Juan and Santa Fe. Not for the first time since the turn of the year, I decided to ask new questions in selection rather than fall back on the same old answers. Not for the first time, there was some unrest in the media. After the Dublin game in the Six Nations, I had been criticised for making a dozen changes for the following match against Italy, with some people accusing me of disrespecting our opponents. I had laughed off the accusation because it was plainly ridiculous: no one gets far in top-level sports coaching by treating other teams with contempt. My job was to piece together a World Cup squad as well as a winning Test side and that selection was a step along the way. So too were the decisions around the tour party.

So often, the reporting in Britain and Ireland has focused on the big-name players left out of a team rather than on the fresh talent drafted into it. For all my problems with aspects of the media back in New Zealand over the years, I think the broadcasters and writers there take a more positive approach in this area and are generally more interested in unfamiliar faces being promoted into the Super Rugby sides or the All Blacks. In Wales, especially, it was different: at times, I felt it was easier to add new faces to the existing group rather than force someone to make way for them – to pick a squad of thirty-six or thirty-seven rather than thirty-one or thirty-two. Was it a sad indictment, tinkering with selection policy purely in an effort to generate a feelgood factor in the press? Maybe, but that's the way I saw it.

For the trip to the Americas, I left out the vast majority of the players who had emptied themselves of energy with the Lions a year previously yet still backed up in the autumn internationals and the Six Nations. There was no Leigh Halfpenny or Liam Williams or Jonathan Davies; no Ken Owens or Justin Tipuric or Alun Wyn Jones. I took Ross Moriarty because his Lions tour had been cut so short by injury. George North went too because he had suffered his disappointments in New Zealand and needed to prove a point. Typically, Dan Biggar also wanted a seat on the plane, but I insisted that he take a break. He wasn't happy: he would run through a wall for you every day of the week. But Dan had just agreed a move to the English Premiership with Northampton and I wanted him to be in the best place to make a go of it. And besides, there were other No 10s demanding some attention.

Would I have taken the same approach had we been playing the All Blacks rather than the Pumas? It would have been difficult without causing no end of self-inflicted pain. Go in light at Eden Park and you're likely to ship seventy points. Without belittling the Argentines for a second, it isn't quite the same down there. I had an opportunity to cast an eye over a significant number of relatively inexperienced players: almost twenty of them were still in the single-figure-caps category, from the hookers Elliott Dee and Ryan Elias, through the props Wyn Jones and Adam Beard, to the scrum-halves Aled Davies and Tomos Williams and the centres Hadleigh Parkes and Owen Watkin. There were joint captains in Cory Hill and Ellis Jenkins – another experiment – and both of them justified the faith placed in them. I promised every tourist some game time and delivered on the pledge, despite some robust discussions in selection. Across the three games there were twenty-five different starters. The policy generated its own energy and we came home with three victories. What was more, I knew there were a good number of front-line internationals back in Wales, watching our performances on television and thinking: 'Jeez, we've got our work cut out here.' Suddenly, there was a serious push on some of our more established players. Which was exactly what I wanted. When the elite squad reconvened for the autumn internationals, I could almost smell the apprehension. There was no comfort zone for anyone now: the senior men, even those with masses of Lions experience, knew they were under pressure from the junior ranks and almost to a man, they reacted positively to the challenge.

Sadly, the Lion King himself was no longer a member of our pride. Sam Warburton was gone. About a month after our return from South America, my long-term captain announced his retirement from all rugby, explaining that the physical wear and tear of life as a completely committed back-rower at the top end of an unrelentingly demanding sport had left him no choice. It was a massive call for Sam, who had not yet reached the age of thirty, but if I'm being frank, I was not surprised when he phoned me to say he had made his decision and that there would be no second thoughts. I knew how hard he had struggled to overcome serious neck and knee injuries. I also knew that he had been considering his options as far back as 2017. I was disappointed to lose him, of course. He had been one of the standard bearers of a new generation of professional players – a group of individuals devoted to their craft, people with the strength of character to convince their colleagues to embrace a modern code of discipline and behaviour in pursuit of the game's great prizes. Just as he had a winning way with referees, Sam had a priceless ability to strike the right notes in the team room. There was still an element of tribalism about the Wales set-up when I appointed Sam a few weeks before his twenty-third birthday and dealing with it wasn't easy for him. He was seen as 'the coach's choice', as a Cardiff Blues man through and through, and there were those from other regions, notably amid the Ospreys contingent, who were a little reluctant to devote themselves to him until he had proved his worth. But by and large, he won people round through his honesty and dedication. It took a special player to achieve that at so young an age. Few people could have managed it.

At twenty-nine, he still had more to give. But I understood his decision. His body had taken a serious hammering over the years, to the extent that the WRU had granted him a six-month sabbatical on full pay and extended it to a full year in recognition of his efforts in the national shirt. He had embarked on pre-season training with an eye on returning for the autumn Tests, realised quite quickly that things were wrong and felt he had no option but to bite the bullet. 'I don't want to see you retire,' I said to him during that phone call, 'but the most important things are your health and your family.' And I meant it. We are talking here about people with thirty, forty and fifty years of life ahead of them. What do we know about the long-term effects of rugby on their wellbeing? Not enough. The sport has done the right thing in recognising the issues around concussion, but what about the impacts of hip and knee replacements, of serious neck problems? Every time I hear someone say that professional players earn a very good living, I say they deserve everything they get. They also have the right to call it a day at the moment of their choosing, for their own reasons.

With Alun Wyn Jones taking on the captaincy and some of the younger players – the tight-head prop Dillon Lewis, for instance – building strongly on their efforts during the tour, the autumn series was good for us: four victories from four against Scotland, Australia, Tonga and South Africa, taking our winning streak to nine – the longest since Graham Henry, my fellow New Zealander, strung together a ten-game run back in 1999. I was certainly relieved to find a way past the Wallabies, given our bitterly frustrating record of narrow failures against them. It was hardly a free-running classic, but Dan Biggar came off the bench to nail the late penalty that allowed us to win the day by the old-fashioned margin of 9–6. Rugby's history books are crammed with players who proved weak under pressure as the clock ticked down. Dan is made of different stuff. He wanted to start that game, just as he wants to start every game when Wales take the field. Not for the first time or the last, he held his nerve and made it work for the team.

Yet even more than the win over the Australians, I took encouragement from the subsequent performances against Tonga and South Africa. For years, we had struggled to beat so-called 'developing' or 'second-tier' nations in autumn Tests on home soil. Sometimes, we hadn't beaten them at all. There was a 16–16 draw against Fiji in 2010 and a 26–19 loss to Samoa two years later. Between 2014 and 2017, our autumn international victories over Fiji, Japan and Georgia were by a grand aggregate margin of fourteen points. Our previous meeting with the Tongans in 2013 had ended in a 17–7 win, achieved only after a scoreless dogfight of a second half. This time, it was different. A team full of bright young things ran in ten tries in a 74–24 triumph. It was the kind of scoreline delivered by the All Blacks on a ruthless day and it said something about the level we had reached, not as a team but as a squad.

A week later, we saw off a Springbok side brimming with big names: Willie le Roux, Cheslin Kolbe and Handré Pollard;

Malcolm Marx, Franco Mostert and Duane Vermeulen. The most satisfying moment came not when Tomas Francis and Liam Williams set the tone with early tries, or when Dan Biggar delivered two more of his 'off the bench' penalties to secure our 20–11 win, but when I picked up some after-match intelligence from one of the tour liaison officers. Standing outside the Springbok changing room as their inquest began, he heard their highly capable coach, Rassie Erasmus, say: 'I told you before we came on this trip that this would be our hardest game, our most physical game.' It was music to my ears. Over the previous three weeks, the Boks had won in Edinburgh and Paris, and lost by a single point at Twickenham in a game they should have won comfortably. To be singled out by Rassie was more proof that we were on a good track.

So much so, in fact, that before the start of the 2019 Six Nations, I decided to deliver a 'watch out for Wales' message to the wider rugby public. There's no better way of doing that than saying your piece in front of a room full of journalists, and as I'd been invited to the annual Rugby Union Writers' Club dinner in central London, the opportunity was heaven-sent. Sarah Mockford, the editor of *Rugby World* magazine and the chair of the organisation, asked me if I'd join two or three other guests in a brief Q&A session. One of those guests was my old flatmate and fellow Waikato forward John Mitchell, now on the England coaching panel as defence specialist. Even better! I was late on stage, not because I wanted to make a grand entrance but because I was in the toilet when the panel was introduced. Just about my first utterance went something like this: 'If we beat France in our opening game, we'll win the title.' John's face was quite a picture, but I wasn't joking. Far from it. I honestly believed we would be crowned champions if we emerged from Paris with a result. I was also confident that my words would be faithfully reported in the press, under banner headlines. Which they were. Just for once, I was the master of my own publicity.

If some people wondered if I had set myself up for a fall, there was some method in the madness. I wanted to send out an upbeat message to the Wales players and fire a shot at our opponents. The results were immediate. At one point during the dinner, Johnny Sexton appeared on the same stage to receive an award in recognition of his trophy-winning efforts for Leinster and Ireland in 2018. 'It'll be a waste of time playing the Six Nations,' he told the audience. 'Warren has already told us who'll be winning it.' Result. Even though Johnny was being ironic, he was playing the game I hoped he would play. My words had registered. It was the same story when we began our preparations for the tournament. The players drew strength from the fact that I'd been prepared to back them in public rather than behind closed doors. When I went further by telling them that I felt they could win the World Cup as well as the Six Nations, it really resonated with them. I remember saying to Liam Williams, who was in the middle of a hot spell in England with Saracens: 'You know, I'm sitting here visualising you winning the

Premiership, the European Champions Cup, the Grand Slam and the World Cup. That'll be a first.' As a motivational tool, it was perfect. By the end of the domestic season, the first three of those predictions had come true.

Not that every member of the squad was feeling as good about life as Liam, who had established himself as a near-automatic starter, either at full-back or on the wing. After a training session ahead of the France match, the Scarlets tight-head prop Samson Lee approached me. 'What do I have to do to get back in the match squad?' he asked. With the World Cup only a few months distant, I could understand his concern. Samson had spent the last couple of campaigns struggling with injury, and during that time Dillon Lewis had come on in leaps and bounds. I didn't respond immediately. Instead, I thought about it over lunch. When the conversation resumed, I said: 'Help me out here, Samson. What am I going to say to Dillon if I pick you ahead of him and he comes up to me wanting to know what he's done wrong? Because I won't have an answer for him.' It wasn't an easy moment, but I'm pretty sure that by the end of our little chat, Samson understood that in a team sport, it can never be about one individual and his personal perspective. There is always someone else in the equation, with a perspective of his own.

To many people, my bold statement at the London dinner must have seemed pretty daft at half-time on opening night in Paris. The French were very good indeed in that forty minutes, with their power game on the maximum setting (they were massive up front, their pack weighing 50 kg more than ours) and their off-loads going to hand despite the wet conditions. Louis Picamoles, a No 8 who takes an awful lot of stopping when he gets himself on the front foot, scored an early try, and that was followed by a score from the wing Yoann Huget, an equally powerful proposition in his own way. At the break, they were 16–0 up. It could have been even worse: had Morgan Parra kicked his goals, they would have been miles out of sight. There was, to say the least, some work to do in the changing room, but with only a quarter of an hour to play with, there was no point over-complicating the message.

'Score first,' I said. 'That's the key. Whatever happens, we have to be the next to score, even if it's a penalty or a drop goal. Do that and there's a way back.'

Did I really feel we had it in us? Absolutely I did, even though we would need the biggest comeback in Six Nations history to win the game. Despite our early problems, Liam Williams had been one of the most threatening players on the field. Alongside him in the back three were George North and Josh Adams, and I was certain they could hurt the French if we could just work them into space. As it turned out, we *did* score first, Josh breaking into open field and presenting Tomos Williams with a try on his tournament debut. Then George took over, capitalising on mistakes by Huget and the giant second-rower Sebastien Vahaamahina to see us home 24–19. As the game swung our way, you could see the belief drain from the faces of the home players. By the end, their faith in themselves had completely evaporated. That was the difference. 'The French are looking for confidence,' I told the media afterwards. 'We've forgotten how to lose.'

I suppose some would dismiss that comment as a glib one-liner, trotted out for want of something better to say. But in reality, it had substance. Ever since the Lions tour, when those involved proved that a rough start in a high-stakes environment did not necessarily have to be terminal, I had prioritised mindset and attitude above virtually everything else. The All Blacks were the benchmark when it came to maintaining discipline under pressure and being ruthless in taking opportunities in the final quarters of matches, when it really mattered. I wanted us to raise our level in the mental side of rugby because our long record of losing tight contests late in the day proved there was a problem to be addressed. Does success breed success? Only if you work at it – and we were definitely working. By winning in France in the way we did, we showed that we were developing the toughness necessary to head for the World Cup with legitimate ambitions.

The big tournament in Japan was at the forefront of my mind as the Six Nations unfolded. We took thirty-one players to France and stayed together in Nice before travelling down to Rome for the game with Italy the following weekend, with everyone playing a full role not just in training, but in the pre-match warm-ups too. Why? Because we would be taking thirty-one to Japan and I wanted us to have an early dry run. I made a lot of changes for the Italy game and spent a restless night on the eve of the match wondering if I had overdone it, but again, this was exactly the kind of situation I would face at the World Cup. Happily, we ground out a 26–15 victory on the back of second-half tries from Josh Adams and Owen Watkin and some flawless kicking from Dan Biggar and Gareth Anscombe. It was hardly a vintage performance, but the job was done.

Next up: England. The Arch-Enemy. At home. In a fortnight. Ever since that third Lions Test against the All Blacks in Auckland in 2017, when we cracked after an extreme spell of ball-in-play lasting fully six minutes and allowed them to score the opening try, I had put long periods of high-intensity training at the heart of our squad sessions. In the first week of preparation before the England game, the players ran themselves into the ground. Looking back, I was on the brink of pushing them too hard. But at the same time, I was able to say: 'England aren't training as hard as us. No one trains as hard as us. They have no idea who's turning up to play them. Not a clue.' And I doubled down on it, time and time again. 'They don't have a clue. They have no idea.' It was almost a chant. Within days, the players were using the same words among themselves.

I reinforced the message in the second week, but there was also talk of strategy. I emphasised discipline, about bringing our fitness to bear on the contest, about dominating the aerial game, about keeping the ball on the park and making England run rather than allowing them to build off the scrums and line-outs they saw as their comfort blankets.

I knew that their entire game was based around Billy Vunipola, Ben Youngs and Owen Farrell – around Nos 8, 9 and 10 – and that if we could disrupt them there and break the link, we would win. So instead of putting width on the ball early, we attacked them through the middle. Sam Warburton, sitting in the television commentary box, expressed some bewilderment at our close-quarters approach, but the penny dropped with him as our ascendancy grew after the break. We went after Vunipola in numbers, stopped Youngs running off the rucks and piled the heat on Farrell. In short, we stopped them at source. If Steve Borthwick, my coaching colleague in New Zealand in 2017, had been spending three hours a day concocting new line-out routines, he'd been wasting his time. England didn't have more than three or four throws all match and by the time Cory Hill scored a wonderful try after a long attack of twenty-odd phases, they knew they were on the slide. Josh Adams added another try two minutes from time to wrap it up 21–13. It was a rewarding moment for everyone involved.

There were also some 'moments' afterwards. Alan Phillips, our team manager, was informed that instead of participating fully in the after-match function, the England contingent would be making a quick getaway straight after the speeches. This was a bit rich – after defeats at Twickenham, we had often hung around for an hour and a half, waiting for the England players to fulfil their commercial commitments in the private boxes – and Alan said so with a degree of force. Happy, he was not. When I finally made it into the banqueting venue, there were no replays of the game on the screens dotted around the room. What I didn't realise until later was that England had gone to Gareth Davies, the chairman of the Welsh Rugby Union, and asked for the television sets to be switched off. If I'd known it at the time, I would have hit the roof. I'd had my nose rubbed in it on more than one occasion up the road in London. Here in Cardiff, such behaviour was suddenly deemed improper. What a joke. When you lose in rugby, you should lose well.

In truth though, nothing could ruin the day for those who hold Welsh rugby close to their hearts. Least of all the supporters. Wales is probably the most intense of all rugby environments, a union nation enveloped in its own history, and just occasionally, the past is allowed to take precedence over the present. After the Lions tour in 2017, I attended a dinner and found myself talking to one of the Welsh players who had tasted victory over the All Blacks under Carwyn James and John Dawes in 1971. 'I watched the last Test at home and when the final whistle blew, I jumped up and shouted "yessss"', he told me. I felt really happy that our success in squaring the series had brought him such pleasure. And then he said: 'We're still the only team to have won a Lions Test series down there in New Zealand.' I sat back and thought: 'Oh my God.' But that incident was a rarity during my years working with the Wales team. Ninety-nine per cent of the time, I was able to draw on the unconditional backing of the overwhelming majority of the rugby public – backing that helped the coaches and players through the difficult spells and played a key part in generating momentum on the field. When the massed ranks of that 74,000-strong choir start singing the team home, there is no feeling to match it.

The rush of energy and inspiration was still there a fortnight later when we met the Scots at Murrayfield. We were really good in the first half, Josh Adams continuing his hot streak with an early try and Jonathan Davies adding another to give us a nine-point lead at the break. It was enough. Scotland found ways to break up the game in the second half, but our defensive effort, led by Hadleigh Parkes and Justin Tipuric, restricted our opponents to a single try from Darcy Graham and earned us an 18–11 victory. Afterwards, Hadleigh talked about the 'amazing' spirit of camaraderie in the team. As a coach, you take some satisfaction from such sentiments. You could have a team full of world-beaters, cutting-edge tactics and the best conditioning programme in the world. But without a sense of togetherness, it wouldn't mean a thing.

Eighty minutes away from another Grand Slam, it was time to look at the long-range weather forecast. Under the rules of the tournament, the roof at our Principality Stadium could not be shut unless both sides agreed, and it was important to work out how Ireland might address the issue. I have to be honest here: right the way through my time in Wales, I not only took the view that we should always play indoors, but also felt that the most influential figures on the union should have been far more vocal in supporting that opinion.

They should have been saying: 'We have a roof and we're going to use it.' No other union in world rugby would have been so reticent on the subject, so willing to allow other countries to dictate the terms of engagement, and it was a frequent source of frustration. But when Ireland asked for the roof to be opened, I was not exactly broken-hearted. We were looking at a wet Test and given the way the Irish were shaping their game under Joe Schmidt, I was happily surprised. 'This suits us,' I thought, 'so just for once, I think I'll shut up about the roof.' At one point, with the rain coming down in torrents and the forecast worsening by the hour, some WRU officials started talking about closing the roof on safety grounds. My response: 'No, no, no . . . let's leave it.'

The Australian referee Angus Gardner had been awarded the game and he asked to do some pre-match training at our Vale of Glamorgan base. The weather was so grim, he was desperate for an indoor venue! During the anthems, I saw him peering up at the sky in what looked to me like bewilderment. If I'd been asked to read his thoughts, I'd have made a good stab at it. He wouldn't have been the first person to say to himself: 'What the hell are we doing here, playing in a monsoon when there's a roof available?'

We started like a side with a big prize within reach and scored early through Hadleigh Parkes, who latched on to an intelligent 'scoring kick' from Gareth Anscombe. The two of them were excellent right the way through the match, Gareth's accuracy from the tee and Hadleigh's outstanding try-saving tackle on Jacob Stockdale being the most obvious highlights in a dominant performance, during which we accumulated twenty-five points without reply until, in the final seconds, we conceded a try to Jordan Larmour that could not have been less relevant in the great scheme of things. Did the Slam mean more to me than those of 2008 and 2012? It's difficult to say. There was a sentimental dimension because I knew it was my final Six Nations with the team I'd grown to love and I was swept away by the jubilation of the supporters. But comparisons are always difficult. All I can say is that I could not conceivably have wished for a better outcome.

While I took enormous satisfaction from our achievement, I was as pleased for our captain as I was for myself. Alun Wyn Jones had been a member of the Wales pack for a couple of years when I arrived in the country and was clearly a player with a long-term future at international level. But I had seen him grow so much as a competitor in the years since, it was almost as if he had become another person entirely. Right from the start, I saw him as an incredible trainer. There has been no drop-off. During a session, he does not simply run from one station to the next. He sprints, flat out, each and every time. He always wants to be the first man there. That commitment allows me to say to the other players: 'There's your challenge. Get there ahead of him.' At first, he was something of a handful. Unusually feisty even in rugby terms, he was more than capable of starting a fight on the practice field. Sometimes, he could be a little negative. Sometimes, there was the hint of a bully about him. That

PRIDE AND PASSION

was my perception back then. Right now, I see him as one
of the true greats of Welsh rugby – a terrific leader and a
wonderfully consistent performer, almost to the level of the
England and Lions legend Martin Johnson. There are simi-
larities between them, but in a way I see Alun Wyn's
achievement as even more extraordinary because while
Johnson had the advantage of playing for a hugely successful
club side in Leicester, the Ospreys have rarely looked like
delivering to the same degree. Outside of the Test environment, Alun Wyn's road has been harder.

His captaincy skills have matured along with every other
aspect of his rugby. Clear and concise in his own mind, there
were times in the early days when his comments seemed a
little random and left-field to others, and it wasn't always
easy for his fellow players to get a handle on him. Now, he
has a phenomenal connection with his colleagues. He is
fiercely loyal, he flatly refuses to be treated differently to the
other members of the side (although he's recently become
better at understanding and looking after his own body) and
unlike some other Wales players over the last eleven years,
he takes full responsibility for his own shortcomings rather
than seeking to place the blame elsewhere. You have to be
straight with him: I always had the sense that if I lost his
trust, it would have gone for good. But if a coach is fair and
honest with him, as I always tried to be, he's a prize asset.
One of Alun Wyn's little rituals before a game is to shake
everyone by the hand. When he reached me, he always said:
'Thanks for the opportunity.' I will miss those moments.

350

No sooner had the Grand Slam celebrations ended than there was renewed interest in my career plans. There was a lot of comment in the press about me coaching the British and Irish Lions in South Africa in 2021 and the speculation was correct. A third successive stint as head coach, completing the set of southern hemisphere tours? It will be a huge honour. If someone had told me during my rough and ready introduction to coaching with the Galwegians club that I would one day be bracketed with Sir Ian McGeechan in any facet of rugby union, let alone this one, I would have laughed all the way to the nearest pub.

But news of my other move, back home to Waikato to run the Chiefs in Super Rugby, did not leak out. Most pundits had expected me to stay in the international game, linking me with England and France, among others. My thoughts were running in a very different direction. When the Chiefs offered me the chance to return to my roots, adding that they were happy for me to take a year's break on Lions business, it made complete sense to agree terms. My mum Kay, who had spent a long time living in New South Wales, was heading back to Hamilton to be nearer her family. So too was my sister Micharn, who had also been in Australia. The Gatland clan, together again in Mooloo country? Nothing could be more enticing. Home is where the heart is, after all – even if a little piece of my heart will always remain in Wales.

14

CHASING THE PERFECT SUNRISE

Almost a year before the start of the 2019 Rugby World Cup, I flew to Japan on a reconnaissance mission of the venues where we would be playing and preparing for our matches, from the southern cities of Oita and Kumamoto on Kyushu island to the cluster of venues around Tokyo–Yokohama, via our initial training base of Kitakyushu and the 45,000-capacity City of Toyota Stadium, where we would face Georgia in our opening match. It was typhoon season. On my return, I mentioned to a Welsh journalist that there was every chance of the tournament being affected – quite possibly badly affected – by the weather. That remark appears to have earned me a new nickname: 'The Prophet.' If only I'd been wrong.

It is often said that sports people live in a 'bubble'. I'm not sure this is entirely fair – I don't believe for a second that I'm the only person in rugby who makes an effort to keep pace with the news – but if there was a bubble mentality at the World Cup, it was blown away by the devastating 130 mph winds of Typhoon Hagibis, which ripped through the main Japanese island of Honshu on the weekend of the final round of pool matches, triggering a tornado and an earthquake in the process and killing more than eighty people. It scared me, even though I wasn't directly impacted. We were due to play our final group game against Uruguay in Kumamoto, where the weather was stunningly beautiful, but I followed the unfolding events on television with a growing sense of fear for the millions who were not so fortunate.

The conditions knocked the competition completely off balance. Three games were cancelled under tournament rules, including the New Zealand–Italy match in Toyota City – a decision that denied the Italians their chance, albeit a fanciful one, of beating the All Blacks and qualifying for the knockout stage for the first time in their history. There was also the prospect of the Japan–Scotland game in Yokohama being scrapped, and as this was a true winner-take-all contest, the consequences would have been severe. So severe, in fact, that some of rugby's leading policy makers could have found themselves in court. Happily, the weather eased and the match went ahead. Famously, in Japan's case; infamously, in the case of the Scots.

There was no doubt in my mind that the decisions made by the organisers as the typhoon neared landfall were fully justified. They had no choice in the matter, on basic safety grounds. But it is also true to say that everyone was a little nervous about the rigidity of the fixture schedule, even before the meteorologists started talking about the threat of a typhoon. For teams with a realistic prospect of reaching the knockout phase, the thought of missing out on a bonus-point victory against weaker opposition was the stuff of nightmares. Quite easily, it could have made the difference between qualification and going home. This was not lost on Sergio Parisse, the great Italy No 8 who would have run down the curtain on a fabulous international career by facing the All Blacks. 'If New Zealand had needed four or five points against us, the game would not have been cancelled,' he said after missing out on his grand finale. It was a loaded remark and it generated a good deal of discomfort among the governing class. Was he right? I guess we'll never know. What I will say is that there could, and probably should, have been a better contingency plan.

The lesson, which needs to be learned over and over again, is that even the best-laid plans are vulnerable to unfortunate turns of events. Early in our summer camp, where we were looking to reintroduce some key personnel who had missed the Grand Slam campaign, we lost Taulupe Faletau to another serious injury. It was such an innocuous thing. On the training field at the Vale, he picked up the ball from the back of a ruck, ran thirty or forty metres down the pitch and was brought down from behind by Josh Adams, who fell on him and accidentally drove his shoulder into the ground. Taulupe would have been tackled like that thousands of times down the years. This time, he broke his clavicle. And that was it. We would be going to the World Cup without a two-tour Lions No 8. On the positive side, we were no strangers to being without him and knew how to cope. It is also true to say that having missed so much rugby, he was still a fair way off from a conditioning point of view. The GPS readouts told us that much and I think it shocked him to discover just how far behind the others he had dropped. But he had been showing some of the old magic during those initial sessions, some of the X-factor stuff that had put him in the front rank of international back-rowers. We would miss him, for sure.

Then there was Gareth Anscombe's injury. Equally innocuous, equally unforeseen. I've been around this game long enough to assume that something will go wrong some-where as you head into a big tournament, but I didn't anticipate losing Gareth in the way we did. It happened about twenty minutes into the opening warm-up game against England at Twickenham: a midfield break, not so much as a finger laid upon him, a sidestep . . . and down he went. Because it wasn't a contact injury, Gareth thought he had simply jarred his knee and decided to run it off, staying on the field for another thirteen minutes. As it turned out, he had damaged both his meniscus and his cruciate ligament. It wasn't just an 'out of the World Cup' injury; it was a 'rest of the season' injury.

Inevitably, there was a lot of finger-pointing and general criticism flying around in the press, with people demanding to know why we allowed him to remain on the pitch. My answer is that I always put myself in the hands of the medics, not being a doctor myself. If a player says to them 'I'm a bit sore but I can move around okay' and they're happy with that, so am I. If they send me a message saying 'he's no good', off he comes. It is also worth pointing out that Gareth didn't make things worse by staying on. The injury had happened and there was no easy repair job to be done. If we'd made a wrong call and cost him a World Cup place because of it, I would be the first to hold up my hands. The reality is that his World Cup chances were over the moment he hit the grass.

On the subject of things not going to plan, I have to admit that we missed our mark in the warm-up matches, although not by as much as some people made out. We were pretty poor in the first twenty minutes of that opening game against England: slow off the line, a little lethargic, more than a little ragged. But even though we lost 33–19, there was nothing much between the sides after our bad start. Alun Wyn Jones, for one, was philosophical about the defeat, our first in fifteen games. 'I wouldn't say it publicly,' he told me afterwards, 'but this may not be the worst thing for us. It gets that winning-run "monkey" off our backs. And anyway, I've been in teams that have lost by forty or fifty points here after a bad start. This time, we didn't capitulate. We stayed calm and tried to find a way back into it.'

Things were different a week later, when we played England in front of our own crowd in Cardiff. If we'd pulled back emotionally at Twickenham – as I've already argued, you can't reach deep into your spirit every time you play a game of rugby – we were properly pumped up for the return and emerged with a 13–6 victory. Just as we had in the Six Nations, we did a job on England at Nos 8, 9 and 10, which is very much the key to beating them. Equally pleasing was the fact that we sharpened our game in the areas that had been blunt at Twickenham, especially in the front row, where the tackle and carry counts showed a marked improvement in the space of seven days. England introduced seven Lions off the bench while we had to run Aaron Shingler, a back-rower, in the second row and Elliot Dee, a hooker, on the flank. Yet we held out. It was a massive restatement of our powers of resilience.

It said plenty for our fitness too, indicating that our conditioning work had left us in the best possible place to push hard at the World Cup. There had been two camps overseas: the first at altitude in Switzerland, the second at sea level in Turkey. We felt the Swiss trip would replicate our previous visits to Poland, while the second trip would stress-test the players in ways that were simply not possible in Wales, even in high summer. Research pointed us in the direction of the Gloria Sports complex in Belek, in the Antalya province of south-western Turkey. There were two pitches, an athletics track, indoor and outdoor pools, multiple gyms, luxury rooms – everything required of a top-end training environment plus a few added extras, all for 90 Euros per player per day, including three square meals and unlimited water. Talk about value for money. The heat and humidity meant that the players were operating at 40-plus degrees, which was well into the red level. Anything hotter would have been dangerous, but the conditioning team – Huw Bennett, John Ashby, Ryan Chambers and the omnipresent Paul Stridgeon – were incredibly precise in their planning. It still came as a shock to the players' systems, though. 'Bobby' had ideas about revealing the training profiles in advance, then had second thoughts. He didn't want to run the risk of someone falling ill in anticipation!

There were two preparatory games left before our departure for Japan, both of them against Ireland. We experimented in selection for the first of them and lost 22–17. I knew it would be my last game in front of our home crowd and it would have meant a lot to go out with a win, but there were more important things on my mind. Certain players needed game time, certain combinations needed to be welded together. Also, there were last-minute decisions on World Cup selection to nail down, notably in the tight-five department. One of the big calls was at lock, where Cory Hill was still recovering from long-term injury. The medics were optimistic about his chances: they had taken advice from their colleagues in the Wales football set-up, who had treated a player with a similar stress fracture in the leg and got him back on the field within a month. Therefore, we decided to stick with him and take Aaron Shingler as cover. The other difficult choice was in the prop department. Rob Evans was the senior loose-head specialist in many respects, but he had been under the surgeon's knife himself and had precious little rugby behind him. We felt we needed five durable props who had enough in the tank to go full-tilt through the tournament, and as young Rhys Carre, a newcomer to the group, had the best fitness levels of any contender, the last place went to him. I gave Rob the bad news – these things are so painful, especially around a World Cup – and was proud of the way he took it. Immediately, he was on WhatsApp, wishing his colleagues the very best of luck. It spoke volumes for his character and my respect for him went through the roof.

A few days later, we were in Dublin for the last of our run-outs. This was not a comfortable afternoon, by any measure. The way Ireland dominated us in the second half to win 19–10 – how they choked us at close quarters, commanded the breakdown, and monopolised territory and possession – was a significant disappointment. There was something wrong somewhere that needed putting to bed and I thought I knew what it was. In the dressing room afterwards, I chose my words carefully. 'Look, I'm not going to be over-critical,' I told the players, 'but was there an element of some of you subconsciously thinking *I want to make sure I get myself on the plane, so no injuries*? I don't want an answer, but I need to pose the question.' Sure enough, a couple of players nodded, as though to confirm my suspicion. Not for the first time, it was Jonathan Davies who showed real guts in facing up to his own shortcomings. 'I was probably a bit like that,' he admitted to me. 'I missed the last World Cup through injury and in the back of my mind I didn't want it happening again.' It's not what you want to hear as a coach, but you understand it. I told him I wasn't one to hold that sort of thing against a player. If he is honest, he gets more credit from me than if he tries to hide something.

At least our flight to Japan took off on time, although we lost Adam Beard, a real prospect in the second row, to appendicitis during the motorway journey to Heathrow. (Adam was sent straight back to Wales for the necessary treatment and joined us a few days later, albeit 8 kg lighter than we wanted him to be.) After a couple of days in Tokyo, during which some of the players headed for Disneyland – unaccompanied by their head coach, I should add – we travelled down to Kitakyushu for what amounted to a final camp. On arrival, I couldn't believe my eyes. It was like stepping out in Cardiff on match day: Wales flags and posters everywhere, countless people dressed in red rugby jerseys. When we held an open training session, the entrance queue stretched for half a mile and 15,000 locals filled the stands. They sang 'Hen Wlad Fy Nhadau' and 'Calon Lan' in full-throated unison, which was no mean achievement. I spent a dozen years perfecting my own rendition of the national anthem and when the tournament began, I realised I was still only 90 per cent there.

If I found the Kitakyushu stadium experience humbling, it was also difficult. Really difficult. A couple of days before the open training, I received a text message from Julie Paterson, the Welsh Rugby Union operations manager, saying she needed to talk to me. When I rang her Julie told me that she and Martyn Phillips, the chief executive, were on their way to Japan and would be arriving within 24 hours. Why? Because there were allegations that Rob Howley, my friend and coaching partner of such long standing, had breached betting regulations and was facing an investigation. My heart sank. I was grateful to Julie for giving me the heads up, but I knew the next few hours were going to be painful. I told Alan Phillips, our team manager, of the situation and we decided it was only fair that Rob should hear the news from us, his closest colleagues. It was not an easy meeting. In fact, it was deeply upsetting.

Martyn and Julie gave me more details on the Sunday, then saw Rob themselves on the Monday and told him he would be heading back to Wales without further ado. The situation was surreal. Somehow, Rob found the strength and composure to play his part in the open training – the way he handled it from a professional point of view was remark-able – but he was not in the room that evening when the players were presented with their World Cup caps. He didn't feel it appropriate to attend. Only then did a few of the squad suspect that something was wrong, although no one outside a very small circle knew the details.

There was a lot going through my mind. First and fore-most, I felt the coaching team had a duty of care towards Rob. Martyn was planning to hold a press conference on the Wednesday and we all wanted to keep the flow of infor-mation under control until then. At the same time, I needed a replacement as attack coach. I met with a group of the most senior players – Alun Wyn Jones, naturally, along with

Ken Owens, Dan Biggar, Hadleigh Parkes, Jonathan Davies and Liam Williams – and gave them a full account of the position in which we now found ourselves, stressing the sensitivity of the situation and asking them to keep it to themselves as far as they were able. There were three obvious candidates to fill the vacancy: Alex King, my fly-half during the Wasps days, had been involved with Wales during my absence with the Lions in 2017 and given a very good account of himself; Matt Sherratt, who was an influential member of the coaching panel at Ospreys; and Stephen Jones, a World Cup No 10 and multi-Test Lion who was preparing to join the Wales set-up under my fellow New Zealander and successor as head coach, Wayne Pivac. The players said they would be happy with any of the three, but as several of them had played alongside Stephen and developed a deep respect for him, they saw no reason not to go for the 'next man in'. I made the necessary calls and Stephen headed for the airport.

One problem may have been solved but I was still all over the place. The same went for Alan. When we had a farewell drink with Rob – a sombre occasion, to say the least – Alan became very emotional. The players quickly picked up on how quiet we were, and while some knew more than others, everyone took on extra responsibility in holding things together. The news leaked out in Wales before Martyn's press conference, as it was bound to do: the moment there is a vague sense of something happening, journalists make phone calls to their contacts, text messages start flying back and forth and before you know it, the cat is out of the bag. I was relieved when Martyn held his briefing and did a brilliant job in saying the right things in the right places. Indeed, I had nothing but admiration for the way the WRU people conducted themselves in acting with great speed, clarity and openness. There was no ducking or diving, no misinformation or hiding behind process. And the best thing of all was the support Rob received from his fellow coaches, the Wales players and a host of others in the union community. So many people reached out to him. I will always feel proud of how the Wales rugby family reacted.

There was more to enjoy when the rugby finally broke out, especially as we started our opening pool match against Georgia in Toyota City with a hiss and a roar. Yes, we were expected to win, but with only two fit locks in the squad, I knew we would have to scrum well against a formidable set-piece unit if we were to come through unscathed. Looking back now, I was more nervous before Georgia than I was before our next game against the Wallabies. It's the 'banana skin' syndrome. There had already been controversy over the refereeing of high tackles and that increased the chances of yellow cards, not to mention red ones. The early loss of a key player can transform straightforward games against unfamiliar opposition into something far more complicated. I wanted this over and done with, frankly.

We did a lot of scrum work in the build-up and it paid off. We were secure in that department, which allowed us to dictate the pace and shape of the contest and gave our back-rowers the freedom to express themselves. Justin Tipuric was outstanding on the open-side flank, Josh Navidi was not far behind at No 8, and by half-time we had created four tries and opened up a 29-point lead. There was a higher level of physicality from the Georgians after the break and the four second-half tries were split between the teams, but all things considered, I was content with a 43–14 scoreline.

Every side in the tournament faced a quick turnaround somewhere and ours was now. We had a recovery day after Georgia, then a four-day lead-in to Australia. The last thing we needed was the unexpected. It was more than a little frustrating, then, that our plans for the eve-of-match captain's run were disrupted by an accident on the motorway that delayed our arrival at the Tokyo Stadium. This may seem like a small thing – I don't suppose there is a single soul living in Tokyo, of all places, who has not experienced the delights of a traffic jam – but nerves are easily frayed so close to a big game. Once again, the players shrugged their shoulders and went about their business with a minimum of fuss. The only lingering issue was Hadleigh Parkes, who had broken a bone in his hand against Georgia. We decided he would be good to go, but took the precaution of promoting Owen Watkin to the bench as direct cover and leaving Leigh Halfpenny out of the party. Funnily enough, Leigh's old full-back rival Kurtley Beale was also demoted, in his case from starter to substitute. This surprised me, but when I looked at the Wallaby selection as a whole, I formed the view that they were worried about our kicking game.

For the second time in a few days, we started brilliantly. Dan Biggar dropped an early goal, Hadleigh made light of his orthopaedic hassle by touching down from a high kick to the corner, Gareth Davies performed his party trick by intercepting a pass from his opposite number Will Genia and sprinting clear for a second try. Even though the Wallabies managed a score of their own through Adam Ashley-Cooper – we felt Justin Tipuric had been taken out in the build-up, but while we were proved correct afterwards we were in a minority at the time – a 23–8 interval advantage over such dangerous opponents was more than satisfactory. Especially as we'd conceded only a couple of penalties, the kind of statistic that counts in a game of such magnitude.

My half-time message was completely positive, but I stressed that we couldn't spend forty minutes sitting on a lead against a team like Australia. 'We absolutely have to keep playing,' I said, telling myself at the end that I'd delivered all the right words. What happened? The first penalties in the second half went against us and we didn't have a ruck of our own for sixteen minutes. In possession terms, we were not merely looking at a shortage; we were experiencing a drought. I was struggling to believe how decisively the indicators had swung against us, but there was no doubting the evidence. The Wallabies were putting us under enormous pressure, and with tries from Dane Haylett-Petty and Michael Hooper, they closed the gap to four points. Hooper's score looked like being particularly debilitating for us because it came after a long, exhausting siege in which our players tackled themselves stupid. When we were penalised at a scrum almost immediately, I wondered whether the Wallabies would reject the kick at goal, set themselves up deep in our 22 and go for the throat. Fortunately, they played safe and took the three points. 'I don't think that's the worst decision for us,' Robin McBryde muttered in my ear. He was right. The only further score was a penalty from our own Rhys Patchell and with some passionate defence in the closing minutes, which demonstrated just how much the players wanted it, we held on. The pool was now under our control.

Michael Cheika, the Wallaby coach, was almost spitting with fury. He was angry about the refereeing of the scrum, angry about a penalty decision against his centre Samu Kerevi, angry about lots of things. On the pitch after the final whistle, I saw him giving a television interview about six or seven metres away. He saw me too, but he didn't acknowledge me. Instead, he looked away, which I thought was pretty rude. I would certainly have done things differently if I'd been the losing coach, but I suppose it's a case of each to his own.

It had been an extraordinary match all round, not least because Alun Wyn Jones had won his 130th cap and set a new all-time record for international appearances in a Wales shirt. I knew he was thinking of his father, a great influence and supporter, who had died in 2016, and I wanted to strike the right note. In the team meeting before kick-off, I had talked about the contact area and the massive threat posed by the Wallaby flankers before saying: 'Alun Wyn, you're breaking a great record and it's a big day for you and your family. I know how proud your dad would have been. Hopefully, we can make it a special day too.' He welled up at that and became very emotional. Then, in the changing shed, he came up to me and said: 'It's alright, Warren. I'm back in the room now.' It was his way of saying that all the personal stuff had been consigned to its proper place and he was in the zone. And as usual, he shook my hand and thanked me for the opportunity. He played so well, fantastically well, especially when the heat was on us. I think he made twenty-five tackles and while he may have missed a few along the way, it was an outstanding performance. Under the circumstances, I was quite happy to say to him and his colleagues after the game: 'Right, it's ten days before Fiji. Don't be stupid about it, but you deserve a drink.' We stuck some money behind the hotel bar and joined the players in rugby's most traditional form of rest and recuperation.

There was no possibility of me underestimating our next opponents, the Fijians: if they hadn't knocked Wales out of the World Cup in 2007, I might never have been offered the head coach's job. More to the immediate point, they had given the Wallabies plenty of problems in their opening match and possessed more than their fair share of amazing rugby athletes, from Josua Tuisova, Semi Radradra and Levani Botia up front, to Leone Nakarawa, Peceli Yato and Viliame Mata in the pack. They were more capable than they once were of lasting eighty minutes, which meant they had the potential to hit us from any area of the field at any stage of the contest, and they could afford to throw the kitchen sink at us. Having come up just a little short against Australia and inexplicably imploded against Uruguay, they had this one opportunity in Oita to rescue something from a campaign that had promised much. I believed we would beat them if we worked them hard in the tight five, showed discipline at the breakdown and defended intelligently by not buying their dummies and restricting their off-loading game. And that was how it turned out. We had a rough start, conceding two tries in the opening ten minutes, but those scores were something else: a Jonah Lomu-type finish from Tuisova in the right corner and a fine finish from Kini Murimurivalu from Radradra's brilliant long pass. There isn't a side on the planet who wouldn't have struggled to protect their line against those assaults. It was a question of us responding by attacking Fiji in our own way and after manufacturing a hat-trick of tries for Josh Adams, one of our highest-performing players, and another for Liam Williams, we made it home by a dozen points, 29–17.

Our chief concern in the aftermath surrounded Dan Biggar, who finished a distant second in a collision with Liam Williams under a high ball and was off the field before the hour mark. We didn't bother with the HIA process, even though Dan, being Dan, would have been back on the field like a shot given half a chance. Instead, we opted for a straight withdrawal. He had taken a big knock during the Wallaby game, after which he felt a long way short of his best, and a part of me wondered whether this might be one too many. If I'm honest, I was worried that his tournament might be over. We talked to World Rugby's medical advisors, we had him scanned, then we called in an independent concussion specialist from Australia who had done a lot of work around the Australian Rules Football scene. He spoke to Dan on a couple of occasions and if he had not been comfortable with his situation, I'd have drawn the line. No return-to-play protocols, no more World Cup. But the specialist gave us the go-ahead to keep Dan in the mix for the knockout stage to come.

Was I overreacting? Absolutely not. Why? Because I completely understood the importance of the issue. Rugby is full of rumours and whispers about coaches playing fast and loose with the guidelines concerning head injuries, but that's not the way I do things. After George North suffered a couple of heavy knocks in our Six Nations match with England in Cardiff in 2015, the New Zealand-based news organisation Fairfax Media published a piece suggesting that I had insisted on him staying on the field. This was serious stuff, not least because it portrayed our doctor Geoff Davies and our medical manager Prav Mathema in a bad light as well as questioning my motives. As there was absolutely no truth behind the allegation – I would never have acted in such a way – the WRU threw its full weight behind the demand for an apology. I travelled all the way to Wellington for the mediation and I went on the offensive. In fact, I gave those publishers hell. The apology was duly secured.

By coincidence, George was the second of our concerns following the Fiji victory. He had only half a dozen touches in the match and his influence was minimal compared to Josh's, let alone those of Tuisova and Radradra, who, in a blinding individual performance, carried the ball nineteen times and beat seven defenders in making 140 metres. Our target for George was between fifteen and twenty involvements, because when he hits that mark, he scores tries. Six was not the figure we had in mind. So when we faced Uruguay with a much-changed team for our final pool game in Kumamoto, it was a big chance for Hallam Amos on the wing. Had he really taken his opportunity, there would have been an interesting selection debate ahead of the quarter-final.

Hallam could have scored three or four tries against the South Americans, but the gods failed to smile on him. It wasn't his fault entirely: our timing as a back line was not great, there were too many imprecise passes, the depth of support running left something to be desired. As a result, we wasted some big scoring chances in the opening fifteen minutes and then started playing too much rugby in the wrong areas of the field and turning over the ball. We kicked eleven times in the whole game. Against the very top sides, I would expect us to kick on between twenty-five and thirty-five occasions. It underlines once again how easy it is to lose control against the so-called 'weaker' nations, especially when they are as brave and tenacious as the Uruguayans turned out to be. I certainly did not expect them to be within a point of us at the break, but equally, I was never worried about the result. Our firepower gave us three second-half tries in a 35–13 victory and if Shaun Edwards was less than jubilant about the concession of a goal-line siege score late in the game, this was nothing new. Shaun takes it personally when the All Blacks break his defensive system, let alone the Uruguayans.

And so to the knockout phase and a quarter-final in Oita against France that in some ways was reasonably straight-forward in terms of preparation and in others extremely challenging. Indeed, there was a tantalising element of light and shade about all four knockout ties, starting with the England–Australia match. Eddie Jones' team was well rested following the weather-driven cancellation of their final pool game with the French (who were therefore equally blessed on the recuperative front) and had won ten of their last dozen matches with the Wallabies, but no international coach in the world looks at a team sheet featuring Kurtley Beale, Samu Kerevi, Will Genia, David Pocock and Michael Hooper and enjoys an uninterrupted night's sleep. As recently as mid-August, Michael Cheika's men had stuck half a dozen tries and forty-seven points on the New Zealanders in Perth. These people were nobody's fools. For their part, the All Blacks had lost two of their previous three meetings with Ireland and gone into *Full Metal Jacket* mode in winning the other. As for the Springboks and Japan . . . who knew anything for sure? Remember Brighton in 2015? More to the point, there were the Brave Blossoms' victories over Ireland and Scotland at this tournament to consider.

This is my way of saying that whatever the form book may say, tournament rugby of the sudden-death variety is a different beast to anything else in the sport. We knew that tactically speaking, the French would hit us with tight pods of heavy runners orchestrated by Antoine Dupont at half-back (a player, by the way, who could be quite something over the next two World Cup cycles). We also knew they would really come after us at scrum time. What French side doesn't go hell for leather at the set-piece, the emotional centrepiece of their rugby? What we didn't know was how their flair players – Maxime Medard, Damian Penaud, Virimi Vakatawa, Gael Fickou, Romain Ntamack and the new long-striding flanker Charles Ollivon – would attack us, especially with Dupont pushing the buttons. Preparing for that side of their game was difficult and hand on heart, I cannot say I was completely surprised to see us struggling to hold them in the opening ten minutes, during which they scored two tries, one of them converted. They looked seriously threatening in open field, none more so than Vakatawa. Here was the France of romance and legend, of Blanco and Saint-Andre and Dominici, and we were on the wrong end of it.

Thankfully, young Aaron Wainwright gave us something to cling to by sprinting clear for a try and cutting the deficit to five manageable points. It was an act of pure opportunism and it illustrated the depth of his rugby instinct. Like many coaches, I take the greatest pleasure in identifying and fast-tracking players of unusual talent. Not all such players succeed in meeting the demands of international rugby, but when someone like Aaron passes the examination in such an unforgiving environment and justifies the faith placed in him, the feeling of satisfaction is something to treasure. Aaron came late to the game, celebrated his twenty-second birthday during the tournament, and with that try, he announced himself to the widest of rugby audiences. He's a quick learner, a talented ball player, and a terrific athlete – a modern-day No 6 with a huge future. He will make mistakes for some time to come, but being like a sponge in soaking up information, he tends not to make the same ones twice. The complete trust I placed in him against France was handsomely repaid.

That try would not be his last major involvement in proceedings. With Aaron at the forefront of things, I felt we were generating momentum in the second quarter. As we were also staying on the right side of the referee, Jaco Peyper of South Africa, I had visions of us reaching the interval with a narrow advantage. Then we lost Josh Navidi to injury, which was bad news. When his replacement, Ross Moriarty, immediately made the same miserable trudge to the touch-line – not because he too was crocked, but because he hit Fickou high and was punished with the inevitable yellow card – we were rocked back on our heels. This was the last thing we needed, especially as Vakatawa scored a try while we were playing a man short. From 12–10 down and exerting some control, we turned round 19–10 down and in a degree of strife. I can't say I was best pleased with Ross, but he acknowledged his error and brought some energy to the field on his return.

Just as I had in Paris during the opening round of the Six Nations, I spent the break emphasising the importance of scoring first in the second half. Camille Lopez, on for Ntamack at No 10, attempted to deny us that comfort with a drop-goal, but missed the target. If I'm honest, I wasn't too disappointed to see Lopez on the field – not because he is a soft touch, but because his appearance suggested that France were looking to defend what they had by kicking away possession. It was at this point that their biggest physical specimen, the lock Sebastien Vahaamahina, lost his head and did his best to remove Aaron Wainwright's into the bargain by smashing an elbow into his jaw. The full gravity of the offence was not apparent at first, but once it was shown on the big screen in all its gory detail, there was only one outcome, a red card. One of the first things that struck me, to coin a phrase, was how 'old school' Vahaamahina's act had been. Thirty years ago, when I was playing for Waikato and the All Blacks, he would probably have been allowed to remain on the field. But quite a lot has changed over the course of three decades, in rugby as in every other walk of life. Players are professionals nowadays. They often play indoors, their every move is captured onscreen, they don't put boots on bodies at the rucks, they don't indulge in mass brawls when the close-quarter stuff gets a little tasty and there are no recent examples of a prop forward drinking aftershave at a post-match banquet – or anywhere else, for that matter. You might have thought some, if not all, of this would have dawned on Vahaamahina, but he did what he did and paid a heavy price. The second thing that flashed into my mind? The irony of it all. In 2011, we had lost a World Cup semi-final to France largely because of a red card. Here, one round earlier, we had every chance of winning a knockout tie against the same opposition in eerily similar circumstances. It took us until the seventy-fifth minute, but we got there in the end through a close-range touchdown from – who else? – Ross Moriarty. We hadn't played at all well and I was the first to admit it. In fact, I told the media afterwards that the better side had lost. But as we were the ones still in the competition, I was happy to settle for that. The alternative would have been far less palatable.

Jonathan Davies, our most experienced centre by a very long way, had missed the France game through injury, but I was able to name him for the semi-final against South Africa in Yokohama. This was a big bonus: in crunch fixtures at the end of a tournament, a two-tour British and Irish Test Lion with seventy-odd caps' worth of know-how is a priceless asset. Unfortunately, I was not so fortunate with Liam Williams and Josh Navidi, both of whom had been operating at a high level through the competition. They were nowhere near fit enough to face the Springboks, who, apart from the wing Cheslin Kolbe, would be at full strength. There was not a lengthy discussion about selection, however. I had no fears about Leigh Halfpenny at full-back, while Ross Moriarty's ultra-physical streak would be more than handy against the likes of Duane Vermeulen, Pieter-Steph du Toit and the other powerhouses in the South African pack.

Unlike the French, with all their unfathomables, there was nothing mysterious about the Boks. They would run their wraparound plays off Faf de Klerk at scrum-half, there would be lots of box-kicking from the same source and when the ball reached Handré Pollard at No 10, he would swing that mighty boot of his in search of territory. The previous day on the same patch of grass, England had turned in an outstanding display to beat the All Blacks – the first World Cup defeat suffered by New Zealand since the last-eight stage of the 2007 World Cup. They had produced fast ball from the breakdown, generated great line speed in defence, played in the right areas thanks to a masterful performance from George Ford at fly-half and asked unfamiliar questions of opponents who had no immediate answers. It was impressive, that's for sure: an object lesson in how to beat the reigning champions. But I knew that to beat the Springboks, we would have to be impressive in a different way.

This would be a 50–50 game, decided by the tiniest margins. A zero-sum game, if you like. In many matches, slight errors in handling or positioning and small concessions at the scrum or in the tackle area do not, in the final analysis, count for much. There are other games where every failure, no matter how infinitesimal, is a body blow of enormous significance. I believed this semi-final would turn out to be of the latter variety and so it proved. It was massively attritional, a battle not of yards but of inches. And we could have won: in fact, after Josh Adams continued his scoring streak by touching down in the left corner, and Leigh Halfpenny had made the difficult conversion, drawing us level at 16–16 with a quarter of an hour left, I felt we *would* win.

A good many people probably felt we were half-crazy to choose a scrum, rather than an attacking five-metre line-out or a simple shot at the sticks, when we were awarded a penalty at the end of a long assault on the Springbok line. But we were unanimous in the coaching box that this was the prime option and we made sure the message reached Alun Wyn Jones on the pitch. The field position was perfect and with a solid platform, we had the pace and the skills to eradicate our seven-point deficit in one move and push on towards victory. The Springboks had been ahead for most of the match but were just beginning to feel some heat. If we could get this right, they would be sick to the pits of their stomachs. And we did get it right. Our execution was spot on. Once again, we were showing guts and application in finding ways to stay in the fight against opponents we could not hope to dominate at close quarters and bring it down to a one-score game in the last few minutes.

Sadly for us, the decisive moments then went against us: a penalty against Alun Wyn for not releasing under pressure from the turnover specialist Francois Louw, followed by another as the Springboks set up their trademark driving maul off the line-out. That gave Pollard a shot to win the game, and win it he did. There was no way back for us. It was over.

My thoughts? Sadness and disappointment, of course. I had felt in my bones that there was a strong possibility of ending my time with Wales as I had started it, with a huge match against England. How I would have loved the occasion. There was a slight sense of frustration too. Whatever happened at that fateful maul on seventy-four minutes, it wasn't particularly clear or obvious. It seemed to me that if any Wales players were off their feet, as the referee Jérôme Garcès appeared to indicate, it was because Duane Vermeulen created the situation by going to ground first. But these calls are part and parcel of rugby and I can't say I felt any burning injustice about the way things ended. Neither was I in the mood to be hyper-critical of my own players. We could have been a little more decisive in controlling the aerial game and made different decisions when we gained ascendancy towards the end. We should certainly have made Damian de Allende, the outstanding Springbok centre, work harder for his try early in the second half. But could I really have asked for more from the team? I don't believe so.

If I had wanted to feel sorry for myself, I could have lamented the absence of so many quality players, from Taulupe Faletau, Gareth Anscombe and Cory Hill to Liam Williams and Josh Navidi. Yet if there were moments during the run-up to the semi-final when I found myself yearning for the luxury of a full-strength squad, my overriding feeling afterwards was one of pride. Pride in the fact that we had punched so far above our weight – not just at this tournament, but for so many years leading into it. Pride in the spirit of togetherness we had shown. Pride in the way we had represented a great rugby nation and given the supporters so much to cheer about and to cherish. I put all this into words in the dressing room after the game, congratulating the players on how far they had travelled as a team. It was only natural that they were shattered by defeat, but they were by no means broken beyond repair. They will come again and wherever I may be in the world of rugby, I will enjoy watching them do it.

After saying my piece, I walked along the corridor to the South African changing room and shared a beer with the winners. Then it was back to the hotel – an hour's drive from the stadium – and one more drink in the bar before bed. I was drained, mentally and emotionally, and hurting just a little. But I slept well in the knowledge that we had fought a good fight and emerged with honour. I first learned the importance of those values at Eastern Suburbs Rugby Club as a five-year-old boy with no boots. However much the game may have been transformed in the half-century since, some things will never change.

ACKNOWLEDGEMENTS

I would firstly like to acknowledge Chris Hewett, my ghost writer, for his patience and humour while writing my book. I admired and respected Chris when he was a sports journalist for the *Independent*. I always felt confident in his discretion when speaking off the record that he would never betray a trust. There are not many like that left in the sport. His sense of humour and the laughs we had during our many chats made this whole process enjoyable. I was also very thankful for his knowledge and the lengths he went to research my career and games I was involved in.

I would also like to thank the team at Headline, especially Jonathan Taylor, the book's publisher, for their belief in me writing my autobiography and their guidance through the process.

Lastly, I would like to say a massive thank you to my wife Trudi for pushing me to do this autobiography and for spending many hours proofreading, sitting in on sessions with Chris and I, and liasing with the publishers. It is something we have talked about doing for years and now it has

come to fruition I am so grateful that our family will have
this history of our life together sitting on the bookshelf at
our home in Waihi Beach to share with future generations
in the coming years.

PICTURE CREDITS

Page 14: Dave Lintott/Shutterstock (top); INPHO/Dan Sheridan (bottom)

Page 15: INPHO/Billy Stickland

Page 16: Chris Harris/WPA Pool/Getty Images (top); David Davies/PA Archive/PA Images (middle); Andrew Matthews/PA Archive/PA Images (bottom)

Page 17: Colorsport/Shutterstock (top); Shutterstock (middle and bottom)

Page 18: Simon Baker/Shutterstock

Page 19: Andrew Fosker/Shutterstock (top); Ross Land/AP/Shutterstock (middle); Mike Chapman/Shutterstock (bottom)

Page 20: Jonathan Brady/EPA/Shutterstock (top); Shutterstock (middle); Huw Evans/Shutterstock (bottom)

Page 21: Kieran McManus/BPI/Shutterstock

Page 22: Kieran McManus/BPI/Shutterstock

Page 23: Adam Davy/PA Wire/PA Images (top left); INPHO/Craig Mercer (top right); Tadashi Miyamoto/AFLO/Press Association Images (middle); Christophe Simon/AFP via Getty Images (bottom)

Page 24: David Ramos - World Rugby/World Rugby via Getty Images (top); Shaun Botterill/Getty Images (middle); Kyodo News via Getty Images (bottom)